‚Back in the West'

Baltische Studien zur Erziehungs- und Sozialwissenschaft

Herausgegeben von Gerd-Bodo von Carlsburg,
Algirdas Gaižutis und Airi Liimets

Band 25

PETER LANG
EDITION

Airi-Alina Allaste (ed.)

‚Back in the West'

Changing Lifestyles in Transforming Societies

PETER LANG
EDITION

Bibliographic Information published by the Deutsche Nationalbibliothek
The Deutsche Nationalbibliothek lists this publication in the Deutsche Nationalbibliografie; detailed bibliographic data is available in the internet at http://dnb.d-nb.de.

Library of Congress Cataloging-in-Publication Data

Back in the West : changing lifestyles in transforming societies / Airi-Alina Allaste (ed.).
pages cm. — (Baltische Studien zur Erziehungs- und Sozialwissenschaft ; Band 25)
ISBN 978-3-631-63465-3
1. Lifestyles—Former Soviet republics. 2. Group identity—Former Soviet republics. 3. Post-communism—Former Soviet republics. 4. Former Soviet republics—Social conditions—21st century. 5. Europe, Eastern—Social conditions—1989- I. Allaste, Airi-Alina.
HQ2044.F6B33 2013
305—dc23

2013004776

ISSN 1434-8748
ISBN 978-3-631-63465-3

Peter Lang Edition is an Imprint of Peter Lang GmbH

Peter Lang – Frankfurt am Main · Berlin · Bruxelles · New York · Oxford · Warszawa · Wien

www.peterlang.de

Acknowledgements

This book has been published with the support of research grant SF0130111s08 of the Estonia Governmental Scientific Research Support Scheme 'Changes in the attitudes and lifestyles of Estonian population in 1985-2013: horizontal stratification'. The lifestyle choices and the manifestation of lifestyles are analysed through the processes taken place in different fields of practice as well as in the interactions of social space and time. The analyses of longer trends are based on the data of population surveys conducted since 1985. Particular aspects of lifestyles have been analysed using qualitative methods and in-depth analyses. Chapters of this book have been discussed jointly in regular seminars where authors have been participating.

In addition to authors, many people we would like to acknowledge have contributed to the book. The chapters of the book were reviewed by Aet Annist, Laura Assmuth, Jakob Demant, Rachel Herring, Mervi Ilmonen, Johanna Lilius, Raili Marling, Irina Novikova, Andu Rämmer and Andra Siibak. We are also grateful to Aino Ugaste, Gertrud Kasemaa, Mare Müürsepp and Erle Rikmann for their valuable suggestions at seminars as well as to Daniel Warren for proofreading and Aivar Joorik for the lay-out of the book. We are grateful to all of them for their contribution. Last but not least, we would also like to give thanks to all people who have participated in various quantitative and qualitative studies, which constitute the empirical bases for the chapters of this book.

Airi-Alina Allaste

Contents

Lifestyles in former socialist society

Airi-Alina Allaste, Andy Bennett

This chapter argues for the importance of the concept of lifestyle in the process of identity formation in former socialist societies. Economically, culturally and in terms of media influence, former socialist countries became part of a world order that emerged in the West during the late 1980s and early 1990s. Whereas the Soviet-type regimes strived for an homogenisation of their populations with regard to lifestyle, the post-socialist transformation made them participants in a global lifestyle market. Yet while in Western societies the establishment of a plurality of lifestyles has been a longer process, for former socialist countries the lifestyle market opened up in parallel with the building up of modern society by governing life(styles). The idea of citizens as autonomous contract-making individuals did not emerge from capitalism of its own accord; it has been the subject of struggles over ways of life and the distribution of freedoms over two and half centuries of capitalist development (Sulkunen 2009). However, former socialist countries – including Estonia – missed the most relevant developments of the twentieth century, starting from the 1960s, and have adopted a contemporary lifestyle only in last two decades.

Strongly associated with the 'cultural turn', lifestyle has become a key term in the critical analysis and interpretation of socio-cultural identities – both individual and collective – in contemporary social settings. The concept of lifestyle as it is used in this chapter as well as in the book in its entirety is not a narrow descriptor for the targeting of taste groups by the cultural industries (see Reimer 1995). We consider the concept of lifestyle as having critical currency in sociological theory and empirical research (Chaney 1996), and use it in reference to individuals' choices in all life domains, taking our starting point from Giddens (1991: 5) definition of lifestyles as 'social practices and ways of living adopted by individuals that reflect personal, group, and socioeconomic identities'. Identity cannot be regarded as an unproblematic reflection of socio-economic circumstances – notably class, community and education. Identity is also a product of reflexively inscribed lifestyle projects that draw upon the physical and symbolic resources of the media and cultural industries. Lifestyle bespeaks a new means of understanding the way in which identities are created, maintained and articulated on an everyday level (Bennett 2005). Through lifestyle projects, individuals forge new forms of socio-cultural association that transcend straightforward notions of identity as inherently produced by and bound up with a given local socio-economic context.

When individuals choose their careers, mates or the networks to which they belong, they are influenced by rapid technological developments, economic uncertainty and other ongoing changes in society. On the other hand, through their choices they also construct new social realities. Emerging lifestyles and new ways of integration exist objectively, are recognised by society and might become, to some extent, new forces for social change. In former Soviet societies – which are described as transition or transforming societies – the interrelation between lifestyles and the process of social change might be more obvious than in Western societies.

Concept of lifestyle

The interest in lifestyles as a sociological concept is frequently related to social, economic and cultural changes that are associated with the latter twentieth century – the period from the 1960s and 1970s onwards. While the classical theories for explaining and interpreting society dealt with vertical stratification (upper, middle and lower class), based on access to resources and occupational status, increasing social mobility and rapid individualisation created a situation in which the traditional models were no longer adequate for representing society (Beck 1992; Bögenhold 2001; Friedland and Mohr 2004; Chan and Goldthorpe 2004; Alexander 2007). A new multidimensional approach was needed, one that was both sensitive to and able to incorporate a new schema based around the interweaving of the terms of lifestyles, social differentiation and horizontal stratification. By the term 'lifestyle', we mean an acquired pattern of attitudes and behaviours that is in some way consistent throughout an individual's life, or in a particular domain of life (Lawson and Todd 2002). As Chaney (2002) argues, contemporary societies are characterised by an increasing plurality of lifestyle choices and constantly diversifying ways of living. Thus, he suggests, it is increasingly difficult to conceptualise everyday cultural life in terms of class background or associated binaries such as 'subculture' and 'dominant culture'. It is rather the case that societies are now increasingly complex in terms of the array of lifestyle preferences and orientations that they produce. The concept of *lifestyle* can be traced back to the beginning of the twentieth century, notably in the work of Weber (1978 [1922]). Influenced by new patterns of consumption emerging across the major European cities during the late nineteenth and early twentieth centuries, Weber challenged Marx's model of economic determinism by arguing that new models of consumption were facilitating the rise of status groups whose claims to social position were not merely based on actual wealth but on the perception of wealth and status that could be effected through lifestyles based around modes of consumption. Weber's work was highly influential on two other sociologists, Veblen and Simmel, whose work was focused on urban culture in the early twentieth century.

Veblen's (1994 [1924]) work was based in the United States, and concentrated upon the wealthy middle classes who had made their money from trade and manufacturing. According to Veblen, this new leisure class attempted to mimic the lifestyles of the European upper classes. Veblen referred to this as 'conspicuous consumption', a term he used to describe the ways in which acts of consumption are used to construct particular lifestyles, which in turn are intended to give out particular messages and create particular images of how individuals want to be perceived by others.

Like Veblen, Simmel was also interested in studying how individuals used their practices of consumption as a way of making social statements about themselves (see Frisby and Featherstone 1997). Much of Simmel's work was conducted in Berlin at the turn of the century. The Berlin of this era was a classic example of an early modern metropolis. Chaney maintains that, in the work of Simmel, 'the metropolis is seen as the focus of new forms of civilised life; it is therefore a world of taste and discrimination in which consumption is overwhelmingly more important than production' (1996: 51).

According to Simmel, the relative anonymity of individuals in the metropolis was isolating, but at the same time provided a driving force for individuals to mark themselves out from the crowd, to create new forms of urban identity – and in this respect, it was the act of consumption that provided the key to the construction of identity. Thus, as Chaney explains:

> Sociologically, the metropolis is mediated through symbolism – it is a lifeworld in which symbols mutually refer in ever more complex layers of association and in which the play of meanings can only be understood reflexively and as a constant process of innovation. The increasingly differentiated world of goods of modernity is not a simple process of enrichment, but neither is it straightforward alienation. The cultural terrain of the metropolis simultaneously offers new potentials for individuals to enhance their subjectivity (1996: 51).

Lifestyle subsequently became more readily associated with market research. According to Reimer, the concept of lifestyle was of particular use to market researchers, as it 'could be used as a more sophisticated instrument than traditional socio-economic background factors to identify segments of buyers' (1995: 122). In the late twentieth century, however, lifestyle again began to be used as a sociological model, particularly in work focusing on social identity. In 1979, French sociologist Pierre Bourdieu introduced his concept of the interplay of lifestyles and social differentiation (Bourdieu 1984 [1979]). According to

Bourdieu, social reality comprises an objective social structure – the space of social positions (vertical axis) – and a subjective structure – the space of lifestyles (horizontal axis). Bourdieu's study focused on France in the 1970s, but several recent studies based on Bourdieu's model (*e.g.* see Koch 1996; Dahl 1997; Hjellbrekke 2000; Roselund 2000; Kivelä and Siisiäinen 2007) have confirmed the universality of his concept. In the last few decades, the interest in lifestyles has increased, and the interplay of lifestyle choices and social differentiation has been a topic of discussions by several Western scholars. Ulrich Beck stresses that today the class- and origin-based determination of a person's life course has diminished, as rapidly social change multiplies the possible life courses and mobility options available, providing 'kits for possible biographic combinations' (Beck 1992: 217). Over the last twenty years, the concept of lifestyle has been developed further by several researchers (*e.g.* see Giddens 1991; Beck, Giddens and Lash 1994; Chaney, 1996). Lifestyles are formed by consumption patterns in the broadest meaning of the word, including work and family behaviour, housing strategies, social networks, recreation and leisure activities, cultural consumption and taste, and other status-related activities that include everyday consumption, like habits of dress, eating and so on (Giddens 1991; Zukin and Maguire 2004). Giddens stresses that lifestyle is not something forced upon an individual; it implies choices, instead of fixed identity positions based on class, community and tradition. Indeed, according to Giddens, lifestyles can be regarded as a product of a new phase of social life, which he refers to as reflexive modernity. Giddens (1991, 1994) describes how the process of reflexive modernity creates multiple choices and options, thus having considerable effect on the lifestyles that individuals construct for themselves. Furthermore, the more the traditions loosen their hold, the more individuals are forced to make their own choices among a diversity of local and global options. While making these choices, an individual has to consider several external factors, such as the influence of the social group, cultural norms and role models, economic assets and so on. Choices are inevitable – or, using Giddens' words, 'we have no choice but to choose' (1991: 81). Giddens stresses the dual nature of lifestyles. In other words, if one wishes to belong to a specific group or stratum, it is necessary to adopt the lifestyle approved and endorsed by the group (*e.g.* place of residence, car, children's school, way of spending one's leisure time). In turn, adopting the lifestyle of a certain group makes one opt for future choices in order not to be excluded from the group. Further important insights regarding lifestyle are offered in the work of Chaney. Like Giddens, Chaney situates lifestyle as a means of charting new forms of social identity, collectivity and belonging in an age where class and attendant forms of tradition exert a weakening hold on the individual. In this way, Chaney considers lifestyles as illustrative of the increasing levels of reflexivity engaged in by individuals in the course of everyday life. Central to Chaney's application of lifestyle is the distinction that he makes between 'ways of life' and 'lifestyles'. Thus, according to Chaney, 'ways of life' are 'typically associated with a more or less stable community [and] displayed in features such as shared norms, rituals, patterns of social order and probably a distinctive dialect' (1996: 92). Lifestyles, on the other hand, are 'creative projects' that rely on 'displays of consumer competence' (1996: 97). Chaney then goes on to suggest that the key to the significance of lifestyles in contemporary consumer societies is the way in which they enable us to understand how individuals use aspects of taste, aesthetics and the symbolic appropriation of physical goods in the formulation of what he refers to as lifestyle 'sites and strategies' (1996: 91). Chaney describes lifestyle *sites* as the 'physical metaphors for the spaces that actors can appropriate and control', while he suggests that *strategies* denote the 'characteristic modes of social engagement, or narratives of identity, in which the actors concerned can embed the metaphors at hand' (1996: 92).

Identity, as it is applied in the chapters featured in this book, is part of the *reflexive project*, which, according to Giddens (1991), is neither stable nor given but processual. From this perspective, because personal identities do not necessarily respond to one's social position, they can therefore not be considered as given or fixed. This type of deconstructionist approach emphasises the impossibility of authentic identities based on a universally shared experience or origin; identities are relational, defined by their difference from something, processual and multiple (Grossberg 1996). Differing profiles of self answer to the various contexts in which the conversation and action of the other is acknowledged. Grossberg draws attention to the distinction between theories of difference and otherness. The latter means that the identity or meaning depends entirely on its relation to or its difference from others. While the theories of difference consider difference itself as given, the theories of otherness assume that difference itself is historically and socially produced, imposed on modern structures of power (Grossberg 1996). Accordingly, together with lifestyle choices and projects of the self, individuals position themselves in society by identification and differentiation. Lifestyles can be seen as forms of social integration that offer an individual a possibility of identification with a social group. And on the contrary, lifestyle may also function as a form of segregation by excluding certain individuals with inappropriate leisure habits, tastes and so on from particular group lifestyles.

As this brief overview illustrates, much of the work published on lifestyle over the last 20 years has concentrated on adapting concept as a framework for our understanding of the impact of socio-economic changes on identity and belonging in Western, developed nations. In this respect, lifestyles are regarded as a product of post-industrialisation and the transformation of former labour-based societies in the West to consumer and leisure-based societies. Central and Eastern European (CEE) countries, on the other hand, have been analysed mainly from a macro perspective. We argue that a focus on lifestyles can contribute an important set of theoretical and empirical tools for explaining these societies. Below, we provide a short overview of how the main theoretical discussions reviewed in the first section of this chapter can be applied to former socialist societies. We begin with an overview of the theories of transition and transformation as key approaches to explaining these societies, and then go on illustrate what an investigation of lifestyles and identities can contribute to our understanding of social change in these societies.

Transition societies and cultures, and the new models of stratification

Change is a pervasive part of social life, and there are no societies without change. Transitology, a research branch concerned with 'transition societies', is a relatively new approach that first emerged in the 1970s, when it focused on processes in Southern European and Latin American societies. After the fall of the Berlin Wall, the concept also gained critical currency in studies of the Central and Eastern European (CEE) countries. Transition societies are defined as former socialist countries undergoing a process of democratisation. The term refers to a situation in which the political structure is changing from a single-party rule to a parliamentary system, administrative institutions are being reorganised, central planning is changing to a capitalist free market economy and a society of shortages is changing to a consumer society. Modernist transitology makes a clear distinction between closed economies and open market economies. In the political sphere, the one party-state under communism was contrasted with the Western democratic pluralist party system.

On the individual level, an individual under communism (*homo sovieticus*) contrasts with the rationally calculating and autonomously acting individual (*home economicus*) characteristic of modern societies (Blokker 2005). While, in Western modernist societies, the agent of change has been the *bourgeoisie* of private owners and change has been a longer process, in transition societies it is 'designed capitalism' and 'functional elites' that are the agents of change. Modernist thinking has been based on the assumption that 'if you create the proper institutions, they will shape the individuals that occupy them so that individual behaviour will confirm to institutional constraints and imperatives' (Eyal *et al.* 1998). As a result of this process, one characteristic of a transition society is the discrepancy between the speed of institutional reform and the slowness of cultural changes and liminality – the sense of being in between the two social orders. One of the most prominent researchers of post-communist transition societies, Piotr Sztompka, describes the situation as parallel existence of old and new cultures:

> On one side there was pervasive, historically inherited repertoire of cultural rules, shaped under the influence of the old communist regime and its characteristic 'habitus' /.../ characterised by acceptance of state paternalism, anti-elitism, anti-intellectualism and opportunistic double standards – common practice of evading rules imposed by the regime /.../ On the other hand there were seeds of completely different culture, functionally demanded by the new democratic and capitalist institutions (Sztompka 2004: 172).

The process can also be understood in Raymond Williams' (1980) terms of residual and emergent forms of culture. While some parts of society's culture, at any given time, continue to be practised on the basis of previous social formations and historic cultural models, other parts are being added continuously through new experiences and from the repertoire of externally available meanings, values and practices, while still others are becoming obsolete (Williams 1980). The new framework of values has been theorised by Michael Kennedy as 'transition culture', which is focused on forward movement, emphasising the fundamentally opposed positions of socialism and capitalism, and stressing the normative superiority of the latter. Kennedy defines transition culture as 'mobilising culture organised around certain logical and normative oppositions, valuations of expertise, and interpretations of history that provide a basic framework through which actors undertake strategic action to realise their needs and wishes' (Kennedy 2002: 9). 'Transition culture' can be interpreted also as a hegemonic set of values in new capitalist societies that influence the whole society. Thus, although societies characterised by transition culture continue to be pluralistic and diverse in terms of the different cultural traits they encompass, materialistic values and professional success are highly prioritised and promoted as standards to be strived for by all individuals.

A different approach to changes in former socialist countries is to focus more on the process and dynamics of change than on the destination. Social change is not seen primarily as a transition from one order to another, but as a transformation – as rearrangements, reconfigurations and recombinations that yield new interweavings of the multiple social logics that are modern society (Stark and Bruszt 1998: 7). Former socialist countries are not seen through the dualism of capitalism/socialism, but capitalisms are perceived as plural. This approach stresses the emergence of a distinctively CEE capitalism, and the focus is not on the destination (a capitalist society), but rather which trajectory is taken and how transformations happen (1998: 7).

It has been argued that macro-level changes and neo-liberalisation have created structural conditions for a new class society (*e.g.* Saar 2011), or even that former communist countries have never been classless societies (*e.g.* Vonderau and Schröder 2008). Without neglecting the idea of emerging new classes, social stratification and a growing discrepancy between different parts of the population in former Soviet societies, we would like to stress the cultural as well as the structural aspects of the social when approaching these processes.

As early as the mid-twentieth century, German sociologists referred to the inadequacy of the classical model of stratification and the need for studies on the cultural aspects of stratification and the role of lifestyle choices (Geiger 1949: 146). The debates about different concepts of social stratification re-emerged in the last decades of the twentieth century when the attention to lifestyles as one of the key concepts in sociology increased considerably (Cockerham, Rutten and Abel 1997). Danielsen (1991) sees the growing interest in lifestyle studies as a sign of a new paradigm for sociological analysis of modern societies that reflects current trends of individualisation, integration and disintegration. In the academic literature, one can find several debates about whether the classical concept of vertical stratification is still optimal, whether it has become obsolete and should be substituted by a new stratification model based on lifestyles, or whether these two approaches should be treated as complementary (*e.g.* Soerensen 1991; Clark and Lipset 1991; Clark, Lipset and Rempel 1993; Pakulski 1993). Due to the fact that in transition societies all changes have occurred at hyper-speed, and new frameworks of values have influenced all levels of society, it is possible that the cultural aspects might have had even wider impact than in Western societies. By analysing a society according to lifestyle criteria, a different image of the society could be created, in which elements of lifestyle demarcate the social groups, but also distinguish a specific group from other groups.

This discussion of transition societies has focused mainly on the end-state of the transition in the form of the Western-type democratic market economy, with attention to formal procedural institutions in the 1990s (Blokker 2004). However, focusing on transformations has expanded to encompass an exploration of macro-level cultural aspects over the last decade. By contrast, far less attention has been paid to the everyday cultures, identities of people and lifestyles in these societies. As the research informing the subsequent chapters in this book illustrates, although their trajectories of socio-economic transition and transformation have been quite different from those of Western nations, the former socialist countries increasingly are orientated towards consumerism and leisure as planned economies give way to privatisation and the free market economy. On the other hand, only part of the population has the means to invest in successful self-projects, whereas other groups have restricted opportunities to influence their individual strategies. Lifestyle concepts and theories developed by Western sociologists can be used to study socio-economic and cultural changes occurring in the former socialist countries, but new frameworks need to be developed that more closely describe the experience of these countries. The following discussion will refer mostly to evidence relating to Estonia, but many of these characteristics are also relevant for other CEE countries.

The cultural context of Estonia compared with Western societies

The changes outlined above, which have occurred in everyday culture and thus in the ways individuals frame their identity, have played a significant role in the transformation of post-socialist societies. Since Soviet ideas, identities and behavioural patterns proved incompatible with the new capitalist societies, people were expected to change quickly, concurrently with the macro-level changes. The majority of the older Soviet and pre-Soviet generations (for whom changing identities and lifestyles was not an easy process) were excluded from the public sphere, and relevant positions in society were taken over by the younger generation (those in their twenties). 'Winners' and 'losers' are metaphors used widely when describing Eastern European societies, both in academic writing and public discussion (*e.g.* see Vonderau and Schröder 2008). Indeed, the part of the population in these countries who found themselves in the 'looser' position had to find solutions to the new problems they faced – including redundancies and/or the need to retrain or face loss of income. In the Estonian context, a now term widely used is 'winner generation', referring to people born in the 1960s (with ethnic differences – see below) who, since the 1990s, have often had the best opportunities to climb the ladder of the structural hierarchy, and consequently the greatest freedom in terms of lifestyle choices.

While the 1990s saw limited material options, which severely restricted the lives of the majority of people in Estonia and other transition countries, economic growth at the turn of the new century widened consumption opportunities and lifestyle choices (see also Hansson's article in this book). Today, Estonia can be characterised by several differences and contrasts within its small society, which makes it an interesting case of exploration of lifestyle choices and different opportunities. Before moving on to discuss these, it should be noted that a number of theorists and researchers in Western countries have also argued that wide differences in access to lifestyle resources and opportunities continue to exist in the West, and that the gap may, in fact, be widening. This point has been argued extensively in some of the work dealing with young people and transitions in the United Kingdom (*e.g.* see Shildrick and MacDonald 2006). However, given the unprecedented rate of socio-economic and cultural change in the former Soviet countries, and the very uneven ways in which these changes have impacted the social strata, it is reasonable to assume that inequality in relation to lifestyle choice and opportunity will be radically more extreme in these settings.

As stated above, the winners of transformation processes in society were those who were young in the 1990s. In 1992, Estonia had the youngest prime minister in Europe. Mart Laar was only 32 at the time of his appointment, and many other relevant positions were taken by people in their twenties. Private businesses were most often established by the younger generation and, compared with Western countries, access to governmental positions was also easier for young people. In the longer term, these developments served to produce a discourse of young people as winners. Early achievements and success became an obligation for young people; in contrast to the Western world, where it is common for people in their thirties to still be studying, young people in the former Soviet countries are expected to have a successful career in their twenties.

The stark generational difference in mentality and lifestyle continues to be a reality in these countries, and we can still speak about new and old cultures in Sztompka's (2004) terms. Indeed, this generational divide in lifestyle has been accentuated further by more recent developments. Thus, during the last decade, the transition culture of the CEE countries has begun to be replaced in part by the network society, with the effect that the younger generation today is widely influenced by global popular and consumer culture. As such, these individuals are increasingly plugged into global trends in lifestyle marketing that are increasingly intergenerational. Thus, as theorists such as Featherstone and Hepworth (1995) and McHugh (2003) observe, an awareness of the uni-age appeal of fashion and style, music, tourism and various other forms of popular leisure has led to marketing strategies that target different age groups in increasingly subtle ways. In CEE countries, it is too early to speak about similar tendencies. As the comparative study of Estonia, Latvia and the Czech Republic shows, young people in all of these countries are global-minded, and their self-identification is based on similar hobbies, tastes and cultural consumption. Older generations – especially ethnic minorities – tend to be characterised by nostalgia and deprivation of their world-view (Kalmus and Vihalemm 2008). Thus a part of the population is excluded from the uni-age lifestyle market.

In Estonia (as in some other countries – for example, Latvia), the process of transition has also had an ethnic dimension. One of the most important aims was the restoration of national independence, and one-third of the population who were not ethnic Estonians lost their status compared with Soviet times. Estonia's 1992 Citizenship Law was based on the principle of restoring the citizenship of pre-World War II Estonian citizens and their descendants. The implementation of this principle left a majority of the country's Russian-speakers without citizenship, as they most often had either moved to the country during the decades of Soviet rule, or were the children (or even grandchildren) of people who had done so. The Russian-speaking minority became disadvantaged in several ways: relative economic deprivation, spatial segregation of the population and a weaker position on the labour market as compared with ethnic Estonians. Members of the ethnic majority and minority groups had partly dissimilar challenges to face when it came to coping with transitions (Kalmus and Vihalemm 2008), as well as different structural and cultural conditions for their lifestyle choices. Whereas ethnic Estonians were initiators of social change, many Russian-speakers perceived changes in the society as being imposed from outside and as threatening their identity. Because of their insecure position in society, their opportunities for lifestyle choices became relatively restricted. While the younger generation of Russian-speakers in Estonia today is global-minded and oriented towards a lifestyle market similar to ethnic Estonians, the largest difference within national groups remain between the middle-age generations. Russian-speaking youngsters differ from their parents to a greater extent than young Estonians do from theirs. During the transition period, Estonians in the 26–45 years age bracket have been more receptive to processes of resocialisation (Vihalemm and Kalmus 2008). This can be explained by the notion that the 'winner generation' has been more successful at adopting the new culture, and within this generation ethnic Estonians have been the real 'winners' compared with their Russian-speaking counterparts. It might be speculated that uni-age consumption trends similar to Western countries have been at least partly taken over the 'winner generation'; middle-aged Estonians are taking the lead in setting examples about how to manage and reflect lifestyle choices as an indicator of social status. At the same time, we cannot speak about widespread changes in this respect so long as the socio-economic dislocations that currently generate lifestyle inequality in the post-Soviet region continue to act as an exclusionary barrier for significant sections of society. Emerging after an era of hardship and austerity associated with the Soviet Union, during the early years after socialism cultural consumption was regarded as part of becoming a contemporary 'normal' person (see also Pilvre in this book). There was a strong urge to become different from *homo sovieticus* and become a 'Western person'. Especially during the 1990s, everything that came from the West was celebrated, but being part of Western consumer culture is still important today. This, combined with the pressure of needing to have a successful career while still relatively young has produced a 'show-off' mentality (Allaste 2008), which means that young people who may not be successful enough at least try to appear as if they are. This entails these individuals presenting themselves as being materially better off than they actually are, and engaging in practices of conspicuous consumption – that is, paying a lot of attention to those parts of their lifestyle that are visible to others. It might be argued that this would 'facilitate their rise of status based on perception of wealth', using the argumentations of Weber (1978[1922]), and can be seen as 'conspicuous consumption to give out particular message and create particular image', relying on Veblen. However, in a transition society it is not always the case of coherent lifestyles as a basis for status, but rather adopting a show-off strategy in the hope of gaining status.

During Soviet times, alternative lifestyles in Estonia (for example, gay culture, music subcultures or religious movements) were strictly limited to the private and underground spheres, and thus were invisible in public. After the restoration of the country's independence, the creation of a coherent national culture was prioritised by most ethnic Estonians. Consequently, distinctive lifestyles and subcultures have only very recently started to become visible in society, and are still not taken for granted as aspects of Estonian society. This is in contrast to Western nations, where both the diversity of lifestyles and their cultural practices are well established, largely tolerated and in some cases increasingly incorporated into more mainstream notions of culture and everyday life. For example, stylistically distinctive youth cultures began to emerge in a broader sense during the mid-1950s as the post-war Western youth market took hold and provided young people with endless opportunities to consume and appropriate objects, images and texts specifically produced to appeal to people between the ages of 15 and 25 (Chambers 1985; Bennett 2000). This was the beginning of a form of conspicuous lifestyle consumption among youth that has continued to spread and diversify in Western nations, and has played a significant role in the cultural transformation of these nations over the past six decades. But while subcultures in Western societies today are associated with consumer networks, in Estonian society, distinctive lifestyles tend to be associated with somewhat naïve enthusiasm – similar to Western societies in the 1960s. In Eastern Europe, subcultures or lifestyle movements diverging from the mainstream are more active in creating an identity for their members, since distinction is primarily seen as potential to change society. On the other hand, in the more established mainstream society, differences are perceived as more frightening and threatening (and perhaps even as ridiculous), compared with more multicultural environments.

It might be argued that, in general, lifestyles in a former Soviet country might have a less significant role than they do in Western societies. Even though younger generations of ethnic Estonians and Russian-speakers have similar world-views, ethnic groups in Estonia are too separated in everyday culture for their differences to be bridged by lifestyles choices and similar tastes. Older generations are excluded from the inter-generational lifestyle market both because of their mentality and due to economic restrictions. Distinctive lifestyles, subcultures and movements can be seen as forms of social integration within the groups, but they are more separated from wider societies than they are in Western countries. In post-Soviet countries, widespread cultural transformations are just beginning to occur, and it is not currently clear what trajectory they will take in the coming years.

Contextualising lifestyle trends in Estonia

The first part of this book focuses on linkages between long-term macrosocietal trends, and personal choices and attitudes. The first two chapters discuss the changes in subjective well-being and values during the period from Soviet stagnation in 1985, through liberal market democracy, to the outbreak of economic recession in 2008. Adaptation to macro-level changes and personal lifestyle choices can be measured by outcomes, namely life satisfaction and subjective well-being – a term referring to a person's self-evaluation of the state of his/her life situation at a particular point in time. The main questions focused upon in the chapter by Hansson concern the extent to which the significant *turning points* on both the society and individual levels are reflected in the changes in subjective well-being, and the impact of attitudes towards different lifestyle choices on well-being outcomes. The study reveals that it is possible to distinguish between two different periods: a period of transition shock – that is, the first years after the fall of the Soviet regime – characterised by significant decline in well-being; and a period of economic stabilisation, characterised by a steady increase in well-being. Above all, the satisfaction with one's financial situation clearly reflects the changes that have taken place in Estonian economy – a rapid decline in the beginning of the 1990s has been followed by an upward trend since the mid-1990s. While in the early 1990s subjective well-being was largely associated with destiny and good luck, over the last 15 years the perception of life control and understanding of individual responsibility has constantly increased; today, the majority of people emphasise the importance of personal efforts and life choices over the role of destiny. The latter could be interpreted through increasing individualisation and acknowledging of the importance of lifestyle choices.

It is claimed that Western societies have turned towards post-materialistic values in the 1970s; the welfare level achieved by that time in the West granted considerable material security to wide sections of the population. In Eastern Europe, the economic base today is still not strong enough for post-materialistic values, and since people from these countries have perceived their social environment as very unstable over the last decades, priority has been given to values related to deficiency needs such as security. Besides, some values (such as universalism and solidarity) remind people of slogans from the hegemonic ideological system characteristic of the former social order. Abstract and universalistic notions of solidarity and collective interests from Soviet times have been replaced by notions individual interest and success, and during the transition period the position of Estonia shifted even more in the direction of materialistic values. The chapter by Raudsepp, Heinla and Tart focuses on the dynamics of value patterns in Estonia from 1985 to 2008. During this time, the importance of friends, self-education and physical fitness is central to the values that have grown most significantly. It is possible to interpret these as recourses for survival in the intensifying competition. Other values that have grown steadily from 1985 to 2008 include family and material well-being. The transition from socialism to liberal capitalism has strengthened the importance of close relationships and individual self-development at the same time.

The change from socialism to capitalism in Estonia was related to the reconstruction of the national state; this linked the systemic change to 'restoration' of the pre-World War II Republic of Estonia, occupied afterwards by the Soviet Union. Particular values, which were associated with the First Republic, have also been expressed in the social order and lifestyle choices. Paadam and Ojamäe's chapter on residential cultures discusses the continuity of a residential preference for a single-family house, with a reference to the First Republic, which remained a dominant home ideal throughout the turbulent twentieth century and its multiple societal ruptures. The drawbacks of the former socialist system, characterised by limited residential choices, have not caused permanent discontinuities, or remarkable changes, in prevalent individual preferences, despite the diversity of alternative lifestyle possibilities emerging in contemporary residential markets. The chapter analyses the single-family residence as a cultural heritage that is sustained and continuously reinvented as a mode of resident identity-building under distinct circumstances of individual lives and societal structural conditions.

The longing for the First Republic was accompanied by an idealisation of the gender order of the 1930s – and, accordingly, promotion of conservative values and neo-traditional gender identities. The chapter by Pilvre provides an overview of Estonian society in the 1990s, paying special attention to the changing gender order looming in the background of discussions in preceding chapters. This chapter analyses how the lifestyle magazine *Mees* (*Man*) both reflected and constructed the gender order, and other changing values and attitudes in Estonian society. Lifestyle magazines are among the primary sites where ideals of gender identity in a certain culture and era are most intensely constructed. The first Estonian lifestyle magazine for men was published in an era in which masculine identity changed rapidly, as Estonia entered the market economy and the consumer society of the 1990s. *Mees* could be interpreted as the lifestyle manual for an era, and a milestone of changing gender order in a transition society where many of the further trends in the dominant gender ideology are presented. This chapter gives an analytical overview of the magazine, which was an attempt to offer men the possibility of consciously contemplating or constructing a gender identity through readership.

Lifestyle choices and identities in transforming society

While the Estonia of the 1990s could have been described as a transition society, the most accurate term for the current state of play could be a 'transforming society'. Referring to previous theories (Stark and Bruszt 1998), this focuses on a transformation process, but in addition recognises Estonia as an active agent in this process. During the twenty-first century, the transition society has gradually been replaced in Estonia by the network society (Lauristin 2012). Estonia is no longer merely copying Western society; it is part of various networks and relationships, and in turn influences processes elsewhere. Contemporary intercultural transformation processes continuously shape the identities and lifestyles of individuals in all European societies. The opening up of a Europe with advanced European Union (EU)-related institutional arrangements, moving across cultures from East to West as well as increasingly from West to East, is becoming the European reality. European societies are conjoined in the transformation through multi-layered cultural exchanges in various fields (Paadam, Ojamäe and Siilak 2012: 214). Together with global processes of technological, economic and political development, all of these changes offer new opportunities for lifestyles on a growing scale (see also Beck and Beck-Gernsheim 1995; Beck and Beck-Gernsheim 2009 [2002]; Giddens 1995; Refsing 1998). Personal experiences of diversifying lifestyles are manifested in the construction of identities as continuous processes.

The second part of the book focuses on contemporary lifestyle choices and identities in Estonia, which are often integrated with other cultures by intercultural relationships, places of residence or translocal networks. In the globalising circumstances, there is an increased possibility for permanently or temporarily working abroad, participation in global communities or meeting partners with different cultural backgrounds. This particularly concerns Estonia after its accession to the European Union, and clearly affects individuals' perspectives regarding their conduct in different fields. Contemporary cross-cultural mobility enables increasing internationalisation of individuals' private lives. However, cross-cultural couples face the additional challenge of (re)organising their lives in a relationship influenced by different cultural identities. The chapter by Paadam, Siilak and Ojamäe focuses on the construction of identities within the process of home creation by culturally mixed couples residing in Estonia. The chapter shows how individual experiences reflect a diversifying palette of modern residential dispositions on the broader scale of the housing field, as well as how partners adapt to and (re)create their homes under new socio-cultural circumstances with a focus on home design, while their tastes, habits and preferences are being influenced by their (current) lifestyles as well as distinct previous cultural experiences.

The transition culture in Estonia that has emphasised materialistic values and professional success still influences people's mentality, and people migrating to Western Europe find themselves in a very different environment. As stated before, post-materialistic values prevail in Western societies, and many welfare states are culturally softer and much more family-, community- and relations-centred compared with former Soviet countries. The chapter by Pajumets and Hearn focuses on couples who have moved from Estonia to Western Europe because of the female party's professional career. While unpaid private domain activities might be a relatively acknowledged lifestyle choice for men in Western Europe, in post-socialist countries masculinity is almost always equated with full-time paid work. The specific focus of the chapter is on the career women's (re)constructions of their domestic husbands' masculine identities, and the links between those micro-political pursuits and more macro-level processes such as freedom of movement, regional economic inequalities and changes in the gender order in the enlarged Europe and the global West more generally.

In the contemporary network society of which Estonia is a part, belonging and communication are not determined by face-to-face contact only, but often take place via the internet. People spend more and more of their time online, which influences their lifestyles and identities. The chapter by Tiidenberg is not specifically about lifestyles in a former Soviet country, but investigates a translocal community where participation is not limited by the country of residence. There is a specific focus on the ways bloggers reflect on their experiences, and how online interactions and the sense of belonging to a community relay the various *narratives of self* that become braided into their identity. This chapter contributes to the understanding of the internet as a space for identity work and construction of social reality.

However, some groups in former socialist countries are not integrated into the global living environment, and their lifestyles are limited by local circumstances. In contrast to the intercultural or translocal lifestyles explored in the previous chapters, Kadri Aavik focuses on the reality of the everyday lives of Russian-speaking women and their restricted lifestyle choices. Narratives of

Russian-speaking women provide a good insight into the impact of transition on the market economy, with new institutional settings coinciding with personal lifestyles – especially in relation to career opportunities. The personal stories offered by these women illustrate the gradual downward mobility, or the upward and downward fluctuations, in careers of women with higher education and good Estonian language proficiency. These skills have not guaranteed stable work opportunities for women in the Estonian labour market in relation to the profession they have studied. In most of cases, the interviewed women have had to choose between accepting less-qualified, low-paid jobs or staying unemployed for at least some time. Although the impact of gender on their career choices is visible in their stories, they do not explicitly express it as one of the reasons for their disadvantaged situation. Belonging to the Russian-speaking community, in contrast, is often used as an explanation for poor opportunities, and in the case of older respondents, age is considered another restrictive factor. According to an existing meta-narrative in the society, Russian-speaking women are considered 'ideal workers' for unskilled jobs. Women with higher education who could expect better choices on the labour market rarely challenge this 'hegemonic metanarrative', as they do not see substantial opportunities for themselves.

Even though there is remarkable diversity among people's choices and opportunities, unpredictable risk factors originating from global trends affect all strata of society. Late modernity's urgency of lifestyle choices brings forward a change in politics, and different social movements have strengthened their position by taking the initiative in finding solutions to global problems (Beck 1992; Giddens 1991). The chapter by Allaste and Lagerspetz focuses on alternative lifestyle choices, and deals with attempts to establish eco-villages in Estonia, which deliberately seek ecologically sustainable, non-hierarchical organisation and intimacy among the participants. The choice to live in alternative communities is both global and local at the same time. Estonian eco-village activism has been influenced by the international eco-village movement's views on ecology and community, and by its New Age-impacted spirituality. By forming alternative lifestyle communities, eco-village activists seek to denounce the capitalist consumer society.

'Late modern' society is a context within which individuals have increased autonomy and choices regarding morality and lifestyle at their disposal. In addition to fundamental choices involving career, marriage and alternative lifestyles, there are also choices concerning leisure habits and consumption preferences. As attempts to discipline people's habits in consumer capitalism are unlikely to succeed (Sulkunen 2009), regulation of consumption – for example, of alcohol use – relies mostly on cultural grounds such as habits and rituals. The chapter by

Kobin explores the distinctive character of socially accepted alcohol-consumption practices and attitudes among young adults in Estonia. Estonia could be described as a country with a 'dry'/Nordic drinking culture. However, the Estonian alcohol culture is showing signs of becoming a 'mixed' culture, where 'Nordic' drinking practices are accompanied by more 'Southern' ones. It might be interpreted as a result of transition from a former socialist country to a country characterised by a free-market economy, access to the internet and travelling, the diffusion of Western hedonistic lifestyles and values, and their integration into youth cultures – including the marketing of alcohol and drinking practices in the media.

While in the 1990s Estonian social scientists were discussing 'the return to the Western world' – after the book of the same name by Lauristin and Vihalemm (1997) was published – now it is possible to conclude that Estonia has arrived at its destination. However, even though our title is now 'Back in the West', it is hardly the same West from which we departed after World War II. In addition, people's everyday lives are also rather different from those in contemporary capitalist societies. Although global trends influence people's lifestyles, local specifics have not lost their importance. This book is about lifestyles in Estonian society, but should be interpreted as a case study representing the majority of CEE countries. Possible lifestyles and identities in all the new capitalist societies have a number of distinctive characteristics compared with societies in the West.

References

Allaste, A.-A. (2008). 'Elustiilid ja väärtused.' [Lifestyles and Values]. Sutrop, M., Pisike, T. (eds.) *Mõtestatud Eesti - ühiseid väärtuseid hoides*. Tallinn: Eesti Keele Sihtasutus, 123-129.

Beck, U. (1992). *Risk Society: Towards a New Modernity*. London: Sage Publications.

Beck, U. and Beck-Gernsheim, E. (1995). *The Normal Chaos of Love*. Cambridge: Polity Press.

Beck, U. and Beck-Gernsheim, E. (2009 [2002]). *Individualization: Institutionalized Individualism and its Social and Political Consequences*. London: Sage.

Beck, U., Giddens, A. and Lash, S. (1994). *Reflexive Modernization: Politics, Traditions and Aesthetics in the Modern Social Order*. Stanford, CA: Stanford University Press.

Bennett, A. (2000). *Popular Music and Youth Culture: Music, Identity and Place*. Basingstoke: Macmillan.

Bennett, A. (2005). *Culture and Everyday Life*. London: Sage.

Blokker, P. (2005). 'Post-Communist modernization, transition studies and diversity in Europe.' *European Journal of Social Theory*, 8(4): 503-525.

Bögenhold, D. (2001). 'Social inequality and the sociology of lifestyle: Material and cultural aspects of social stratification.' *American Journal of Economics and Sociology*, 60(4): 829–847.

Bourdieu, P. (1984). *Distinction: A Source Critique of the Judgement of Taste*. London: Routledge.

Bourdieu, P. (1989 [1979]). *Distinctions: A Social Analysis of the Judgement of Taste*. London: Routledge.

Chambers, I. (1985). *Urban Rhythms: Pop Music and Popular Culture*. Basingstoke: Macmillan.

Chaney, D. (1996). *Lifestyles*. London: Routledge.

Chaney, D. (2002). *Cultural Change and Everyday Life*. Basingstoke: Palgrave.

Clark, T. N. and Lipset, S. M. (1991). 'Are social classes dying?' *International Sociology*, 6(4): 397-410.

Clark, T. N., Lipset, S. M. and Remperl, M. (1993). 'The declining political significance of social class.' *International Sociology*, 8(3): 293-316.

Cockerham, W. C., Rutten, A. and Abel, T. (1997). 'Conceptualizing contemporary health lifestyles: moving beyond Weber.' *The Sociological Quarterly*, 38: 321-42.

Dahl, H. (1997). *Hvis din nabo var en bil. En bog om livsstil*. Kubenhavn: Akademisk Förlag.

Danielsen, A. (2004). 'Lifestyles, class and the field of Fluidum.' *Report from the 1st National Conference of Sociology*, 3, Oslo: 851-872.

Eyal, G., Szeleneyi, I. and Townsley, E. (1998). *Capitalism Without Capitalists: The New Ruling Elites in Eastern Europe*. London: Verso.

Featherstone, M. and Hepworth, M. (1991). 'The Mask of Ageing and the Postmodern Life Course.' Featherstone, M., Hepworth, M. and Turner, B.S. (eds.) *The Body: Social Process and Cultural Theory*. London: Sage.

Frisby, D. and Featherstone, M. (1997). *Simmel on Culture: Selected Writings*. London: Sage.

Geiger, T. (1949). *Die Klassengesellschaft im Schmelztiegel*. Köln-Hagen: Kiepenheuer.

Giddens, A. (1991). *Modernity and Self Identity*. Cambridge: Polity Press.

Grossberg, L. (1996). 'Identity and cultural studies – is that all there is?' Hall, S. and Du Gay, P. (eds.) *Questions of Cultural Identity*. London: Sage.

Hjellbrekke, J. (2000). *Studying Mobility Trajectories in the Norwegian Social Space*. Bergen: University of Bergen, Department of Sociology.

Kalmus, V. and Vihalemm, T. (2008). 'Patterns of continuity and disruption.' *Young*, 16 (3): 251-278.

Kennedy, M. D. (2002). *Cultural Formations of Post-Communism: Emancipation, Transition, Nation, and War*. Minneapolis, MN: University of Minnesota Press.

Kivelä, P. and Siisiäinen, M. (2007). 'Sosiaalinen pääoma ja verkostot – teoriasta empiriaan.' [Social capital and networks – from theory to empirical material] Alanen, L., Salminen, V.-M. and Siisiäinen, M. (eds.) *Sosiaalinen pääoma ja paikalliset käntät*. Jyväskylä: Jyväskylän yliopistopaino.

Koch, M. (1996). 'Class and taste: Bourdieu's contribution to the analysis of social structure and social space.' *International Journal of Contemporary Sociology*, 33(2): 187-202.

Lauristin, M. (2012). 'Eestlaste kultuurisuhte muutused liikumisel siirdeühiskonnast võrguühiskonda.' [Changes in attitudes towards culture on the way from transition society to network society]. Aarelaid-Tart, A. (ed.) *Nullindate kultuur I, teise laine tulemine*. Tallinn: Acta Universitatis Tallinnensis: Socialia.

Lauristin, M. and Vihalemm, P. (eds.) (1997). *Return to the Western World.* Tartu: Tartu University Press.

McHugh, K. E. (2003). 'Three faces of ageism: society, image and place.' *Ageing and Society*, 23(2): 165-185.

Paadam, K., Ojamäe, L. and Siilak, K. (2012). 'Cross-cultural exchanges: intimate relationships and transforming societies.' Miller, R. and Day, G. (eds.) *The Evolution of European Identities: Biographical Approaches.* London: Palgrave Macmillan, 211-232.

Pakulski, J. (1993). 'The dying class or Marxist class theory?' *International Sociology*, 8(3): 279-292.

Refsing K. (1998). 'Gender identity and gender role patterns in cross-cultural marriages: the Japanese-Danish case.' Breger, R. and Hill, R. (eds.) *Cross-Cultural Marriage: Identity and Choice*. Oxford: Berg, 193-208.

Reimer, B. (1995). 'Youth and modern lifestyles.' Fornäs, J. and Bolin, G. (eds.) *Youth Culture in Late Modernity*. London: Sage.

Saar, E. (ed.) (2011). *Towards a Normal Stratification Order: Actual and Perceived Social Stratification in post-Socialist Estonia*. Frankfurt: Peter Lang.

Shildrick, T. and MacDonald, R. (2006). 'In defence of subculture: young people, leisure and social divisions.' *Journal of Youth Studies*, 9(2): 125-140.

Soerensen, A.B. (1991). 'On the usefulness of class analysis in research on social mobility and socioeconomic inequality.' *Acta Sociologica*, 34: 71-87.

Stark, D. and Bruszt, L. (1998). *Postsocialist Pathways: Transforming Politics and Property in East Central Europe.* Cambridge: Cambridge University Press.

Sulkunen, P. (2009). *The Saturated Society: Governing Risk and Lifestyles in Consumer Culture.* London: Sage.

Sztompka, P. (2004). 'The trauma of social change: a case of postcommunist societies.' Alexander, J. C., Eyerman, R., Giesen, B., Smelser, N. J. and Sztompka, P. (eds.) *Cultural Trauma and Collective Identity.* Berkeley, CA: University of California Press, 155-195.

Veblen, T. (1994 [1924]). *The Theory of the Leisure Class: An Economic Study of Institutions*. New York: Mentor Books.

Vihalemm, T. and Kalmus, V. (2008). 'Mental structures in transition culture: differentiating patterns of identities and values in Estonia'. *East European Politics and Societies*, 22(4): 901-927.

Vonderau, A. and Schröder, I. W. (eds.) (2008). *Changing Economies and Changing Identities in Postsocialist Eastern Europe.* Berlin: LIT Verlag.

Weber, M. (1978 [1922]). 'The distribution of power within the political community: class, status, party.' Weber, M. *Economy and Society: An Outline of Interpretive Sociology.* Berkeley, CA: University of California Press.

Williams, R. (1980). *Problems in Materialism and Culture*. London: New Left Books/Verso.

Zukin, S. and Smith Maguire, J. (2004). 'Consumers and consumption.' *Annual Review of Sociology*, 30: 173-197.

PART I

CONTEXTUALISING LIFESTYLE TRENDS IN ESTONIA

From plan to market: major trends in life satisfaction and subjective well-being

Leeni Hansson

Introduction

Since the late 1980s, the post-socialist countries of Central and Eastern European, as well as the countries of the former Soviet Union, have undergone a process of radical political and economic reforms. Estonia, like other Baltic countries, witnessed several transitions – from totalitarianism to democracy, from a centrally planned economy to a free-market economy, from a society characterised by shortage economy to a consuming society (Lauristin and Vihalemm 1997; Keller and Vihalemm 2003). The main challenge of the period was to build up new institutions of an independent state and to change the ineffective plan economy, which was characterised by high centrality and low freedom of choice, into modern Western-style market economy. Social scientists have referred to the period of transitions as 'returning to the Western world' (Lauristin and Vihalemm 1997) or returning to the 'consuming West' (Keller and Vihalemm 2003).

In the beginning, the collapse of the Soviet political and economic system created high expectations, as the new social order and free market were expected to generate economic growth and consumer freedom, and accordingly, increase well-being. However, most of the studies dealing with transition countries have revealed that contrary to the expectations, the populations of these countries had to pay for the macro-level socio-economic transformation with their well-being (Easterlin 2009; Zagorski 2011; Selezneva 2011; Ainsaar 2011; Abbott and Wallace 2012). In these countries, the mean subjective well-being scores which, in the 1980s, were already lower than in Western countries, decreased in the early 1990s. The share of people who considered themselves the losers of transition was rather high, and only a small share of people perceived themselves as the winners (Narusk and Hansson 1999).

It is well known that different countries and country groups passed through transition reforms at different speeds and with different success. For example, comparative studies have revealed that, compared to other former Soviet countries, the transition strategies of the three Baltic states – Estonia, Latvia and Lithuania – were relatively successful, and compared to the early 1990s, by the end of the 1990s their macroeconomic indicators had significantly improved (Hamm *et al.* 2012; Abbott and Wallace 2012). However, despite positive macro-level economic development, the Eurostat data showed that in the Baltic countries, real wages were still lower than at the end of the 1980s. Thus, in spite of the fact that macro-economic indicators were improving, on the everyday level, adaptation to the reforms was a rather painful experience characterised not only by a breakdown of conventional practices and lifestyles, but also by rising economic inequality (Easterlin 2009). Accordingly, while speaking of the 1990s we can speak of a certain turning point that made many people find solutions to new problems they had to face, like the loss of a job or need for requalification, loss of income and the need for changes in the structure of the family budget, changes in accustomed lifestyles, *etc.*

Unlike the 1990s, the turn of the century was characterised by the positive macroeconomic changes that resulted in stable and fast economic growth and significant improvement of the labour market situation (Eamets 2011). For instance, instead of unemployment problems characteristic of many 'old' European countries, the unemployment rate in Estonia was amongst the lowest in EU and several branches of economy experienced labour shortage. Positive changes in the labour market, in turn, resulted in improvement in material security and the living standard of the population (Trumm and Kasearu 2009). Consequently, the increase in material security had a positive impact on consumption opportunities and lifestyle choices, including the access to more expensive leisure activities such as travelling and spending one's vacation away from home (*ibid.*). Furthermore, according to the survey conducted by the World Bank in 2006, the Baltic countries, with Estonia on top, belonged to the group of new EU member states where, compared with the late 1980s, populations were more satisfied with the economic situation. However, the world financial crisis and recession hit the three Baltic countries, including Estonia, harder than the 'old' European countries.

The complexity of the period of transition from plan to market makes it most interesting to explore in more detail the extent to which the macro-level radical changes of the period were reflected in life satisfaction and subjective well-being. Examining Estonia as an example representing former Soviet countries, the present article will focus on the changes in subjective well-being related to different historical periods of time – from the last decade of the Soviet regime to the end of the first decade of the present century. The main research questions are: (1) What happened to individual well-being during the period of transition? (2) To what extent did the turning points brought about by macro-level changes influence subjective well-being? (3) To what extent were individual preferences and attitudes towards life choices related to subjective well-being?

The study is based on the data collected within five nationally representative population surveys 'Work, Family, and Leisure' (WFL), carried out since 1985 with circa five-year intervals till 2008. Due to fast and extensive changes in the political and economic system of the country, the years in which the population surveys were conducted were not just five points of time, but the years also denoted significant turns in Estonian society and turning points in the everyday life of Estonian people. As independent statehood was restored in Estonia in 1991, the WFL survey of 1985 was conducted when the country was still part of the Soviet Union. The early 1990s in Estonia – the first years of independence – were characterised by radical political reforms and an unstable economic situation. Similar states of affairs were characteristic of the majority of Eastern European countries. The favorable economic trends of the late 1990s and early 2000s, particularly Estonia's acceptance into the European Union in 2004 brought about significant improvements to the economic situation of Estonian people. The last survey in the WFL series was carried out at the end of 2008 – the period of world economic and financial crises; however, the social impact of this recession was not yet fully experienced in Estonia.

Understanding subjective well-being

Adaptation to macro-level changes and the outcomes of personal decisions and choices can be measured by general life satisfaction and level of subjective well-being. By the term *subjective well-being* we mean an individual's personal assessment of the state of his or her life situation at a particular point of time (Veenhoven 1991; Diener and Diener 1995). The term 'subjective well-being' is often used interchangeably with the terms like life satisfaction and happiness (Ervasti and Venetoklis 2010).

The concept of subjective well-being was first developed in psychology, but it has gained increasing interest in economics and sociology as well. Among psychologists, the studies on subjective well-being have a long tradition, especially studies with the focus on the relationship between personality traits and well-being. Economists have traditionally been interested in the effect of objective economic factors on well-being, such as employment status, income, consumption patterns, *etc.* (see Easterlin 2001, Stutzer and Frey 2003; Ferrer-i-Carbonell 2005). Sociologists in turn have mostly been interested in the relationship between subjective well-being and social context (Böhnke 2007; Kroll 2011, *etc.*). Today we can also speak of an interdisciplinary approach in the studies on subjective well-being that is situated on the edge of psychology, sociology and economics (Selezneva 2011).

Until the turn of the present century, the studies on subjective well-being were mostly based on empirical data regarding developed Western countries (*e.g.* Easterlin 2001, Hansson *et al.* 2005). Due to the limited number of representative datasets, the number of studies on well-being in the post-socialist countries was scarce. As the situation in the post-socialist countries is very different from the one in developed Western countries, it was understood that the conclusions on subjective well-being determinants found for developed Western countries could not be automatically transformed to the post-socialist countries (Selezneva 2011). The understanding resulted in the increasing interest of the well-being studies concerning the countries of Central and Eastern Europe as well as the countries that had gained independence from the former Soviet Union (Easterlin 2009; Ainsaar 2011; Zagorski 2011; Abbott *et al.* 2011, *etc.*). Eastern and Central European countries and the former Soviet countries do not form a homogeneous cluster, as these countries differ by political and historical background and cultural values, as well as by the speed and outcome of reforms (Selezneva 2011). Accordingly, it is most interesting to compare how different transition paths have influenced subjective well-being on the individual level.

In comparative studies, the cross-country differences in well-being are mainly explained by country characteristics and resources that countries possess to meet the needs of the population (*e.g.* Veenhoven and Kalmijn 2003; Böhnke 2007; Minkov 2009). The most commonly used macro-level indicators by which the general well-being of a population is measured are the human development index, GDP per capita, purchasing power, employment and unemployment rates, social expenditure policies, housing and environmental conditions, life expectancy, *etc.* National human development reports and studies by the Word Bank can be named as the best examples of well-being studies using national macro-level indicators. However, several authors (*e.g.* van Praag *et al.* 2003; Easterlin 2009; Abbott and Wallace 2012, *etc.)* have argued that macro-level indicators are often weakly associated with people's experiences and perceptions, and do not fully reflect their sense of subjective well-being. According to Erik Allardt's approach, general well-being is related to objective resources and subjective assessments in the dimensions of having (material resources), loving (social relationships), and being (needs related to personal development) (Allardt 1993). Therefore, positive changes in macro-level indicators of a country, for instance improvement of general economic situation or improvement in (un)employment rates do not necessarily mean symmetrical changes in life satisfaction and subjective well-being on the individual level (D'Acci 2011).

A separate approach to well-being research was developed according to which well-being should be studies by asking people how they actually feel. In subjective well-being studies, for instance in cross-national comparative studies like the World Value Surveys, the European Social Survey (waves 1 and 2) and the Eurobarometer Surveys, subjective well-being is measured with a single-item variable of self-reported life satisfaction (see Lucas and Donnellan 2012). However, several studies (*e.g.* van Praag *et al.* 2003; Stutzer and Frey 2006) have found that subjective well-being is influenced by various factors like having a stimulating and secure job, stable family life, supportive informal network, level of income, acceptable standard of living, *etc*. Accordingly, several authors have suggested that subjective well-being should not be dealt with as a single-item measure of satisfaction with life but rather as a multi-dimensional construct or 'an umbrella term' (van Praag *et al.* 2003; Diener 2006; Easterlin 2009; Chmiel *et al.* 2012) that comprises both overall life satisfaction as well as satisfaction with different domains of life. The studies on subjective well-being (that in addition to general life satisfaction measures, have also included domain satisfaction measures) have used different sets of domain indicators, but most commonly used components of multi-item well-being measures are satisfaction with financial situation, satisfaction with work/job, and satisfaction with family life (see Cummins 1996; van Praag *et al.* 2003; Selezneva 2011, *etc.*).

Thus, the most frequently used domain variable in subjective well-being studies and the key component of a multi-item well-being measure is satisfaction with one's financial situation. Furthermore, satisfaction with financial situation is considered a better predictor of subjective well-being than the objective measure of income (Ferrer-i-Carbonell 2005; Ervasti and Venetoklis 2010; Abbott *et al.* 2011). However, several studies have revealed that the correlation between financial satisfaction and subjective well-being is stronger in countries with lower GDP and weaker in economically developed countries (Diener and Diener 1995). And second, in the majority of cases satisfaction with financial situation depends on earlier experience or on social surroundings and reference group, *i.e.* on the feeling that a person is (is not) as well off as his/her co-workers, peers, friends, kin, or as (s)he expected to be (Abbott and Wallace 2012).

Thus, satisfaction with financial situation is closely, but not exclusively, related to subjective well-being. A strong relationship between work/job satisfaction and subjective well-being has also received considerable attention (for an overview, see Heller *et al.* 2002). First of all, the studies have shown that there is a significant well-being gap between the labour market participants and those outside of the labour force (Clark 2009; Ervasti and Venetoklis 2010; Selezneva 2011). It is shown that paid work not only provides the funds for making a normal living, improving living conditions and choosing preferable lifestyle options, but also provides a certain social status and feeling of belonging (Headey

2008). Furthermore, in the post-socialist countries in particular, it is possible to observe a certain stigmatisation of individuals out of the labour force (Selezneva 2011).

The third important key component often used in the measures of subjective well-being is satisfaction with family life and personal relationships (Diener and Diener 1995; Pinquart and Silbereisen 2010). According to several studies, married individuals are more satisfied with their lives and report higher level of subjective well-being than individuals who were never married, who in turn report greater life satisfaction than individuals after marriage or partnership dissolution, *i.e.*, divorced, separated, or widowed persons (Stutzer and Frey 2006; Soons and Kalmijn 2009).

In the studies of the 1990s, satisfaction with leisure and satisfaction with housing conditions were rarely used as components of multi-item well-being measures. However, in the latest studies (Sagiv and Schwartz 2000; Snir and Harpaz 2002; Pinquart and Silbereisen 2010) satisfaction with leisure has gained more attention, and it has also been included in the compound subjective well-being measure as one of the important life domains.

In Diener's (1984) conceptual model of subjective well-being, all components can be considered as correlated. However, there are two different correlation patterns observed. The *bottom-up model* says that the level of subjective well-being is determined by the level of satisfaction with individual life domains. The *top-down model*, in contrast, implies that individuals who, due to specific personality characteristics, experience a higher level of general subjective well-being, also feel more satisfied with specific life domains (for more detail, see Chmiel *et al.* 2012).

The latest studies have posed a discussion as to whether satisfaction with different life domains has a cumulative effect on subjective well-being. One school of research suggests that if an individual is mainly focused on one of the domains of life, for example a person is either highly work-oriented or family-oriented, (s)he may only need success in this particular life domain to be satisfied with life (Cummins 1996; Plagnol and Scott 2011). On the other hand, individuals may compensate for the lack of success in one domain by deriving satisfaction from additional commitment in other domains (Snir and Harpaz 2002; Rojas 2006). Thus, we can look at subjective well-being as a socially constructed phenomenon.

The dominant theory of subjective well-being characteristic of the studies of the 1970 and 1980s – the *set-point theory* – suggested that well-being is associated first of all with personality traits, and therefore adult persons have more or less stable level of subjective well-being. Accordingly, the set-point theory suggests that different circumstances, life events and individual life-style choices can produce only temporary changes in well-being level (for a review, see Clark *et al.* 2008). The studies of the late 1990s and early 2000s based on representative data have contested the set-point theory. These studies have revealed that personality is not the only factor influencing well-being but a variety of contextual and situational factors, especially significant *turning points*, either on societal level or on the individual level can also bring about significant changes in the level of subjective well-being (Headey 2008; Plagnol and Scott 2011).

The use of the term 'turning point' differs between authors. Wheaton and Gotlib (1997) define a turning point as a change in direction in the life course that *'has the long-term impact of altering the probability of life destinations'* (Wheaton and Gotlib 1997: 5). Thus, according to the definition above, turning points could refer both to society level changes as well as to the normative life events, such as graduating from a university, getting or changing a job, becoming a parent, moving to another country, *etc.* as such transitions also involve adjustment to new social roles and alter the life trajectories (Headey *et al.* 2010).

Today, there seems to be a broad consensus in the research literature indicating that transition from one social order to another lowers the level of well-being and life satisfaction (for an overview, see Dabalen and Paul 2011). In the one hand, it is explained by growing inequality of income or incomplete adaptation of certain population groups (the elderly, minority groups, *etc.*), and on the other hand, by the fact that the subjective well-being level reacts more strongly to negative news than to positive ones (Selezneva 2011).

Methods and data

In the present study, I used the data from five nationally representative mailed surveys on general living conditions 'Work, Family, and Leisure' (WFL) conducted in Estonia from 1985 to 2008 with ca 5-year intervals. Thus, the WFL surveys cover the time span from the Soviet period, through the period of reacquisition of independent statehood and radical political and economic reforms that brought about significant economic decline to the period of economic recovery and accession to the European Union. The primary advantage of using the WFL data is that the data of the five surveys are comparable, and allow the conducting of dynamic analyses of continuities and changes in life satisfaction and subjective well-being over a rather long period of time – 23 years. The surveys also recorded demographic characteristics and respondents' opinions on important aspects of a life, work-related and family-related values and beliefs, motivational goals, *etc.* The size of the samples of the WFL surveys averaged from 1500-2000 individuals per survey. As the 1985 survey sample contained only individuals in active employment (in the USSR for the working age population employment was obligatory), for the present study the samples of all WFL surveys were restricted to actively employed prime age (25-65) respondents.

As was mentioned in the majority of comparative surveys, subjective well-being is explored by a single item measure – self-reported general satisfaction with life. The WFL survey question concerning general life satisfaction was nearly identical to the one used in the World Value Survey: *How satisfied are you with your life, all things considered?*, the responses ranging from 1 = *not satisfied at all* to 5 = *completely satisfied.* In addition, in the WFL surveys, each set of questions on a certain life domain included satisfaction questions. Thus, it was possible to observe how satisfied the respondents were with their family life, job, financial situation, housing conditions, and leisure in different periods of time. For the analysis, a compound measure of subjective well-being was constructed by summarising the variable of general life satisfaction, and five domain satisfaction items. Accordingly, the compound measure varies from 6 to 30; in which lower scores indicate lower level of subjective well-being, and higher scores signify higher level of well-being.

Respondents' attitudes towards their future life prospects were measured by agreement or disagreement responses to two statements: (1) *What my life will be like depends only on me*, and (2) *A person's life is determined mainly by destiny.*

In the analysis, the main accent was put not on the levels of satisfaction but on the changes in life satisfaction and subjective well-being. It has to be brought to notice that the WFL survey of 2008 was conducted before the impact of the financial crises was felt in Estonia.

Changing life satisfaction and domain satisfaction

It is common knowledge that the Soviet system was characterised by full employment, free education and healthcare and relatively low level of economic inequality. According to the Soviet ideology, the members of the society were expected to be satisfied with the regime and with their lives. On the other hand, the Soviet system was characterised by bureaucratic order, suppressed human rights, low level of personal freedom, and limited options of lifestyle choice that together with shortage of housing and even indispensable commodities made it difficult to be satisfied. Accordingly, the fall of the Soviet regime and regaining independence created high expectations and were supported by the majority of population. However, high expectations were soon replaced by disillusionment caused by unexpected negative outcomes of transformation.

In the present study my main interest was to explore to what extent the macro-level socio-economic changes related to transition from a Soviet economy to a free-market economy affected subjective well-being of Estonian people. In the first step, I tried to measure how strongly the changes in life satisfaction and satisfaction with major domains of life – family life, job, housing conditions, financial situation, and leisure time – were associated with the turning points in the Estonian society. And second, using the composed measure of general subjective well-being time trends in well-being in various population groups were analysed.

The period of 'transition shock'

The analysis of the data of the five WFL surveys revealed that in the period under review – from the mid-1980s to the end of the first decade of the present century – it was possible to differentiate between two well-defined periods characterised by different trends in subjective well-being. The first period – from the 'Singing Revolution'[1] of the late-1980s to the mid-1990s – was characterised as the period of dismantling the institutions of the Soviet system and laying foundation of the newly independent state (Lauristin and Vihalemm 1997). However, as Estonia had chosen a neo-liberal path of reforms and individuals were left to their own devices, on the individual level the decade was perceived as a period of transition shock characterised by significant decline both in general life satisfaction as well as in satisfaction with several life domains. For instance, while in the mid-1980s, 46 percent of respondents reported that in general terms they were satisfied with their lives, then by 1993 the share of respondents satisfied with life had fallen to 31 percent.

The majority of studies have shown that satisfaction with one's financial situation is positively related to general life satisfaction and it is used as one of the main components of subjective well-being measures. Most significant changes in satisfaction with one's financial situation took also place between the mid 1980s and early 1990s while the share of respondents satisfied with financial situation fell from over 30 percent in 1985 to as low as 8 percent in 1993. Furthermore, in 1993 the majority of respondents mentioned that economic constraints and shortage of money were their major personal problems.

As mentioned above, reforms of the transition period brought about radical changes in the labour market structures with an increase in the rates of unemployment and underemployment. Considering the modification of the labour market, changes in employment relations, mismatches between the qualifications of the employees and the qualifications required by the job, and growing insecurity quite characteristic of the early 1990s, it is surprising that compared

1 The 'Singing Revolution' is a name commonly used for peaceful mass events that took place between 1987 and 1991, and that lead to the restoration of independent statehood of Estonia.

to the mid-1980s, during the period of the 'transition shock', the share of respondents who described themselves as satisfied with their jobs had not decreased.

In the Soviet period, satisfaction with housing conditions was the second lowest after satisfaction with financial situation. Relatively low satisfaction with housing conditions can be explained by the fact that under the Soviet regime free housing market did not exist, and housing was administratively distributed and controlled (Paadam 2000, Ojamäe 2009). Accordingly, there was very little people could do to improve their living conditions. The ownership reform, emergence of free housing market and an increase in the options of obtaining a home resulted in a steady increase in the level of satisfaction with housing conditions.

Although in the 1990s there were significant changes in Estonians' family formation patterns and family/household composition, satisfaction with family was another domain that was practically unaffected by the transition period. Thus, one could suggest that in a period of radical changes in the society that had negative impact on several spheres of life, people preferred to relay on traditional and secure values, first of all on the family. On the other hand, the result does not rule out the possibility that the notion of the family has changed, and in the mid-1980s and in the 2000s the family was defined differently.

The decline in the satisfaction with leisure was obviously related to deterioration of the economic situation, as most leisure time activities needed some extra spending.

To conclude, the results of the study showed that in the mid-1980s and early 1990s satisfaction with life was positively associated with satisfaction within each of the five domains, but most distinctly with two life domains – family life and financial situation.

The period of stabilisation

Contrary to the early 1990s, on the macro-level the late 1990s and early 2000s were characterised by stabilisation of economy, considerable improvement of labour market situation, and decreasing uncertainty. Furthermore, among population the raised expectation towards the EU membership (Estonia joined EU in 2004) and hopes for positive outcomes related to accession increased the feeling of security. Accordingly, similar to the results of the Eurobarometer surveys (see Raelo 2009) and European Values Studies (see Ainsaar 2011) the WFL surveys showed that the share of respondents satisfied with their lives increased steadily and by the turn of the century the level of life satisfaction of the mid-1980s' had recovered, and by the end of the decade the share of respondents satisfied with their lives had practically doubled.

It is commonly known that in the countries in transition, people are mostly not satisfied with their income and material situation. However, since the second half of the 1990s, it was possible to notice a certain upward trend in the satisfaction with one's financial situation but it took more than 20 years till satisfaction with financial situation reached the level of the mid-1980s. Accordingly, the satisfaction with financial situation reflected clearly the changes taken place in Estonian economy. Like in the period of transition shock, in the period of stabilisation the changes in the satisfaction with leisure followed the pattern of satisfaction with the financial situation. Obviously, an increase of the economic resources in the 2000s provided a better access to quality leisure. Thus, like satisfaction with financial situation, satisfaction with leisure also followed a U-shape change with a decline in the shock period of most radical reforms, and an increase in the period of stabilisation.

There seemed to be two domains of life where one could not notice any influence of the changes and instability related to the transition period – job and family life. Both in the period of insecurity as well as in the period of stabilisation, satisfaction with these two domains of life was relatively high. At the same time, the association of general life satisfaction and favourable housing conditions increased. Furthermore, in the 2000s, there was a stronger connection between general life satisfaction and satisfaction with housing conditions than with the financial situation.

Figure 1 presents the trends in mean scores for general life satisfaction and five domain satisfactions for different periods of time. As the data indicate, in all five surveys, respondents reported highest level of satisfaction with work and family life, and the lowest level – with financial situation. The mean scores for satisfaction with life as a whole, for major life domains, and the changes in the scores in the period of 1985-2008 are presented in APPENDIX I.

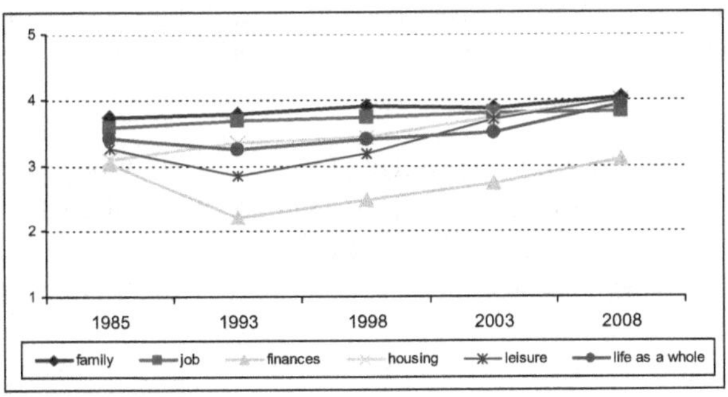

Fig. 1: Satisfaction with life as a whole, and satisfaction with life domains, mean scales for different periods of time (5 = completely satisfied ... 1 = not satisfied at all)

In sum, the present study revealed that the changes in general life satisfaction and the domain specific satisfaction reflect different political and economic processes – turning points that have taken place in the Estonian society since the mid-1980s.

Gender differences in life satisfaction

In the next stage of the analysis, the changes in general life satisfaction and with five domain satisfactions were analysed separately for men and women.

Comparative cross-country studies on gender differences in general life satisfaction have yielded contradictory results. For instance, Inglehart's (1990) study on 16 countries found that among women life satisfaction was somewhat higher than among men. A study by Böhnke and Kohler (2008), in turn, revealed that men are slightly more satisfied with life than women. In the present study, gender differences in satisfaction with life as a whole were insignificant. However, we could observe significant gender differences in satisfaction with several domains of life.

Fig. 2: Changes in the level of satisfaction with job and financial situation among Estonian men and women, mean scores for different periods (5 = fully satisfied ... 1 = not satisfied at all)

The findings of the studies conducted in advanced Western countries (*e.g.* Clark 2009) have shown that, in general, men are less satisfied with work than women. The WFL survey data did not confirm these results, as there were practically no differences between Estonian men and women in their satisfaction with job – neither in the mid-1980s nor in the 2000s. However, Figure 2 presents results of the analysis that might have been hard to predict. Although men and women reported an equally high level of job satisfaction, there were significant gender differences in their satisfaction with financial situation (Figure 2). In all five WFL surveys, women were less satisfied with their financial situation then men, and in the period under observation the gender gap in satisfaction with financial situation even increased, rather than diminished. Furthermore, while in 2008 men reported considerably higher satisfaction with their financial situation than in the mid-1980s; among women the satisfaction with their financial situation was even lower in 2008 than it had been in the mid-1980s. In Estonia women's lower level of satisfaction with income and economic resources can mostly be explained by vertical and horizontal segregation and increasing gender pay gap that according to the Eurostat statistics is the highest among the EU countries (Gender pay gap statistics 2010). Thus, we could say that in Estonia women's contribution to society is still less rewarded than men's contribution.

As to family life, the study revealed that in both time periods – the period of transition shock and the period of stabilisation – men reported a higher level of satisfaction with family life than women. The findings confirm the results of several previous studies carried out in Estonia (*e.g.* Narusk and Kandolin 1997; Gender Equality Monitoring 2005, *etc.*) and can most obviously be explained by a rather traditional approach to family roles that were, and still are, largely prevailing in Estonia, with a persisting belief that the male partner's role in the family is to be a breadwinner, and he has the right to rest at home while the female partner's role is to care for the family and the home regardless of whether she is employed or not.

The survey data provided also another interesting result. Although besides significant differences in the satisfaction with their financial situation, women also reported a lower level of satisfaction with family life and leisure; we could not find any significant differences in their self-reported satisfaction with life as a whole.

Changes in subjective well-being

As mentioned above, some life domains may have different weight for an individual than others. Thus, using the general life satisfaction item and five domain specific items we constructed a general measure of subjective well-being, with 6 indicating the lowest level of well-being and 30 – the highest level.

Figure 3 shows that there were significant changes in the general subjective well-being level in the period from the mid-1980s to the end of the first decade of the present century. The study revealed that the reported levels of subjective well-being declined in the period between the mid-1980s and early 1990, followed by relatively steady increase in the period of economic stabilisation. Thus, concerning the 2000s, we can speak of a considerably higher level of subjective well-being than in the Soviet period, or in the period of radical reforms of the 1990s. As satisfaction with financial situation is considered to be the most important component of a multi-item well-being measure, it is obvious that the unexpected decline in financial satisfaction characteristic of the early 1990s pushed down the general subjective well-being level, and on the contrary – increase in the reported satisfaction with financial situation characteristic of the turn of the century, resulted in increase in subjective well-being.

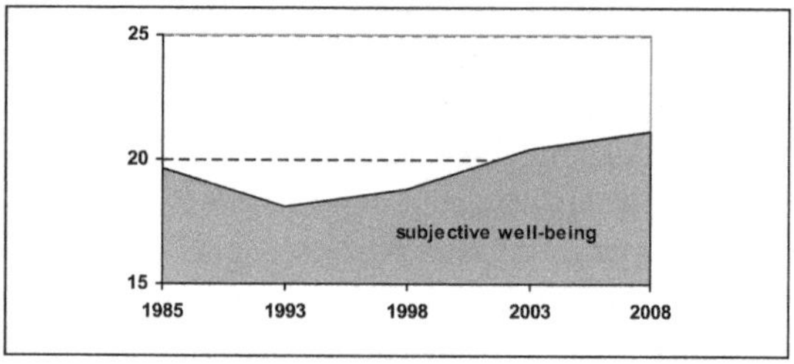

Fig. 3: *Changes in subjective well-being in 1985-2008 (scale 6-30)*

The results of the analyses showed that in all WFL surveys, subjective well-being level of men was somewhat higher than that of women that most likely could be explained by men's higher average income and higher level of satisfaction with their financial situation.

Previous studies (*e.g.* Zagorski 2011) have shown that life satisfaction and well-being deteriorate with age. In the present study, the changes in the effect of age upon well-being were of interest. The analysis revealed that in 1985, there were statistically significant differences in subjective well-being between the age groups but quite unexpectedly it was the older age group (55 and older), who reported the highest level of well-being. In the next two surveys we could observe no significant age-related differences in the level of well-being. However, in the survey of 2008 respondents of the oldest age group report the lowest level of well-being. One possible explanation concerning the changes in the effect of age is that they reflect the processes of adaptation to the radical transformation and a new social context that was easier for younger and usually better educated people, often called 'the generation of the winners' (Narusk and Hansson 1999), and considerably more problematic for the older generation.

One of the interesting results of the study was that in the Soviet period, years of education were not associated with subjective well-being, and there were practically no differences in the well-being level of respondents with different educational backgrounds. However, from the early 1990s onwards higher (university) level education started to play a significant role in the level of subjective well-being. For instance, in the 2000s, the differences in subject well-being of respondents with lower levels of education – basic or secondary education – were not significant, but the differences between the above mentioned two education groups and those with university or college level education were highly significant. On the one hand, the changes in the role of education in the level of subjective well-being reflect the changes in the value of education in the society (see Raudsepp, Tart and Heinla in the present book). On the other hand, in the 1980s, education level was not related to income. In the Soviet economy, wages and salaries were more dependent on the economic sector than on one's qualification or job status. Today the average income of those with a university degree is considerably higher than of those with basic or secondary level education. Furthermore, better educated individuals are usually engaged in more interesting jobs and accordingly report higher satisfaction with job. Thus, we could suggest that objective material conditions and satisfaction with financial situation, as well as job satisfaction are associated with, and raise the subjective well-being level of better educated people.

Attitudes towards life choices

The transition period and the new social order brought about a diversity of new options but also an increasing importance of individuals' choices, aspirations and decisions about their own lives. Giddens (1991) has referred to individuals' decisions for making choices among a diversity of options and taking an active part in shaping their life chances and well-being as *life politics*. Thus, in the next stage of the analysis the focus was shifted from external factors like the changes in the socio-economic context to internal factors like changes in the attitudes towards possible life choices. The survey data of 1993-2008[2] allowed us to explore the extent to which changes in subjective well-being were associated with individual preferences and attitudes, *i.e.* whether Estonian people, while making substantial decisions that might affect their lives, prefer to rely on their own, or they prefer to rely on destiny and good luck.

The analyses revealed that the share of both men and women with the high perception of being their own masters, and who were convinced that their future and realisation of their life goals depended mostly on their own personal choices and decisions had since the early 1990s somewhat increased (among men from 80 to 87 percent, among women from 68 to 78 percent), and the share of individuals with low life control, who presumed that one's life and future were determined by destiny – significantly decreased (among men from 45 to 29 per-

2 In the WFL survey of 1985, the set of questions on individual preferences and attitudes was missing.

cent; among women from 60 to 32 percent). Thus, one could conclude that within the past 15 years, perception of life control and understanding of individual responsibility has increased, and today the majority of people place importance rather on personal efforts and life choices than on destiny and good luck.

When the level of subjective well-being among representatives of the self-confident group and those who place confidence mostly in destiny was compared, one could see that individuals who were oriented towards personal responsibility and their own decisions were more likely to experience a higher level of satisfaction with different domains of life and, accordingly, a higher level of subjective well-being irrespective of the time period. In contrast, relying mainly on good luck and destiny seems to be negatively associated with subjective well-being. One possible explanation of the result is that for self-confident individuals it was easier to adjust to the new demands of the changing social context. On the other hand, the finding might also suggest that individuals, who are well adjusted in the society and experience high level of well-being, are more likely to see their success and achievements as the outcome of their own life style choices and decisions. And on the contrary, low level of subjective well-being is by individuals obviously rarely perceived as the result of their own mistakes or misjudgements of opportunities but willingly related to bad luck – extrinsic forces and unfortunate circumstances.

Conclusion

In Estonia, like in the majority of former socialist countries, the reforms of the late 1980s and early 1990s brought about not only intended but also unintended consequences in many areas of life. In the present study, Estonia was dealt with as an example of former Soviet countries to document the extent to which radical socio-economic reforms of the transition period, which can be dealt with as significant turning points in the society, were reflected in the changes in life satisfaction and subjective well-being on the individual level.

The evidence presented in the article confirms that the level of subjective well-being and the ways in which it is constructed vary markedly in different periods of time characterised by rapidly changing social context. The study indicates that the period of disillusionment, uncertainty and limited choices characteristic of the first decade of transformation, witnessed a significant decline in subjective well-being, whereas the period of stabilisation brought about an increase in well-being.

Some findings of the study support the standard findings in previous subjective well-being research but several results mentioned above deserve a deeper look, in particular, the effect of social changes on satisfaction with different domains of life. For instance, the findings of the study confirm the findings of previous studies (*e.g.* Selezneva 2011) that there is an apparent correlation between satisfaction with material conditions and the subjective well-being level. As satisfaction with one's financial situation is a relative measure, it is usually assessed by comparing it with a reference group of friends, peers, and relatives, or with a reference point of time. Accordingly, in the mid-1980s, *i.e.* in the Soviet period, rather moderate general income level of population was combined with relatively low economic inequality. The low income inequality, in turn, ensured fairly high level of subjective well-being. In the 1990s, the relatively low income level of the majority of population together with the emergence of a well-off reference group, *i.e.* a group of affluent people, was well reflected in the significant decline of subjective well-being. Economic growth and the improvement in average satisfaction with income and material resources, characteristic of the 2000s, brought along an increase in subjective well-being. Two other domain satisfactions – satisfaction with housing conditions and satisfaction with leisure – are also indirectly related to financial situation as only the sufficiency of economic resources can facilitate access to lifestyle choices related to quality leisure and quality housing. Satisfaction with housing conditions and leisure are relatively new components not very often used in subjective well-being measures. However, the present study suggests that the importance of these two domains for general life satisfaction and subjective well-being seems to be increasing.

Comparison of the survey data of different decades revealed that there were only two domains of life – satisfaction with work and satisfaction with family life – in which one could speak of relative stability of satisfaction level, especially in the period from the mid-1980s to the end of the 1990s. Thus, among Estonian people, family and work seem to be basic values subjective well-being is based on, irrespective of time or changes in the social context.

The study confirms that while coming from the Soviet system, some social groups had more difficulties in adaptation to the new social context than others, and in the background of general increase in subjective well-being their well-being level stayed lower than that of the reference groups. In both periods of time – in the period of insecurity as well as in the period of stabilisation – women experienced lower level of subjective well-being than men. Thus, one could conclude that the gender equality policies worked out and introduced in the last decades have apparently not been efficient for increasing the feeling of subjective well-being among women. One interpretation of gender differences in subjective well-being is that the increased gendered pay gap in Estonia today is one of the largest among the EU countries.

According to the set-point theory that is often used as a theoretical basis for the studies carried out in Western countries, the level of subjective well-being is expected to be stable and only briefly influenced by different life events. The present study revealed that there were significant differences in the level of general life satisfaction, several domain satisfactions, and subjective well-being in the surveys carried out in different periods of time that were characterised by major macro-level changes, and significant changes in the everyday life of people. Accordingly, based on the findings one could suggest that for the post-socialist countries, that for a relatively short period of time have come through rapid and essential changes in society, the turning-point approach is a more suitable theoretical basis for analysing subjective well-being data than the stability based set-point theory.

The analysis of the survey data showed that in the context of subjective well-being it is not only structural characteristics but also basic values and attitudes towards life prospects that might play a significant role in general subjective well-being. The data used in the article were random cross sections, therefore most suitable for analysing time trends. However, in developing a deeper understanding of the association between attitudes towards life choices and subjective well-being, qualitative studies are likely to be more useful than the cross-sectional survey data.

References

Abbott, P. and Wallace, C. (2012). 'Rising economic prosperity and social quality: the case of new member states of the European Union.' *Social Indicators Research.* [Online]. Available: http://link.springer.com/article/10.1007/s11205-012-9992-0 (2012, October 18).

Abbott, P., Wallace, C. and Sapsford, R. (2011). 'Surviving the transformation: Social quality in Central Asia and the Caucuses.' *Journal of Happiness Studies*, 12: 199-223.

Ainsaar, M. (2011). 'Changes in the well-being of social groups in the Baltic states from 1990 to 2009.' *Estonian Human Development Report 2010/2011. Baltic Way(s) of Human Development: Twenty Years on.* Tallinn: ECA, 82-87.

Allardt, E. (1993). 'Having, loving, being: An alternative to the Swedish model of welfare research.' Nussbaum, M. C. and Sen, A. K. (eds.) *The Quality of Life.* New York: Oxford University Press, 88-94.

Böhnke, P. (2007). *Policy or Privacy: What Matters most for Individual Well-being? Determinants of life satisfaction in the enlarged Europe.* Discussion Papers. Berlin: Social Science Research Centre.

Böhnke, P. and Kohler, U. (2008). *Well-being and Inequality.* WZB Discussion Paper 2008.

Chmiel, M., Brunner, M., Martin, R., Schalke, D. (2012). 'Revisiting the structure of subjective well-being in middle-aged adults.' *Social Indicators Research*, 106: 109-116.

Clark, A. E. (2009). *Work, Jobs and Well-Being across the Millennium.* OECD Social, Employment and Migration Working Papers, No. 83, OECD Publishing.

Clark, A. E., Diener, E., Böhnke, P. E., Georgellis, Y. and Lucas, R. E. (2008). 'Lags and leads in life satisfaction: A test of the baseline hypothesis.' *Economic Journal*, 118: 222-243.

Cummins, R. A. (1996). 'The domains of life satisfaction: An attempt to order chaos.' *Social Indicators Research*, 38: 303-332.

Dabalen, A. and Paul, S. (2011). *History of events and life-satisfaction in transition countries.* Policy Research Working Paper 5526. The World Bank, Europe and Central Asia Region, Poverty Reduction and Economic Management Sector Unit.

D'Acci, L. (2011). 'Measuring well-being and progress.' *Social Indicators Research,* 104 (1): 47-65.

Diener, E. (1984). 'Subjective well-being.' *Psychological Bulletin*, 95 (3): 542-75.

Diener, E. (2006). 'Guidelines for national indicators of subjective well-being and ill-being.' *Journal of Happiness Studies*, 7: 397-404.

Diener, E. and Diener, M. (1995). 'Cross-cultural correlates of life satisfaction and self-esteem.' *Journal of Personality and Social Psychology*, 68 (4): 653-663.

Eamets, R. (2011). 'Employment, labour market flexibility and the economic crisis in the Baltic States.' *Estonian Human Development Report 2010/2011. Baltic Way(s) of Human Development: Twenty Years on*. Tallinn: ECA, 74-82.

Easterlin, R. A. (2001). 'Income and happiness: towards a unified theory." *The Economic Journal*, 111: 465-484.

Easterlin, R. A. (2009). 'Lost in transition: Life satisfaction on the road to capitalism.' *Journal of Economic Behavior & Organization*, 71 (2): 130-145.

Estonian Human Development Report 2008. (2009). Tallinn: ECA.

Ervasti, H. and Venetoklis, T. (2010). 'Unemployment and subjective well-being: An empirical test of deprivation theory, incentive paradigm and financial strain approach.' *Acta Sociologica: Journal of Nordic Sociological Association,* 53 (2): 119-140.

Ferrer-i-Carbonell, A. (2005). 'Income and Well-being: An Empirical Analysis of the Comparison Income Effect.' *Journal of Public Economics*, 89: 997-1019.

Gender Equality Monitoring 2005. Tallinn: TLU and Ministry of Social Affairs.

Eurostat (2010). *Gender pay gap statistics*. [Online]. Available: http://epp.eurostat.ec.europa.eu/ (2012, October 18).

Giddens, A. (1991). *Modernity and Self-Identity*. London: Polity Press.

Hamm, P., King, L. P. and Stuckler, D. (2012). 'Mass Privatization, State Capacity, and Economic Growth in Post-Communist Countries.' *American Sociological Review,* 77: 295.

Hansson, A., Hillerås, P. and Forsell, Y. (2005). 'Well-being in an adult Swedish population.' *Social Indicators Research*, 74: 313-325.

Headey, B. (2008). 'The set-point theory of well-being: Negative results and consequent revisions.' *Social Indicators Research*, 85: 389-403.

Heller, D., Judge, T. A. and Watson, D. (2002). 'The confounding role of personality and trait affectivity in the relationship between job and life satisfaction.' *Journal of Organizational Behavior*, 23: 815-835.

Inglehart, R. (1990). *Culture Shift in Advanced Industrial Society*. Princeton: Princeton University Press.

Keller, M. and Vihalemm, T. (2003). 'Return to the 'consuming West': Young people's perceptions about consumerization of Estonia.' *Young*, 11 (3): 195-215.

Kroll, C. (2011). 'Different Things Make Different People Happy: Examining Social Capital and Subjective Well-Being by Gender and Parental Status.' *Social Indicators Research*, 104: 157-177.

Lauristin, M. and Vihalemm, P. (1997). 'Recent historical developments in Estonia: Three stages of transition (1987–1997).' Lauristin, M. and Vihalemm, P. (eds.) *Return to the Western World*. Tartu: Tartu University Press, 25-40.

Lucas, R. E. and Donnellan, M. B. (2012). 'Estimating the reliability of single-item life satisfaction measures: Results from four national panel studies.' *Social Indicators Research*, 105 (3): 323-331.

Minkov, M. (2009). 'Predictors of differences in subjective well-being across 97 nations.' *Cross-Cultural Research*, 43 (2): 152-179.

Narusk, A. and Kandolin, I. (1997). 'Social well-being and gender: post-Soviet Estonia and welfare state Finland.' *Scandinavian Journal of Social Welfare*, 6: 127-136.

Narusk, A. and Hansson, L. (1999). *Estonian Families in the 1990s: Winners and Losers*. Tallinn: Estonian Academy Publisher.

Ojamäe, L. (2009). *Making Choices in the Housing Market: Social Construction of Housing Value*. Tallinn: Tallinn University.

Paadam, K. (2000). *Constructing Residence as Home: Homeowners and their Housing Histories*. Tallinn: TPU Press.

Pinquart, M. and. Silbereisen, R. K. (2010). 'Patterns of fulfilment in the domains of work, intimate relationship, and leisure.' *Applied Research in Quality of Life* (2010) 5: 147-164.

Plagnol, A. C. and Scott, J. (2011). 'What Matters for Well-Being: Individual Perceptions of Quality of Life Before and After Important Life Events.' *Applied Research in Quality of Life*, 6: 115-137.

van Praag, B. M. S., Frijters, P. and A. Ferrer-i-Carbonell. (2003). 'The anatomy of subjective well-being.' *Journal of Economic Behavior and Organization*, 51: 29-49.

Raelo, A. (2009). 'Happiness and satisfaction with life.' *Estonian Human Development Report 2008*. Tallinn: ECA, 63-67.

Raudsepp, M., Tart, I. and Heinla, E. (2012). 'Continuity and change of value profiles in 1985-2008.' Allaste, A.-A. (ed.) *Back in the West: Changing Lifestyles in Transforming Societies*. Frankfurt: Peter Lang.

Rojas, M. (2006). 'Life satisfaction and satisfaction in domains of life: Is it a simple relationship?' *Journal of Happiness Studies*, 7: 467-497.

Sagiv, L. and Schwartz, S. H. (2000). 'Value priorities and subjective well-being: direct relations and congruity effects.' *European Journal of Social Psychology*, 30: 177-198.

Selezneva, E. (2011). 'Surveying transitional experience and subjective well-being: Income, work, family.' *Economic Systems*, 35: 139-157.

Snir, R., and Harpaz, I. (2002). 'Work-leisure relations: Leisure orientation and the meaning of work.' *Journal of Leisure Research*, 34: 178-203.

Soons, J. P. and Kalmijn, M. (2009). 'Is marriage more than cohabitation? Well-being differences in 30 European countries.' *Journal of Marriage and Family*, 71: 1141-1157.

Stutzer, A. and Frey, B. S. (2003). *Reported Subjective Well-Being: A Challenge for Economic Theory and Economic Policy*. CREMA: Working Paper 2003-07. [Online]. Available: http://www.crema-research.ch (2012, October 18).

Stutzer, A. and Frey, B. S. (2006). 'Does marriage make people happy, or do happy people marry?' *Journal of Socio-Economics*, 35: 326-347.

Trumm, A. and Kasearu, K. (2009). 'Development of individual quality of life, 1994–2008.' *Estonian Human Development Report 2008.* Tallinn: ECA, 55-62.

Veenhoven, R. (1991). 'Is happiness relative?' *Social Indicators Research*, 24: 1-34.

Veenhoven, R. and Kalmijn, M. (2005). 'Inequality-adjusted happiness in nations: Egalitarianism and Unitarianism married together in a new index of societal performance.' *Journal of Happiness Studies,* 6: 421-455.

Wheaton, B. and Gotlib, I. H. (1997). 'Trajectories and turning points over the life course: Concepts and themes.' Gotlib, I. H. and Wheaton, B. (eds.) *Stress and Adversity over the Life Course: Trajectories and Turning Points*. Cambridge: Cambridge University Press, 1-28.

Zagorski, K. (2011). 'Income and happiness in time of post-communist modernization.' *Social Indicators Research*, 104: 331-349.

Appendix I

Level of satisfaction with life as a whole and with life domains in Estonia in 1985-2008 (means, 5 = fully satisfied ... 1 = not satisfied at all)

	1985	1993	1998	2003	2008	Changes between …	
						1985-2008	lowest - highest
N=	1527	1108	1534	1122	1138		
Satisfaction with…							
family life	3.72	3.78	3.89	3.87	4.03	0.29	0.29
job	3.58	3.67	3.72	3.80	3.82	0.24	0.24
financial situation	3.03	2.23	2.47	2.72	3.10	0.07	0.87
housing conditions	3.10	3.35	3.42	3.72	3.99	0.89	0.89
leisure	3.27	3.18	3.18	3.69	4.00	0.73	0.82
life as a whole	3.41	3.25	3.40	3.50	3.93	0.52	0.68

Continuity and change of value profiles in 1985-2008

Maaris Raudsepp, Indrek Tart, Eda Heinla

Introduction

Recent macro-level changes in Eastern Europe have been described not only as a transition from state regulated socialism to liberal market capitalism, from authoritarian rule to pluralistic democracy (Kennedy 2002), from closed society into a liberal globalised world; but, as more profound civilisational change (Sztompka 1996), metaphorically described as returning to the West (Lauristin and Vihalemm 1997). The unique period of transition from one societal system to another, the destruction of a soviet system of social regulators and overtaking by another set of regulators, makes East European former socialist countries an interesting site for exploring the changing *Zeitgeist* and the interplay of macro-societal and subjective processes.

Values are a psychosocial link between individuals and society, being an aspect of both cultural and personality system (Schwartz 2008), functioning as generalised regulators both on the level of personal life-worlds as well as on the societal/cultural or institutional level. They orient individuals and groups to meaningful goals and to socially acceptable means of attaining these goals. In times of the collapse of the established order of things in the political and social sphere, personal values act as a source of order inside the individual (Szakolczai and Füstös 1998).

According to modernisation theory, economic development, cultural change and political change go together in a coherent and predictable manner (Inglehart 1997). Changes in value priorities accompany and reflect major socio-cultural changes, therefore individual values can be used as markers of macro-social trends and ruptures. But there is also inertia of values. Some aspects of values are stable over time; others change more rapidly. Our chapter focuses on both stable and changing aspects of values in the Estonian context. We are going to discern the dynamics of consensual and divergent value patterns among the Estonian population.

The present chapter focuses on one stream of value measurements among the Estonian population carried out by a team of researchers in the Institute of International and Social Studies during the years 1985 to 2008 (Narusk, Hansson, Kelam and Laidmäe 1999; Arvisto and Heinla 2001; Heinla 2004; Heinla 2009; Heinla and Derman 2010).

We focus on the stability and change of value patterns in Estonia over the period from late socialism (1985) to the first decade of early liberal capitalism (2008). This is a period of systemic societal changes (see Lauristin 1997; Lauristin and Vihalemm 2009). During these years tremendous changes have occurred in the Estonian society in multiple dimensions. On the institutional dimension, Estonia evolved from a country under a Soviet regime to an independent democratic nation state and EU member. On the socio-economic dimension transition from socialist planned economy to liberal market economy took place, accompanied by marketisation of social relations and domination of consumerist lifestyle, essential changes in labour relations and employment, as well as in increasing socio-economic differentiation (Saar 2011). Within the cultural dimension, openness to global influences has grown and many regulative ideas have been replaced. Beside similarities to development of all former socialist East European countries, Estonia's specificity is cultural heterogeneity: one third of its population consists of soviet period immigrants who have different cultural roots. Their integration into the Estonian society has remained an issue (see Vetik 2012).

Conceptualising values

Values are general regulators of social relations and human activities, indicating both the relevant goals (orientations) and socially accepted ways of attaining these goals. In this respect, they function both as shared meanings (promoted by official ideology, dominant representations and discourses) and as individual regulators in personal life worlds. Lifestyle choices are based on and express certain value systems. Changing hierarchies of values reflect changing priorities of life goals in changing societal contexts. Value priorities are formed in the course of primary socialisation and adaptations to the changing societal context. Empirical research of human values has proceeded in several streams.

In studies based on **Ronald Inglehart**'s conceptualisation of values and his revised version of modernisation theory (Inglehart and Baker 2000), values are grouped along two relevant dimensions that characterise polarisation: *traditionalism vs. rationalism/secularism* and *materialism (survival values) vs. postmaterialism (self-expression values)*. The first dimension is related to the process of modernisation; the other to the transition from industrial society to post-industrial societies – which brings a polarisation between the weight accorded to survival and that given to self-expression. Self-expression values give high priority to freedom of speech, environmental protection, tolerance of diversity, trust, social participation, hedonism, self-realisation and quality of life, reflecting a cultural shift that is emerging among generations who have grown up in welfare societies taking survival for granted. The main determinant of postmaterialistic value change is subjective sense of security, which depends on material well-being, social and political stability, high life expectancy and other macro-societal factors.

Western societies turned toward post-materialist values in the 1970s after they achieved a considerable welfare level following World War II. In Eastern Europe the development was more ambiguous. On the one hand, economic development was not so rapid; on the other, certain post-materialist values, *e.g.* social solidarity and general self-development, were propagated as part of the hegemonic ideological system (Inglehart and Baker 2000). The sense of security as the basis for non-materialist values was supported by the system of social guarantees during socialism (minimal income, free education and medical service were available to everyone). According to sociological surveys, the dominant value pattern of late socialism has been characterised as 'pseudo-postmateralistic'. The majority of people were oriented towards social and altruistic values instead of pragmatic and individualistic values (Saarniit 1995). However, such declared supremacy of collective (national) interests over individual ones may reflect a discrepancy between the publicly declared and privately held values (Shlapentokh 1982), differentiation of mythological and pragmatic levels of the Soviet period mentality (Shlapentokh 1985).

The data from World Value Surveys 1981-2007 [Estonia participated in the survey since 1990] and European Value Study enables one to compare the Estonian position with other countries. Similarly to Protestant Western European countries and countries with the experience of Communist rule, Estonia is high up in the dimension of rationalism/secularism (opposed to traditionalism values) and, similar to other Eastern European former socialist countries, low in the dimension of post-materialism, with a relatively high rating of scarcity values (Inglehart and Welzel 2005). Inglehart (2006) explains it by ideological effect of socialist anticlericalism and the experience of material scarcity during socialism. According to Inglehart, low priority of post-materialist values is an obstacle for genuine democracy in former socialist countries.

During the first period of transition (1990-1996) the position of Estonia shifted even more in the direction of materialism, most remarkably among the middle-aged generation (Toomere 2001). Such a shift backwards to survival values reflects the growing sense of insecurity caused by the collapse of the previous political and economic system and growing economic hardships (Inglehart and Baker 2000). Widening consumption opportunities occupied people's attention and supported the development of a materialist orientation.

Another widely used theoretical model of basic human values, as well as instrument of measurement, was elaborated upon by **Shalom H. Schwartz**. He defines values as cognitive/social representations of the important goals or motivations (biological, social interaction and social institutional needs), '...socially approved verbal representations of basic motivations' (Sagiv and Schwartz 2000: 178). As values function as cultural devices aimed at control and social regulation – at the same time, providing a framework for making sense of individual lives (see Raudsepp 2011) – they form distinct patterns in certain macro-social contexts. For example, highly competitive liberal capitalism is characterised by a value pattern high in the individual mastery and group embeddedness, and low in the harmony, intellectual autonomy, and egalitarianism orientations among the culture level values. On the individual level, competitive liberal capitalism promotes a high level of achievement, conformity and power values combined with low importance of universalism and self-direction values (Schwartz 2007). Compared with socialism, the capitalistic system favours the pursuit of self-interest, competitiveness, materialistic values and goals (profit, wealth, possessions), and undermines concern for collectivistic and universalistic values (equality, solidarity, social altruism).

Transition from Soviet period rhetoric to a post-Soviet frame of reference involves a shift in the normative hierarchy of values. Abstract and universalistic notions of universal solidarity, cooperation, collective interests and other social values were replaced by the priority of individualistic values like individual interest, individual effectiveness, success, competition and particular group interests.

Results of several empirical studies (Verkasalo *et al.* 1994; Spini 1997; Schwartz and Bardi 1997; Sagiv and Schwartz 2000) indicate that in the 1990s people faced with a post-socialist reality devalued former rhetorical ideals (fraternity, solidarity, equality, *etc.*) and adopted a value pattern that suits better for adaptation with the harsh reality of early capitalism.

Comparison of value patterns in Estonia and Sweden in 1991-1995 (Lauristin and Vihalemm 1997) showed systematic changes towards the decline of the importance of universalistic values and growing hedonistic and individualistic orientation. More changes were observed among the Estonian Russian-speakers; whereas, values changed in different directions among older and younger Russian speaking respondents in contrast to other more similar changes among different generations of Estonians.

Kalmus and Vihalemm (2004: 34) remarked on the general value change in 1991-2003, stating that more importance had been given to values related to hedonism, close interpersonal relations and self-assertion, or indicators of individual emancipation from previous normative pressures. Individualistic-emancipatory values dominated over collectivistic and universalistic values among young and affluent groups ('winners' of transition) while older respondents assess more highly collectivistic and universalistic values.

An alternative stream of studies seeks to conceptualise **values as life orientations**. A longitudinal survey on the attitudes of the post-war generation carried out in 1966-1991 (*e.g.*Titma 1999; 2002; Titma *et al.* 1996) also included questions on life orientations, inspired by ideas of Kluckhohn (1956). These life orientations were defined as cognitive, emotional and behavioral orientations to main life activities – work, studies, family life, voluntary social activity, hobbies, interaction with friends, and so forth, and were broadly classified as orientation to work, family and leisure). These basic life orientations are interpreted as values – normative beliefs that regulate human activities. Beside relative importance or hierarchy of these values people differ also in terms of underlying meanings of these values (Titma and Paalandi 2001).

Longitudinal analysis revealed high individual stability of the profile of these life orientation values along the lifespan (Titma and Paalandi 1999). However, a radical shift in group-level value priorities was observed already before the perestroika period. In contrast to the 1960-s and 1970s when value priorities were highly stable, in the beginning of 1980s significant inter-cohort shift in value priorities of young people were recorded including a decreasing orientation towards social altruism and general self-development with dramatically increasing orientation toward material well-being and high social position indicated profound transformations in value consciousness (Saarniit 1995: 147). Therefore, a shift from a socialist 'pseudo-post-materialist' orientation to the more pragmatic 'neo-materialistic' survival orientation was already registered among the youth by the 1980s.

A growing openness to Western lifestyle examples as well as consumer goods (*e.g.* through Finnish TV), as well as growing criticism of the socialist system in the media, created a new external frame of reference; welfare capitalist societies became a model for many people, especially youth. The increase in pragmatism and individualism, as well as an emphasis on material and status aspects of work began in the early 1980s and were intensified in the period of perestroika and the collapse of the Soviet system. So the movement from the totalitarian communist value system to the values of modern welfare capitalist society had already begun before the radical change of sociopolitical system. In a sense, young people were pre-adapted (prepared) for the radical system change. At the same time this preparedness was incomplete. Saarniit (1995: 152) notes that young people in Eastern Europe accepted the most obvious values of a modern capitalist welfare society (material well-being, freedom of choice) but have not fully grasped its more hidden aspects (like personal responsibility and initiative).

This stream of studies highlights value changes in two cohorts. Our analysis is going to focus on the tendencies in value consciousness in general population.

Methods and data

Our aim is to reveal the dynamics of the *hierarchy of life values* in the Estonian population and its ethno-linguistic and demographic subgroups during the period from 1985 to 2008.

The research data is based on five representative population surveys 'Work, Family and Leisure' carried out by the sociologists of the Institute of International and Social Studies of Tallinn University. In the surveys identical sets of questions on life values were used. Respondents had to assess on a 5-point Likert scale (from very important to not at all important) the personal importance of the following life values: *family*, *children*, *health*, *close friends*, *faith*, *love*, *professional work*, *varied life (new places, acquaintances, impressions,* etc.*)*, *cultural interests (reading, going to the theatre,* etc.*)*, *economic well-being*, *keeping up-to-date with current affairs*, *creative activities*, *physical fitness, self-education*, *social participation and voluntary activity*, *high social position*, *clean environment (nature)*.

Overall changes in value hierarchies

We expect that changing hierarchies of values reflect shifting priorities of life goals in the changing societal contexts. The overall value ratings and their hierarchy have remained remarkably stable from 1985 to 2008 (see the dynamics of mean ratings in Appendix 2). The general fit of the value ratings is extremely good – values that are high remain high, and vice versa. Even the year-by-year alteration leaves not much room for changing the ranking of items. 1990s are mostly below the total average and 2000s above. Such stability is a support for the conceptualisation of these value items as life values. Value items are forming distinguishable high-low clusters that appear to represent different generalised value domains.

Most highly assessed values over the observed 23 years are *children* and *family* (see Appendix 1), which are also most consensually assessed. These existential values have retained their priority throughout the years of initial socio-economic restructuring crisis in the 1990s, as well as during the later re-stabilisation in the 2000s. Throughout the period the least valued among the presented list of values are *voluntary social activities* and *high social position.*

The hierarchy of shared items of values in all surveys (Appendix 3) is rather stable, and most of the values have not changed their position more than by one rank while only four values have moved by two ranks [*clean nature* and *cultural interests* have moved in the direction of less importance, *love* and *self-education* have become more important by 2008 in comparison with 1985]. Arvisto and Heinla (2001), Heinla (2004; 2009), Heinla and Derman (2010) analysing the changes in mean ratings, recorded some indication of the growing importance of life values interpreted in the Inglehart's postmaterialist framework, but this tendency was not very clearly resolved, along with the growing importance of *creative activities* and *self-education* (as post-materialist values) and similar growth in the importance of *material well-being* (materialist value). Instead of general growth of post-materialism they speak about stabilisation of social processes and differentiation of value patterns.

Family and children have been the top priorities throughout the period for men and women, ethnic Estonians and non-Estonians. Interestingly, these values have changed their positions. Until the end of 1990s children were assessed as most important; in the 2000s the priority was given to family. In the study the meaning of family is not specified – it may mean either family of origin, 'own' family through marriage or cohabitation or family as a symbol (Hansson 2009).

Economic well-being has continuously grown in importance and its estimation has been relatively consensual. This tendency indicates that economic factors remain important to Estonians, reflecting the dominant discourse of the necessity of rapid economic growth as the main road to maximising well-being, typical to modernisation (Inglehart 1997). Dynamics of this value reflects gradual adaptation to capitalist hegemonic ideology with the stress on hedonism and consumerism – material wealth has become a basis for realising all other aims (Inglehart and Baker 2000). This trend of pragmatisation of value consciousness of Estonian youth had already begun in the 1980s (Saarniit 1995; 1997).

Professional work had a rather significant rise in importance in 1998, which diminished thereafter to the level of 1985. Heinla and Derman (2010) explain this by means of the rising unemployment and the diminishing value of *professional* work (compared to any kind of work). Work is a value that most likely changed its meaning as the result of societal transformations. It was an ideologically supported value in the Soviet period when work was an obligation for everyone as a commitment to the common goal and the means of being useful to society and other people. At that time, work was guaranteed to everyone and there was no competitive pressure for hard work and efficient performance.

Through professional work, several motivations could be realised like self-expression, social interaction and gaining social approval (Titma and Paalandi 2001). In a market economic context, the meaning of work has transformed into a means for maintaining one's material well-being (Titma and Helemäe 1996). On the other hand, tradition of protestant work ethics in Estonia promotes the belief in the importance of work in itself.

Most notably the importance of certain values have grown, such as *friends self-education* and *physical fitness*. Heinla (2009) has observed a significant rise in the importance of physical fitness in 2008, especially for the youngest (below 35) age group, men with higher education, women with secondary education, and older women. A possible explanation could be a partial shift to post materialistic self-expression orientation, growing importance of post-materialist lifestyle values in the framework of quality of life motivation (Inglehart 1997). Emphasis on physical fitness – jogging, cycling, concern for food quality, *etc.* – is an indicator of a post materialistic lifestyle, growing valuation of beauty, strength and youthfulness.

But an alternative explanation is also possible – friends, self-education and physical fitness may be resources for survival in intensifying competition, so that their rising importance reflects diversification of survival resources. For example, the growing importance of *physical fitness* may be result of the deterioration of the accessibility of medical service, which induces one to pay more attention to all means for supporting one's health and ability to work. This process is on the level of survival orientation. The fact that the importance of physical fitness has grown both for the youngest and oldest age groups indicates that different processes may be operating behind it.

Titma and Paalandi (2001) note the changing meaning of interaction with friends; that is, during the Soviet period interaction with close friends was a compensatory device for the limited possibilities for political participation and making a professional career. In the new capitalist reality friends have acquired a new meaning, becoming an important social resource (Kazjulja and Roosalu 2011).

The value that has dropped in importance most notably is *faith*. Thus the secularisation process, which began during the socialism, is continuing, and the transitional unstable period of the 1990 only temporarily brought faith to the foreground, probably as a compensatory resource in times of social shattering. Return to religious beliefs in former socialist countries has been related to pervasive insecurity due to the collapse of a social system (Inglehart and Baker 2000). However, in Estonia, religious revival has affected only some segments of society (mostly the Russian speaking minority).

Voluntary social activities and social participation is the only value in the list that can be interpreted as an indicator of collectivism. In the general value hierarchy it steadily occupies one of the last positions. The explanation of its relative subjective unimportance during socialism when it was ideologically promoted has been a challenge for sociologists (Titma and Paalandi 2001). In our study there was a decline of its importance in 1993 compared to 1985 and gradual increase of importance thereafter. Such dynamics could be explained by initial reactivity to ideologically marked value (propagated collectivism in soviet period) and subsequent change of its meaning. Citizen activity was controlled and partly suppressed in the soviet system and, as a consequence, social participation and voluntary social activities obtained negative connotations and have been relatively infrequent in the former socialist countries (Howard 2003; Rämmer 2008), indicating to certain deficit in democracy, which was noted also in some value studies (Schwartz 1997). 'Although overwhelming majorities of the public of former socialist societies endorse democracy as a general goal, they show much lower levels on such underlying qualities as tolerance and the post-materialist valuation of freedom of speech and political participation as goods in themselves. These attributes seem to play a crucial role in the emergence and survival of liberal democracy.' (Inglehart and Baker 2000: 81).

Importance of *clean nature* grew considerably in the 1990s and dropped thereafter to the level of 1985. In the 1990s both Estonians and Russian speakers ranked clean nature 3rd in their value hierarchy, in 1985 and in the 2000s Russian-speakers considered clean nature as relatively less important than members of Estonian-speaking majority. A possible explanation for this temporary rise could be intensive media coverage of the environmental problems and large-scale public protests related to the Soviet central government's plans to start phosphorite mining in Estonia in the late 1980s (the so called 'phosphorite war') (*e.g.* Vogt 2005).

Changing value hierarchies in different groups

Age group differences in life values reflect different underlying processes, related to socialisation and life cycle. Birth cohorts (generations) as units of socialisation are important factors of value change in society (Inglehart 1990). Hypothetically, value priorities that are formed during early socialisation are most stable, generational collective memory retains these value patterns during later changes, forming a basis of generational collective identity. Most sensitive period for stabilisation of personal value hierarchies is the socialisation until 20 years of age. Societal and family context at this period has greatest influence on individual value systems. Generations growing up in stability and affluence have different value priorities compared to generations who grow during wars and social upheavals, which promote feeling of existential insecurity (de Graaf *et al.* 1996). So, the resulting value patterns reflect a relatively stable component of early socialisation, and changing components of continuous adaptation to the changing societal context.

General cultural shift occurs through the mechanism of generation replacement. World value survey results indicate that 'throughout central and eastern Europe, the younger generations place markedly greater emphasis on self-expression values than do the older generations. In the long run, the process of intergenerational population replacement is working to make these values more widespread. Their progress will be greatly enhanced insofar as economic recovery and political stability are attained' (Inglehart and Baker 2000: 84). In Estonia, individual and within-cohort stability of value hierarchies has been recorded in longitudinal studies (Titma 1999). A notable between-cohort value change in the direction of pragmatism and individualism was recorded in the 1980s (Saarniit 1995). Studies using Schwartz's value survey data, have noted intergenerational gap: growing individualism of younger people (hedonistic, consumeristic and self-assertive orientation) and collectivism of older people (Kalmus and Vihalemm 2004). Lilleoja (2012) analysing inter-cohort value differences based on European Value survey 2004-2010, recorded a value shift towards greater individualism (greater importance of self-direction, hedonism, stimulation, achievement) in the cohort born of the 80s, which has been socialised during the sharp societal system change.

Tart (2011) notes that the relationship between values priorities and age is the key factor that is relatively linear. It shows the generally accepted trend that an increase in age results in a higher appreciation of altruism and preservation of *status quo*, whereas younger respondents appreciate more highly the values expressing egoism and openness to change.

In the previous studies of life values, comparison of younger (below 35 years) and older respondents shows systematic differences in value assessments (*children* and *professional work* are more important for older people, *friends*, *love* and *varied life* are more important for the young) (Heinla and Derman 2010). This tendency seems to reflect natural differences in the priorities of natural life course stages. Analysis of rank order of values shows great differences between the youngest (18-34) and oldest (55-74) age groups in the attitude to *nature*, which throughout the years has been more important for older people. This difference reflects probably cohort-specific differences; that is, the experience of national liberation movement intertwined with collective pro-environmental movement during the 'phosphorite war' in the 1980s has been accessible to the oldest cohorts, thus increasing the importance of *clean nature* for them in the 1990s.

Gender/role differentiation intensified in the 1990s with the revival of traditional gender roles and patriarchal gender relations (Pilvre, this volume). The traditional model prescribes men to be more oriented to work and career, and women to family life. Previous analyses (Heinla 2009) confirm this model: women assess *family*, *children*, *health* and *love* consistently more highly than men. For men, *professional work* and *physical fitness* are more important than for women. Consistent gender differences emerged also in the valuation of *self-education* and *cultural interests* which are more important for women. In the subgroup of young women with higher education also *varied life* and *physical fitness* are more important than for men. Such gender asymmetry in the assessment of certain values may reflect either more 'postmaterialist' orientation to self-realisation of women or an alternative strategy of survival. In the longitudinal analysis of work values Rämmer (2011) notes that in the second half of 1990s and in 2004 young women have assessed self-education and self-realisation more highly than young men, interpreting it as a perceived necessity to compete for good jobs in a market economy.

The significance of voluntary activities and *social participation* has become more important for women compared to men in the 2000s. Dynamics of the relative importance of life values during the years indicate that women have begun more to value physical fitness, self-education, relatively less – professional work and cultural interests. Decline of the importance of cultural interests was also characteristic of men (dropping from 8th position in 1985 to 11th position in 2008). Men's value assessments have remained relatively stable, while the rank order of women's values have changed more between 1985 and 2008 than among men.

Changes value hierarchies in ethno-linguistic groups. Home language based differentiation in value priorities and structure have been recorded in different streams of value studies. Several studies based on Schwartz' value model have found substantial differences between value patterns of ethnic Estonians and Russian-speaking Estonian inhabitants. Rudnev and Magun (2010) analysing European Social Surveys 2006-2007, found a relatively large discrepancy (on the dimension of self-enhancement – self-transcendence) between two cultural groups in Estonia – Estonian and Russian-speakers. Such a great difference is unique among European multicultural societies. Value preferences of ethnic Estonians are more similar to the population of Finland, Belgium, Great Britain and Norway than to Russian-speaking co-patriots. On the other hand, Estonian Russian-speakers are more similar to respondents in Russia, Ukraine and Slovakia. Similarly, comparing Estonian value priorities of representative samples with those of Sweden and Finland (Tart 2011), Sweden and Russia (Tart 2008), significant difference in the value structures between majority Estonian speakers and minority Russian-speakers were revealed.

Studies of life orientations (Saarniit 1997) have found that the changes of life values of ethnic Estonians and Russian-speakers have proceeded in similar directions – pragmatisation (growing individualism, material well-being and social status concerns), the main difference being that the changes have been more rapid among young Russian-speakers. More profound and multi-layered value change among Russian-speakers during the transition period compared to Estonians have been recorded in the 1990s and in the 2000s (Kalmus and Vihalemm 2004; 2006; 2008a; b) and have been interpreted by greater objective and subjective pressure on Russian-speakers, who have experienced the societal changes as more dramatic and adjustment more difficult. As a result, they have lost their previously more collective-oriented mindset and have become more self-conscious and self-assertive on the one hand (Sõmer 2011), and have begun to rely more on some self-transcendence type of values (faith) (Vihalemm and Kalmus 2009), on the other.

In the domain of life values research (Heinla and Derman 2010), throughout the years, significant ethnic group difference have maintained in the assessment of *economic well-being* and *professional work* [with Russian-speakers considering it more important than Estonians]. It may be interpreted as being a deficit value due to the more vulnerable position of Russian-speakers on the labour market and their sense of insecurity. The unemployment level has been much higher among Russian-speakers than among Estonians, many Russian-speakers lost their jobs due to restructuring of labour market and new language and citizenship policy in the 1990s. It is remarkable that in groups with secondary education, ethnic differences were greater than among groups with higher education (Heinla and Derman 2010).

Among the young (below 35), the ethnic gap in the assessment of *professional work* increased considerably between 1993 and 1998 and decreased in the 2000s, the importance of *economic well-being* has steadily grown in both ethnic groups. While in previous years there were no ethnic differences in the rating of *social participation*, but in 2008 this value was significantly more important for young ethnic Estonians. Relative social passivity of young Russian-speakers reflects their growing alienation from the Estonian state (see Vetik 2012).

Faith has consistently been of more value for Russian-speakers than for Estonians, being in both groups more highly valued in the 1990s than in the 2000s. Throughout the period, general rank order of values in Russian-speakers has changed more than in Estonians. Most notable changes among Russian-speakers have been increase in the importance of *clean nature* in the 1990s, *self-education* and *physical fitness* on the one hand, and decreasing importance of *professional work* and *cultural interests*, on the other.

Discussion and conclusion

Available empirical data enables us to compare value patterns of Estonians throughout the period of collapse of the state socialism and its transformation into liberal market economy. In the context of significant shifts in political, socio-economic and cultural spheres, our study revealed relative stability of main life orientation profiles. Most notable changes have occurred in the value structures of Estonian Russian-speakers (especially men), women, youngest and oldest age groups. Societal transformations affected the life-worlds of both ethno-linguistic communities, but the changes of political and economic position in the society were more profound for Estonian Russian-speakers.

The importance of several life values – *family, friends, self-education, physical fitness, material well-being* – has steadily grown from 1985 to 2008. This result resonates with the conclusion by studies in Schwartz' tradition which recorded growing importance of hedonism, close relations and self-direction values during 1991-2003 (Kalmus and Vihalemm 2004). Our study shows that transition from socialism to liberal capitalism has strengthened the orientation to the safety of close relationships (affiliation) on the one hand, and individual self-development towards competence and autonomy, related most probably to the growing motivation to increase one's competitive advantage, on the other. In parallel, the increase of the importance of *economic well-being* reflects the overwhelming importance of financial success in the capitalist system and the enlargement of consuming opportunities. This trend coincides with the general predictions on the psychological effects of liberal capitalist system (Schwartz 2007; Kasser *et al.* 2007).

Cultural interests and *faith* have steadily decreased in importance, reflecting the general trend of weakening ties with collective belief systems. In the capitalist system cultural sphere has lost its previously high status in society, which was intentionally supported by the socialist state via dotations into the 'official culture', and unintentionally gained through being one of the few means for expressing oppositional views. Intensified work life in a market economy does not leave as much spare time for realising various cultural interests as it was possible during socialism.

Some values have gone through wave-like dynamics such as *clean nature* and *professional work* which were most highly assessed in the 1990s; whereas, *social participation* took a sharp decline in importance in 2003. Decreasing importance of *clean nature* may reflect the general tendency of devaluing universalistic values and growing pragmatism in the new societal context. After socialism, Estonia has lost highly polluting industrial enterprises, and as a consequence, environmental issues have lost their immediacy and topicality compared to the era of 'phosphorite war' in the 1980s.

If we conceptualise life values in the Inglehart's theoretical framework of bipolar dimensions by dividing them into materialistic (survivalist) and postmaterialistic (self-realisational) values, then the dynamics are not very clear. The greatest shifts occurring among postmaterialist values has been in different directions (increasing importance of *love* and *self-education*, decreasing importance of *clean nature* and *cultural interests*). The importance of *economic well-being* as a materialistic value has been stable for ethnic Estonians and has changed for Estonian Russian-speakers, with decreasing importance in the 1990s and regained importance in the 2000s. Postmaterialist life values measured in this study are consistently more important for women compared to men.

Sztompka (2004) has described the post-communist transition as a traumatogenic social change with all the effects and coping strategies that are characteristic of cultural trauma. Oppositional systems of representations – the so-called old 'bloc culture' shaped under the old regime, and the emerging capitalist culture contradict each other in several dimensions – collectivism vs. individualism, solidarity in poverty vs. competition, egalitarianism vs. meritocratic justice, security vs. risk, reliance on fate vs. emphasis on agency, counting on social support vs. self-reliance, and so on (Sztompka 2004: 172). Probably also a contrast between former images of welfare capitalism (represented by neighbouring Finland) and the harsh reality of early liberal capitalism, realised in Estonia, is relevant here.

Societal transition 'empowers some, and disempowers others' (Kennedy 2002: 300), produces new life opportunities for some, and loss and impoverishment for others. One of the most important consequences of societal transformation has been growing differentiation of life conditions and life opportunities, and a growing gap between, 'winners' and 'losers' of transition (Lauristin 2004; Saar 2011). On the one hand there is society of scarcity (the older, rural, poor group), and on the other – the affluent society of security where survival is taken for granted and which is increasingly regulated by self-realisation values. For the latter group, opportunities to realise a variety of consumption, lifestyle and career choices were opened. In Estonia, significant differences in value assessments between people with different levels of material well-being have been recorded. There is a specific value gap between different income groups indicating that self-assertion values are important for the wealthy; whereas, universalist values (equality, faith) are more important for the poor (Kalmus and Vihalemm 2004).

Previous analyses of life values as interpreted in the framework of materialism-postmaterialism, show growing gaps between different population groups in terms of deficit and postmaterialist values (Arvisto and Heinla 2001), differentiation between old people who live outside the capital (orientation to deficit values) and the young, educated urban affluent group who are oriented towards postmaterialist values (Heinla 2004). During the period from 1985 to 2008 increase of significance of post-materialist orientation has occurred only in the young and wealthy segments of the population (Heinla and Derman 2010). Thus during the observed period there was a mixture of various tendencies. For some groups it was a transition from scarcity to security (with a focus on non-materialist, quality of life issues), and for other groups, a transition from relative security under socialism to scarcity and starvation.

Various approaches to the conceptualisation and measurement of human values – as those by Shalom Schwartz, Ronald Inglehart, and the life values approach, analysed in the present chapter, reveal different and complementary aspects of value-based self-regulation and goal-setting on the societal and individual levels. In Inglehart's terms, post-socialist value orientation can be characterised as secular and survivalist. Studies based on Schwartz's conceptualisation of values have shown how transition from socialism to capitalism has favoured the pursuit of self-interest, competitiveness, materialistic values and goals (profit, wealth, possessions), and undermined concern for collectivistic and universalistic values (equality, solidarity, social altruism). Relative stability of the structure of life values in the context of turbulent societal changes, as demonstrated in the present analysis, indicates the genuine value-ness of the life orientations as stable landmarks. In times of a total collapse of the established order of things, including the political system and the social order of daily routine life, the system of values leading to a major spiritual revival locates the source of order inside the individual. Personal evaluation motivates individual decisions and behavior more than the social (moral) patterns and brought to forefront the similarity of life value hierarchies of 1985 and 2008 that smoothed the turbulence created by traumatic societal change. As the political system in Estonia stagnates, people will continue to search for a more convincing haven of life values.

References

Arvisto, M. and Heinla, E. (2001). 'Eesti elanikkonna väärtushinnangud 1993. ja 1998.aastal.' [Values of the population of Estonia in 1993 and 1998] Heinla, E. (ed.) *Kultuur, elukvaliteet ja väärtushinnangud* [Culture, quality of life and values]. Tallinn: TPÜ Press, 90-109.

de Graaf, N. D. and Evans, G. (1996) 'Why are the young more postmaterialist? A cross-national analysis of individual and contextual influences on postmaterialist values.' *Comparative Political Studies*, 28 (4): 608-636.

Hansson, L. (2009). 'Muutused perekonnakäitumises ja -rollides.'[Changes in family behaviour and roles] Hansson, L. (ed.) *Töö, kodu ja vaba aeg: argielu Eestis aastatel 1985–2009*. [Work, home and leisure: daily life in Estonia in 1985-2009]. Tallinn: TLU Press, 38-70.

Heinla, E. (2004). 'Eluväärtused.' [Values in life] Hansson, L. (ed.) *Valikud ja võimalused. Argielu Eestis aastatel 1993–2003*. [Choices and opportunities. Daily life in Estonia in 1993-2003]. Tallinn: TPÜ Press, 11-24.

Heinla, E. (2009). 'Eluväärtused Eesti taasiseseisvumise künnisel ja majanduskriisi eelõhtul.' [Values in life on the threshold of Estonia regaining independence and on the eve of economic crisis] Hansson, L. (ed.) *Töö, kodu ja vaba aeg. Argielu Eestis aastatel 1985–2008*. [Work, home and leisure. Daily life in Estonia in 1985-2008]. Tallinn: RASI, 17-38.

Heinla, E. and Derman, N. (2010). 'Изменения в ценностной системе населения в период социальной трансформации в Эстонии.' [Changes in the system of values of population during the social transformation of Estonia]. *Sociologicheskiye Issledovaniya*, 3: 50-57.

Howard, M. M. (2003). *The weakness of civil society in post-Communist Europe*. Cambridge: Cambridge University Press.

Inglehart, R. (1990). *Culture Shift in Advanced Industrial Society*. Princeton, NJ: Princeton University Press.

Inglehart, R. (1997). *Modernization and Post-Modernization: Cultural, Economic and Political Change in 43 Societies*. Princeton, NJ: Princeton University Press.

Inglehart, R. and Baker, W. E. (2000), 'Cultural Change, and the Persistence of Traditional Values.' *American Sociological Review*, 65 (1): 19-51.

Inglehart, R. and Welzel, C. (2005). *Modernization, cultural change and democracy*. New York: Cambridge University Press.

Inglehart, R. (2006). 'East European Value Systems in global perspective.' Klingemann, H.-D., Fuchs, D. and Zielonka, J. (eds.) *Democracy and political culture in Eastern Europe*. Routledge, 67-84.

Kalmus, V. and Vihalemm, T. (2004). 'Eesti siirdekultuuri väärtused.' [Values of Estonian transition culture] Kalmus, V., Lauristin, M. and Pruulmann-Vengerfeldt, P. (eds.) *Eesti elavik 21. sajandi algul*. [Estonian experience at the beginning of the 21st century]. Tartu University Press, 31-43.

Kalmus, V. and Vihalemm, T. (2008a). 'Patterns of continuity and disruption: The specificity of young people's mental structures in the three traditional societies.' *East European Politics Societies*, 16 (3): 251-278.

Kalmus, V. and Vihalemm, T. (2008b). 'Cultural differences: identity and values.' *Estonian Human Development Report* 2007, 67-72.

Kalmus, V. and Vihalemm, T. (2006). 'Distinct Mental Structures in Transitional Culture: An Empirical Analysis of Values and Identities in Estonia and Sweden.' *Journal of Baltic Studies*, 37: 94-123.

Kasser, T., Cohn, S., Kanner, A. D. and Ryan, R. M. (2007). 'Some costs of American corporate capitalism: A psychological exploration of value and goal conflicts.' *Psychological Inquiry*, 18 (1): 1-22.

Kazjulja, M. and Roosalu, T. (2011). 'Achieving high level occupational status: The relevance of social network capital.' Saar, E. (ed.) *Towards a normal stratification order. Actual and Perceived Social Stratification in Post-Socialist Estonia*. Peter Lang Publishers House, 219-252.

Kennedy, M. D. (2002). *Cultural Formations of Postcommunism. Emancipation, Transition, Nation, and War*. Minneapolis: University of Minnesota Press.

Kluckhohm, C. (1956). 'Toward a comparison of value emphases in different cultures.' White, L. (ed.) *The state of the social sciences*. Chicago: Chicago University Press, 116-132.

Lauristin, M., Vihalemm, P., Rosengren, K. E. and Weibull, L. (eds.) (1997). *Return to the Western World: Cultural and political perspectives on the Estonian post-communist transition*. Tartu: University of Tartu Press.

Lauristin, M. (2004). 'Eesti ühiskonna kihistumine.' [Stratification in Estonian society]. Kalmus, V., Lauristin, M, and Pruulmann-Vengerfeldt, P. (eds.) *21. sajandi algus: uurimuse 'Mina. Maailm. Meedia' aruanne*. [The beginning of the 21st century: Report on the study 'Me, the World, Media']. Tartu: Tartu University Press, 25-40.

Lauristin, M. and Vihalemm, T. (1997). 'Changing Value Systems: Civilizational Shift Local Differences.' Lauristin, M. and Vihalemm, P. (eds.) *Return to the Western World: Cultural and Political Perspectives on the Estonian Post-Communist Transition*. Tartu University Press, Tartu, 243-263.

Lauristin, M. and Vihalemm, P. (2009). *Estonia's transition to the EU: twenty years on*. Routledge.

Lilleoja, L. and Tart, I. (2011). 'Estonian Basic Value Structures.' Tart, I. (ed.) *Basic Human Values in Estonia and Baltic Sea Countries*. Tartu University Press, 39-62.

Lilleoja, L. (2012). 'Sünnikohortide alusväärtused ja nende muutumine nullindate Eestis.' [Basic values of birth cohorts and their changes in Estonia in the early 2000s] Aarelaid-Tart, A. (ed.) *Nullindate kultuur II: Põlvkondlikud pihtimused*. [The culture of the early 2000s II: confessions of generations]. Tartu: Tartu University Press, 247- 265.

Narusk, A., Hansson, L., Kelam, A. and Laidmäe, V. (1999). 'Changing values and attitudes 1985-1998.' *Estonian Human Development Report*, 30-35.

Raudsepp, M. (2011). 'Values as a Regulative Device of Mind and Culture.' Tart, I. (ed.) *Basic Human Values in Estonia and Baltic Sea Countries*. Tartu University Press , XI(1/2), 69-100.

Rudnev, M. and Magun, V. (2010). 'The Life Values of the Russian Population. Similarities and Differences in Comparison with Other European Countries.' *Sociological Research*, 49(4): 3-57; 51(6): 19-73.

Rämmer, A. (2008). 'Teel tagasi Läände: eestlaste hoiakud ja väärtused post-sovjetlikul ajastul.' [On the way back to the West: Estonians' attitudes and values in the post-soviet period] Rämmer, A. (ed.) *Vaateid teelahkmelt: Sotsioloogia, sotsiaaltöö ja sotsiaalpoliitika aktuaalseid probleeme Eestis*. [Views from the crossroads: Topical problems of sociology, social work and social policy in Estonia]. Tartu University Press, 32- 64.

Rämmer, A. (2011). 'Soolised erinevused sõjajärgse ja võitjate põlvkonna tööväärtustes.' [Gender differences in the work values of the post-war and winners' generation]. *Ariadne lõng* [Ariadne's thread], XI (1/2): 69-100.

Saar, E. (ed.) (2011). *Towards a normal stratification order Actual and Perceived Social Stratification in Post-Socialist Estonia*. Peter Lang Publishers House.

Saarniit, J. (1995). 'Changes in value orientations in youth and their social context.' Tomasi, L. (ed.) *Values and post-soviet youth. The problem of transition*. Milano: Franco Angeli, 141-153.

Saarniit, J. (1997). 'Mitte-eesti noorte väärtusteadvuse spetsiifikast.' [Specific features of value consciousness of non-Estonian adolescents] Järve, P. (ed.) *Vene noored Eestis: sotsioloogiline mosaiik*. [Russian adolescents in Estonia: sociological mosaic]. Tartu: Avita, 69-82.

Sagiv, L., and Schwartz, S. H. (2000). 'Value priorities and subjective well-being: Direct relations and congruity effects.' *European Journal of Social Psychology*, 30(2): 177-198.

Schwartz, S. H. and Bardi. A. (2001). 'Value hierarchies across cultures: Taking a similarities perspective.' *Journal of Cross-Cultural Psychology*, 32: 268-290.

Schwartz, S. H. (1997). 'Influences of adaptation to communist rule on value priorities in Eastern Europe.' *Political Psychology*, 18(2): 385- 410.

Schwartz, S. H. (2007). 'Cultural and individual value correlates of capitalism: A comparative analysis.' *Psychological Inquiry*, 18(1): 52-57.

Schwartz, S. H. (2008) 'Values: cultural and individual.' Van de Vijver, F. J. R., Chasiotis, A. and Breugelmans, S. M. (eds.) *Fundamental questions in cross-cultural psychology*. Cambridge: Cambridge University Press, 463-493.

Shlapentokh, V. (1982). 'The study of values as a social phenomenon: The Soviet case.' *Social Forces* 61(2): 403-417.

Shlapentokh, V. (1985). 'Two levels of public opinion: The Soviet case.' *Public Opinion Quarterly*, 49: 443-459.

Spini, D. (1997). *Valeurs et representations sociales des droits de l homme: Une approche structurale. These*. Universite de Geneve.

Sõmer, M. (2011). 'Heterogeneity of the Estonian Values Space.' Tart, I. (ed.) *Basic Human Values in Estonia and Baltic Sea Countries*. Tartu University Press, 63-87.

Szakolczai, A. and Füstös, L. (1998). 'Value systems in axial moments: A comparative analysis of 24 European countries.' *European Sociological Review*, 14(3): 211-229.

Sztompka, P. (1996). 'Looking back: The year 1989 as a cultural and civilizational break.' *Communist and Post-Communist Studies*, 29(2): 115-129.

Sztompka, P. (2004). 'The trauma of social change. A case of postcommunist societies.' Alexander, J. C., Eyerman, R., Giesen, B., Smelser, N. and Sztompka, P. (eds.) *Cultural Trauma and Collective Identity*. Berkeley, CA: University of California Press, 155-195.

Tart, I. (2008). 'Alusväärtused Eestis – lõimumise ressurss?' [Basic values in Estonia – a resource for integration?] Ainsaar, M. and Kutsar, D. (eds.) *Eesti Euroopa võrdlustes*. [Estonia in European comparisons]. Tallinn: Eesti Vabariigi Sotsiaalministeerium, 101-113.

Tart, I. (2011). 'Basic human values of Sweden, Finland and Estonia. Change and stability of value systems in 1991-2005.' Tart, I. (ed.) *Basic human values in Estonia and Baltic Sea countries*. Tartu: Tartu University Press, 89-110.

Titma, M., Silver, B. D., Vöörmann, R and Johnson, D. (1996). 'The Estonian longitudinal survey.' *International Journal of Sociology*, 26: 76-93.

Titma, M. and Helemäe, L. (1996). 'Occupational values of Estonian generations. International.' *Journal of Sociology*, 26(3): 31-52.

Titma, M., Paalandi; V., Koreinik, K. and Murakas, R. (1999). *Kolmekümneaastaste põlvkonna sotsiaalne portree*. [A social portrait of the thirty-year-olds' generation]. Tartu; Tallinn: Teaduste Akadeemia Kirjastus.

Titma, M. and Paalandi, V. (2001). 'Eluorientatsioonide ealine dünaamika ja seda kujundavad faktorid.' [Age dynamics of life orientations and factors influencing it] Titma, M. (ed.) *Sõjajärgse põlvkonna elutee ja seda kujundanud faktorid*. [Life of the post-war generation and factors shaping it]. Tartu: Tartu University Press, 225-263.

Titma, M. and Roots, A. (2002). 'Eluorientatsioonide kujunemine.' [The development of life orientations] Titma, M. (ed.) *30- ja 50-aastaste põlvkonnad uue aastatuhande künnisel*. [Generations of 30- and 50-year-olds on the threshold of the new millennium]. Tartu: Tartu University Press, 174-205.

Toomere, T. (2001). 'Väärtusorientatsioonide muutused postsotsialistlikes riikides.' [Changes in values in post-socialist countries]. *Akadeemia* 13 (12): 2543-2560.

Verkasalo, M., Daun, A. and Niit, T. (1994). 'Universal values in Estonia, Finland and Sweden.' *Ethnologia Europeae* 24 (2): 101-117.

Vetik, R. (ed.) (2012). *Nation-building in the context of post-communist transformation and globalization. The case of Estonia*. Bern: Peter Lang Verlag.

Vihalemm, T. and Kalmus, V. (2009). 'Cultural Differentiation of the Russian Minority.' *Journal of Baltic Studies*, 40 (1): 95-119.

Vogt, H. (2005). *Between utopia and disillusionment: A narrative of the political transformation in Eastern Europe*. New York: Berghahn Books.

Appendix 1

Assessment of life values by Estonian population in 1985, 1993, 1998, 2003 and 2008, response very important, %

How important are for you....	Abbreviation	year				
		1985	1993	1998	2003	2008
Children, their welfare	Children	76	83	87	83	82
Family	Family	62	76	84	80	85
Health	Health	–	73	81	79	80
Clean, unpolluted nature	Nature	47	66	60	50	49
Love	Love	49	46	57	54	57
Economic well-being	EconWB	37	41	43	47	46
Close friends	Friends	24	34	39	39	43
Professional work	Profwork	26	28	38	28	25
Keeping up-to-date with current affairs (radio, TV, *etc.*)	WEvents	22	21	17	23	–
Self-education	SelfEduc	9	13	18	20	20
Physical fitness	Fitness	13	11	11	14	22
Cultural interests (reading, going to the theatre, movies, *etc.*)	CultIntr	14	13	14	13	14
Varied life	VarLife	14	10	13	11	13
Faith	Faith	–	17	20	7	7
Creative activities (technical, artistic, *etc.*)	Creative	5	5	6	8	–
Voluntary activity, social participation	VolunAc	5	2	3	4	5
High social position	HighPos	–	4	4	4	4

Sources: 'Eesti 2008', 'Eesti 2003', 'Eesti 98', 'Eesti 93', 'Eesti 85', TPÜ RASI

Appendix 2

Mean ratings and standard deviations of life values

	1985	1993	1998	2003	2008
Children, their welfare	4.6 (0.80)	4.8 (0.59)	4.8 (0.57)	4.7 (0.65)	4.7 (0.67)
Family	4.5 (0.80)	4.7 (0.62)	4.8 (0.52)	4.8 (0.53)	4.8 (0.46)
Health	–	4.7 (0.54)	4.8 (0.50)	4.8 (0.53)	4.8 (0.54)
Clean, unpolluted nature	4.3 (0.85)	4.6 (0.61)	4.5 (0.69)	4.4 (0.79)	4.4 (0.75)
Love	4.2 (0.91)	4.2 (0.85)	4.4 (0.78)	4.4 (0.82)	4.4 (0.80)
Economic well-being	4.2 (0.72)	4.2 (0.72)	4.3 (0.71)	4.4 (0.72)	4.4 (0.69)
Close friends	3.8 (1.02)	4.0 (0.93)	4.2 (0.85)	4.1 (0.95)	4.3 (0.83)
Professional work	3.9 (0.89)	3.9 (0.92)	4.1 (0.85)	3.9 (0.97)	3.8 (1.06)
Keeping up-to-date with current affairs (radio, TV, *etc.*)	3.9 (0.87)	3.8 (0.84)	3.7 (0.83)	3.9 (0.98)	–
Self-education	3.3 (1.08)	3.5 (0.93)	3.7 (1.02)	3.7 (1.04)	3.8 (0.98)
Physical fitness	3.4 (1.12)	3.3 (0.97)	3.5 (0.91)	3.5 (1.09)	3.8 (1.03)
Cultural interests (reading, going to the theatre, movies, *etc.*)	3.7 (0.92)	3.5 (0.91)	3.5 (0.93)	3.4 (1.4)	3.4 (1.16)
Varied life	3.2 (1.21)	3.0 (1.10)	3.3 (1.06)	3.0 (1.24)	3.2 (1.22)
Faith	–	2.9 (1.38)	3.1 (1.34)	2.3 (1.27)	2.3 (1.27)
Creative activities (technical, artistic, *etc.*)	2.5 (1.22)	2.6 (1.10)	2.7 (1.08)	2.8 (1.18)	–
Voluntary activity, social participation	2.9 (1.14)	2.3 (0.97)	2.6 (0.98)	2.6 (1.14)	2.7 (1.16)
High social position	–	2.1 (1.16)	2.4 (1.15)	2.1 (1.15)	2.2 (1.16)

***Standard deviation** shows how much variation or 'dispersion' exists from the average. A low standard deviation indicates that the data points tend to be very close to the mean, whereas high standard deviation indicates that the data points are spread out over a large range of values.*

Appendix 3

Rank order of 12 life values that were present in all the surveys throughout 1985-2008 (based on mean ratings)

	1985	1993	1998	2003	2008
Children, their welfare	1	1	1	2	2
Family	2	2	2	1	1
Clean, unpolluted nature	3	3	3	5	4
Love	4	5	4	3	3
Economic well-being	5	4	5	4	5
Close friends	7	6	6	6	6
Professional work	6	7	7	7	7
Self-education	10	8	8	8	8
Cultural interests (reading, going to the theatre, movies, *etc.*)	8	9	9	10	10
Physical fitness	9	10	10	9	9
Varied life	11	11	11	11	11
Voluntary activity, social participation	12	12	12	12	12

Continuities of residential cultures. Re-inventing identities in single-family houses

Katrin Paadam, Liis Ojamäe

Introduction

Single-family housing has remained a dominant home ideal in Estonia throughout the societal ruptures of the disquiet 20th century. This preference had been pervasive despite the severe drawbacks in the actual opportunities to acquire a family house in the conditions of centrally controlled housing provision system and a prevalence of large-scale blocks under state socialism – a legacy continuously and noticeably present in today's housing scene. Likewise, there seems to be an enduring niche for single-family housing in an intensified market supply with, especially, the gradually enlarging scale of the different type of residential offers, which attempt to meet the increasingly diversifying lifestyle-driven demands for individual ways of residing.

The experience sought in single-family houses has been widely observed as a continuous residential preference in an abundance of studies on European societies, as well as across continents (*cf.* Ruonavaara 1996; Ilmonen 2007 on Finland; Vestergaard 2006 on Denmark; Støa 1996 on Norway; Borgegård and Kemeny 2004 on Sweden; Karsten 2007 on Netherlands; Bourdieu 2005 on France; Nicolaides and Wiese 2006 on USA; Kemeny 1992, 1995a on Australia; *etc.*). Although entwined with the meaning of home and often also with the meaning of homeownership there, however, are important differences embedded in the social and cultural histories of societies behind the shaping of this preference.

Appearing in different forms, design and spatial opportunities, single-family houses, while assumed to reflect residents' tastes, but equally their economic capacities, are associated with individuals' performances and self-representations, and are also open to symbolic categorisations of social groups. (Sirgy *et al.* 2005; Æro 2006; Mallett 2004). In general terms, the single-family house in Estonia represents a preferable way of residing, the significance of which builds on characteristics that contrast with a block of flats and, thus, with a distinct cultural prospect for home creation. In this regard, single-family housing may be considered as standing for a residential cultural heritage of particularity, sustained in continuous re-invention of residential and social identities. Hence, while signalling potentially multifarious identities, a single-family house also bespeaks national pride, though mainly as a sign of distinction from the historically defined conditions of the collective way of residing forced on individuals and families by the previous regime.

We propose that the developments in the housing field, which followed the 1990s' transformation with the apparently booming single-family housing preference and can be observed in sprawling new detached housing settlements, had a special symbolic significance in Estonia, fully comprehensible if considered against the societal disruption of the 1940s. The connections forming between the historical contexts of nationalisation and denationalisation of land and housing property allow, on the one hand, tracing and, therefore, understanding the structural consequences of the recent reform on housing relations and a cultural turn reflected on the (re)construction of dispositions towards greater individuality in residential choices, on the other hand. With the normalisation of private ownership of housing with restored pre-occupation ownership rights on the basis, this change denotes alteration of the context of opportunities for the realisation of residential preferences in a dual relationship with the making of the markets. The irruptive single-family housing development opening to visual observation, heavily promoted in 'home of one's own' popular-style market discourse is, however, deceptive when assessed on higher shares of flats in the total of newly constructed dwellings.

While content with single-family housing as a stable preference, we assert appeasement of this boom of preference along with the diversification of offers in the market (Ojamäe and Paadam 2009a). Also, one should not exclude the exceptional cases of becoming a house owner – by inheritance or in the occurrence of unexpected opportunities for house purchasing, as opposed to a mature preferential choice of residence, constructed as part of a long-term individual or family strategy or a biographical plan.

It is, however, argued that the construction and realisation of residential preferences in any of the situations forming in individual lives assume inclination, a dispositional basis having formed within the social experience (Bourdieu 1989 [1979]; Paadam 2003). Furthermore, as asserted elsewhere (Bourdieu 2005; Ojamäe 2009), residential preferences stemming from the perception of the ideal tend to be modified in the process of choosing a residence. Therefore the actual choice might appear as a reflection of the changing ideal or an adjustment to the possible.

Set in the structural context of the evolving Estonian housing field, the discussion of single-family housing as a way of residing of significance draws on two subsequent qualitative studies from 2000 and 2006. The interviews conducted with altogether thirty house owners unfold on different recent phases of restructuring and maturation of relations in the field and in the society. With enquiries into the ways the house-owners conceive of the value and experience of residing in single-family houses, our primary interest centres on the interconnectivities building between individuals' unique experiences and broader cultural images of *a house of one's own.* This is, in particular, in terms of the formation of preferences and actual choices at the changing residential and social circumstances. More specifically, the paper addresses questions on how the shaping of images of a house of one's own can be interpreted in the dramatically constrained conditions for individual choice-making (in the Soviet period), and at moving towards dilated scales of supply of different types of residences in residential markets; how the perceived continuities of a single-family way of residing can be understood as a foundation as well as an aspiration for the (re)construction of identities.

Constructing residential identities and the ways of residing

It has been continuously argued from the earlier works onwards that housing appears as 'a sign of identity' (Gullestad 1984: 152) primarily for the visibility of its form and condition, and often, if not always, subject to judgements on its residents. As easily available to the gaze (Bourdieu 2005), housing alludes its importance both for external categorisations as well as for self-perceptions of individual residents, and thus, for ways they construct their residential and social identities in broader terms (Jenkins 2000; Forrest and Kearns 2001; Clapham 2005; Hauge and Kolstad 2007; Mallett 2004; Karsten 2007; Rapoport 2001). This is, however, known from distinct historical social practices that spatial and physical aspects of housing could concur as inexhaustible or misleading proof for judgements forming upon different cultural and social experiences of the spectators. In this vein, the collectivist ideologically defined housing typology of the past – read from the amount and (low) quality of large-scale urban residential blocks in Estonia – tells little about the residents' current tenure status as owners or their residential preferences of rather the single-family housing as standing for a home ideal (Paadam 2003; Ojamäe and Paadam 2009a and 2009b). Therefore, the residential situations as they open to observation in their physical and spatial structural forms need to be considered within the duality of the genesis of societal structural relations and individuals' dispositions and capacity to act upon the historical, cultural and personal circumstances forming in their lives at a particular time.

Residential buildings and localities of distinct architectural typologies, aesthetics and quality, are by nature of a complex character appearing both as image-provoking (Forrest and Kearns 2001) as well image-influenced (Kauko 2006 on Marwell 2004). Conveying an array of symbolic values and, in particular, those ascribed to home and the related mystification of homeownership (Bourdieu 1989 [1979], 1999 [1972], 2005; Kemeny 1992), the residential buildings and wider settings have been avowed to be central to identity (Hall and Coffey 1999: 6). This understanding is even strengthened in more recent interpretations of contemporary user practices, where residence appears not only as an end in itself but also as a means to an end (Clapham 2005, 2006), and hence, purporting a link with pursued lifestyles and identity construction. Also in this vein, neighbourhoods are becoming increasingly differentiated in terms of their meaning and associated lifestyles (Clapham 2005: 182). Put in a consumer perspective, housing bears upon the symbolic competence of users signifying their social status and, respectively, the identity present in inter-subjective negotiation of values and meanings between members of society or social groups (Chaney 1996: 45).

Patterns of residential consumption emphasising symbolic values are, however, increasingly addressed in conjunction with articulated lifestyles (Kauko 2006: 97 on Kloosterman and Lambregts 2001) suggesting less salient social divisions between individuals' performances (Warde 2005) and greater ambiguity in the observable hierarchies of residential identities. In this light, residential choices are to be increasingly considered a matter of lifestyle choice forming not necessarily in a linear relationship with affordability or even a phase in individual or family lives, as in interpretations of a more traditional nature.

It is argued that contemporary residential choices bespeak reciprocity of individuals' differentiated and more refined needs for spatial consumption also enabling personalised self-expression of tastes for aesthetics and that of the generally rising standard of living (Woodward 2003; Æro 2006; Paadam, Gromark and Ojamäe 2011). As observed elsewhere, the increased importance of aesthetics relates to the decreased importance of housing as shelter (Burnett 1986 on the social history of British housing); which is to the evolvement of welfare conditions supporting individualisation of residential tastes not only along, but within, and occasionally across, social groups. Merging into a diversity of lifestyles, the social and functional, and the physical and symbolic aspects of residence are hardly specified in direct correspondence with tastes identified upon individuals' positioning in social space (as often drawn on Bourdieu).

In order to embrace the complexity of this multilayered interplay of aspects, which inspire action and contribute to the eventual construction of distinct residential identities as well as symbolic categorisations, we have conceived the notion of *ways of residing* (Paadam 2004, 2007). As a dimension of lifestyle constituted in residential and wider social practices, ways of residing unfold as a complex cultural phenomena on the nature of socio-physical relations forming on all interrelated spatial scales of a residence (from immediate private and semi-private spaces in buildings to public spaces of neighbourhoods). A key-issue for understanding ways of residing is to conceive of the linkages building between the socio-physical relations and individuals' differentiated capacities to relate to residence, both on the level of actions as well as aspirations (Paadam 2003). The notion of capacity is derived from Bourdieu's theory of practice (1999 [1972]). Putting equal emphasis on the importance of convertible social, cultural and symbolic dimensions, beside economic aspects in the shaping of human dispositions and actions, it is considered highly relevant for also the study of residence (*cf.* Bourdieu 1998, 2005).

Individual ways of residing, as a dynamic concept, can be analysed in the context of housing careers intertwining with family careers, working careers or activities in other fields, albeit not necessarily as synchronised performances. Sometimes housing careers simply turn out to be what they are (Ruonavaara 1998) or occur by accident (O'Dwyer 1999) or unexpectedly, for the worse, or for the better as, for example, in cases of interference by profound societal transformations (Paadam 2003) or structural changes in the field and individual capacity (Ojamäe 2009) demanding improvisation and adjustment to the circumstances upon the availability of individual capacity (Bourdieu 1994 [1990]). It is, nevertheless, asserted that ways of residing are a consequence of the dual continuously changing relationship between individual endeavours and structural dynamics of institutional conditions (*e.g.* public and market policies) shaped as well by different actor-interests (*e.g.* local governments or property developers) in the field. What is symbolically significant about the experience of residence is its personal nature, often crystallised in the emotive notion of home, which cannot be understood apart from values embedded in collective experience whereby meanings and identities are constructed (*cf.* also Kemeny 1992).

There exist different understandings of home and, more importantly, different ways in which its meaning is being constructed as well as interpreted (Bourdieu 1999 [1972] and 2005; Bachelard 1999 [1957]; Cooper Marcus 1995; Edensor 1997; Dovey 1999; Harris and Davis 2001). Nevertheless, as a social and cultural construct (Lewin 2001: 356; Rowlands and Gurney 2000) home manifests the affiliating bonds to a place and to the experience of a place (Benjamin 1995). Furthermore, the construction of the meaning of home bears upon the collective cultural experience emotionally as well as do unique experiences of individuals of socio-physical relations forming on the complexity of spatial scales of a residence (Paadam 2003). As has been asserted elsewhere, the socially constructed meaning of home is neither a consequence of a purely individualistic nor of a purely social process; it is forming in an interactive process of individual human activity operating in the social context of place (Perkins and Thorns 1999: 130).

It is contended that imageries of home draw largely on the symbolic differentiation of residences, which are believed to enable distinct ways of residing as associated with the potential of buildings and neighbourhoods of particular architectural typology to support preferable lifestyles. A more detailed enquiry into any specific way of residing in any particular type of residence reveal, however, internal diversities in the actual performance of individuals which tend to be connected to different cultural orientation.

Charged with this knowledge, the client request is met as well as promoted in property development and marketing strategies. However, contemporary property development, sales and construction strategies, (re)constructing the criteria of desirable housing, contribute to commodification and homogenisation rather than diversification and personalisation of residential supply (Ojamäe 2010; Bourdieu 2005; *cf.* Perkins *et al.* 2008; Gottdiener 1995). With the exceptions of, for example, gentrified residential districts and converted buildings offering greater personality (Paadam, Gromark and Ojamäe 2011), as well as a few single-family signature buildings, this trend particularly concerns the new sprawling detached housing developments.

The 'house of one's own' – changing structural circumstances and residential cultures

The single-family house – the 'house of one's own' in popular discourse reflecting important symbolic values – has been dominating the scale of residential preferences in Estonia. This also concerns the largest city Tallinn (70% preferring a detached house in 1995, 61% in 2008, *cf.* Tallinna linnaelanike… 1995; Ojamäe and Paadam 2009a), with only a marginal share of detached houses, and larger rather than smaller blocks prevailing in stock since the beginning of the construction of large-scale housing in the early 1960s.[3] The reasons for the persistency of preferential dispositions towards having a house of one's own could be seen as lying in the historical formation of the urban residential scenes related also to relatively late urbanisation (as in Kemeny 1995b) as well as in the personal experience of residents and their perceptions of residential values. With the exception of the centrally located larger public and residential buildings from the early 20th century, the generally relatively low-scale residential blocks

3 The early post-WWII construction substituted the stock damaged during the war with blocks of mild Stalinism (Kalm 2001); as represented in various forms, it never really reached the monumental volume for which it is known (Stalinistlik maja 2012). Aside small blocks and villas of different styles, significantly also the functionalist buildings (Kalm *ibid.*) the Tallinn housing stock predominantly consisted of small-scale wooden blocks at the beginning of the 1930s (Eesti arvudes 1920-1935 1937).

with semi-private gardens characteristic of the built environment from pre-WWII period, as well as family houses of the garden city movement from the end of the 19th century, and increasingly during the first decades of the 20th century in the border areas and outside the city of Tallinn and other larger towns (Bruns 1993: 101-102) have been shaping the image of the city and perceptions of preferential residence. Some of these, initially resort areas, have become parts of the city (*e.g.* Nõmme and Pirita districts in Tallinn), where the family houses, villas or small blocks with private and semi-private gardens continuously shape the urban scene.

It is quite obvious that the consequences of the Soviet period – the enforced change from the capitalist to socialist social system in the 1940s – having fundamentally transformed the functional logic of the society, dramatically affected urban and residential development. After the nationalisation and expropriation of private property, public housing became a dominant tenure form. The non-egalitarian patterns of housing distribution, also characteristic of the CEE-wide state socialist system, having guaranteed residential choices for mainly the top-status people in the social and political state hierarchy (Mandic and Clapham 1996; Gentile and Tammaru 2006) substituted the market-based housing development in Estonia.

During that period, first for the war-damaged housing stock, and increasingly for meeting the housing need of the growing population with a significant in-flow of immigrants from other parts of the Soviet Union, construction of large blocks of flats was prioritised in order to alleviate the housing deficit. However, the housing deficit remained unsolved throughout the period of state socialism (Bruns 1993; Social Trends 2 2001) for there was continuous unavailability of adequate space that would have met families' needs as well as limited opportunities to acquire a preferable type of residence. In these conditions the symbolic value of a single-family house signifying a distinct way of residing was only strengthened.

Nevertheless, the housing deficit made private housing construction possible to some extent, especially during the years 1958-1964, when the share of smaller detached houses made up approximately one fifth of new construction. Although those 'house-owners'[4] were provided with some support by the state (free land, a limited number of long-term loans, Roopalu and Veski 1959), it often meant

4 In the Soviet socialist system ownership of housingproperty was not considered as realty for the state-owned land property. However, as concerned the designated right to use or obligation to invest and maintain the house and the plot, the residents of the private houses could be considered Soviet equivalent to property owners, reinforced as such in the public perception.

considerable private investments and self-help construction. Therefore, the average construction periods lasted more than 10 years. The residential plots were limited to 300-600 m^2 in larger towns, and 700-1200 m^2 in smaller towns and rural settlements, as were the sizes for buildings from 50 to 70 m^2 (1950s-1960s, Roopalu and Veski 1959: 5). Until the 1980s detached houses were usually built without central water and sewage systems and in the 1950s-1970s often without running water.

Despite the shortcomings in the quality of newly built single-family houses built with limited resources and under severe constraints as to space, the aesthetics and planning of these houses had been shaped by the construction culture and traditions from the earlier period (Kalm 2001). These buildings represent a different idea of home from what had been promoted by the Soviet ideology (see also Kannike 2005). Together with small residential blocks from the pre-occupation period they symbolised appreciated ways of residing and an ideal type of residential culture. The symbolic meaning of a family house, especially, as a distinct residential identity had been deeply rooted in the national self-perception and reconstructed in contrast to the expansion of Soviet collectivist-type large-scale monotonous blocks of no appreciated aesthetics or functional character, with no control of residents over the centralised management and maintenance system, the mixed composition of inhabitants, with quite distinct previous residential experiences ultimately affecting the daily residential practices. During that period 'a house of one's own' became, however, a myth in a sense of property ownership and could rather be defined by way of residing as part of a lifestyle people dreamed of (Paadam and Ojamäe 2008).

The property ownership reform at the beginning of the regained independent statehood in the 1990s had also a profound effect on the detached housing sector. Restitution (built before WWII) and privatisation of housing property (former public housing)[5] re-opened, though differentiated prospects for entering the market. Residential construction, having come to almost a standstill during the first years of the 1990s' reconstruction of housing relations, concerned only a limited number of new villas affordable mainly to the *nouveau riche* with economic capacity to self-finance their new residences. The top-market single-family houses which dominated the construction field in the 1990s were peaking with 74% of the new construction in 1997. The development of single-family houses for sale was initiated in 1996-1997. However, due to the economic constraints and the lack of long-term housing loans at that time, old detached houses and summerhouses available for transformation into permanent residences in

5 96% of the dwellings, predominantly in large blocks, are in private ownership (Statistics Estonia) while the owner-occupation rate is 84% (as of 2006, Social Trends 4 2007).

suburban and more distant areas[6] provided a more affordable alternative, but again only for the more economically well-off individuals and families (Elamistingimused 2000).

The situation changed at the beginning of the 2000s along with the turbulent processes in financial and property (construction) markets: during the period of 2000-2007 the annual price increase of residential properties reached 10-30% (Ojamäe 2009), the intensified construction resulted in suburbanisation and sprawling developments around larger towns, especially the capital city of Tallinn, where the suburban population growth has been the fastest (Tammaru *et al.* 2009).[7] The new residential settlements, which had been the main targets of detached housing construction during the boom were characterised by a rather homogeneous contingency of residents of mostly Estonians (86%, *cf.* in Tallinn 54%, in Estonia 68%) and highly qualified specialists whose income per household member was on average 150% higher than the average in Tallinn (Ahas and Silm 2006). In 2005, a wish to have a 'house of one's own' was amongst the most frequently stated reasons for moving and purchasing the property (*ibid.*), which despite the respondents' above the average affordability level has not been accessible at a closer distance to the city where the property prices are relatively higher.

The current stock of family houses is differentiated both by age and quality: 49% of the houses have been built before World War II and 9% after 1991 with older family houses tending to be smaller and of a lower comfort level, especially in the countryside (Elamistingimused 2000). The newer houses of higher quality tend to be owned by households in the highest quintile whereas the share of family houses owned by households of the lowest as well as the highest income quintiles is almost the same (28 and 29% respectively) (Income and Living Conditions 2005). This curious relation points, with insights into the history of the field, as to the restituted property as well the property continuously in the possession of families or the relatively large share of self-built family houses in the Soviet period.

Nevertheless, the ownership of single-family houses with 32% of the total stock per country and only 10% in Tallinn (Statistics Estonia 2012) has remained marginal despite the lasting preference. The assumptions behind the

---

6 A recent study has indicated that the former second homes in Tallinn Metropolitan Area have offered more significant access to detached housing than new residential developments in the region (Leetmaa *et al.* 2012).

7 Although designating a spatially highly visible change of the (sub)urban residential areas, the annual share of new construction during the recent housing boom did not exceed the annual volumes of new construction during Soviet period (see Ojamäe 2009).

state-of-the-art of this particular section in the housing field tend to be complex, but mainly related to economic capacities, the prevalence of blocks in the newly constructed stock and, in the case of Tallinn, undoubtedly, the sprawl.

The qualitative study of house owners

Residential histories – the personal and collective met in biographies

The qualitative enquiry into the perceptions of a single-family house, the construction of dispositions towards this specific way of residing and residential identities built on entire biographical experiences of 30 house owners has been conducted at different periods of the latest reform of relations in the housing field.

The first 16 in-depth interviews involved house owners in mainly the two historical districts acknowledged as neighbourhoods of predominantly detached residences, in Tallinn in 2000. The houses of different size, quality and architectural styles have been obtained by restitution, inheritance or market purchase (see also Paadam 2003).

The second set of 14 in-depth interviews with 17 house owners (couples in 5 cases) were conducted in a new suburban settlement in a small town near Tallinn in 2006. The newly constructed detached and semi-detached houses of neo-functionalist style had been highly fashionable and of symbolic significance at the time of the property (see also Ojamäe 2009).

In 2000 the ownership reform had been almost completed in terms of the restitution of expropriated property to the owners or their legitimate heirs, and privatisation of most of the public housing property. The housing market was developing and the boom was slowly starting to emerge. The mobility had, however, been restricted or postponed for economic reasons for a decade as the long-term housing loans had only shortly become available. The interviewees, having obtained a family house at different pre- and post-transformation periods had not, obviously, foreseen this opportunity to be restored their property rights or the opening of the market. Their more or less matured preference for a family house had rather been realised quite *by accident* due to profound structural changes in the society. The analysis, though, discloses a solid dispositional basis, particularly, the cultural capital shaped within individuals' and families' earlier and present experiences having been driving their aspirations and prepared them for the opportunity to have a house of their own.

In 2006, the housing field was approaching the peak of the market boom. Within a short period, a rapid increase in housing construction as well as of offers in housing and financial markets occurred, accompanied by cheap housing loans. The year 2006, when the acquisition of a house was made possible due to favourable structural conditions, denoted the *fulfilment of a dream* in the interviewees' subjective interpretations. As it appeared, the wish to buy a house was supported by intensified market discourses, making use of appealing residential symbols bearing upon shared cultural memory, as well as dispositions having formed in individual housing histories.

The main difference between the two data sets lies in the particular phase of societal transformation and the ways the interviewees' have acquired their property. The first group while directly influenced by the ownership reform (restitution) was otherwise relatively heterogeneous in terms of the interviewees' socio-economic status, the location, as well as current market value of their property. The second group was more homogeneous and comprised rather 'typical' middle-class buyers of suburban housing. However, neither of the two data sets includes elitist house owners.

The biographical interviews applied in both of the studies are considered to allow deeper insights into interviewees' personal stories, which also reflect the collective experiences of rapidly changing social and economic contexts in Estonia. Bespeaking the interconnectivities between different social systems, they make sense in the formation of contemporary housing and, importantly, in relation to more enduring meaning structures. Interviews are analysed by using a thematic analysis approach focusing on interpretations of the interviewee's accounts on their residential preferences and experiences. While based on two different datasets the chapter seeks to find possible continuities in the construction of the family house ideal and respective residential identities amongst the house owners having acquired their property in different societal periods and in distinct ways.

Residing in a 'house and garden' – a lifestyle-driven preference

An aspiration for a family house can be understood when interpreted on its perceived resourcefulness compared to any other type of residential buildings. This is, primarily, for the opportunities a single-family house is expected to offer on a wide scale of residential space – in a house and the surrounding garden – exclusively for family use. This understanding is powerful in representations of owners of single-family houses independent of the way and time their property has been acquired – either before or unexpectedly after the societal structural transformation and property ownership reform of the 1990s, or in the recently formed, more mature market conditions of mid-2000s.

For both groups of house owners (interviewed respectively in 2000 and 2006) the main categories defining the merits of this specific way of residing are seen to be associated with freedom and privacy - a particular sense of greater autonomy in taking decisions on any aspect of designing and using the space at the disposal of its owners and in the interests of different family members on any of its scales[8]. The sense of privacy sought in a detached house clearly draws upon a cultural image of residence, which contrasts to collective ways of residing in large urban blocks and to a parallel current trend of transparent residing with foggy spatial boundaries between the private and the public.

> **Jaan** (2000): Most of my life I had lived in a house... You see, Estonians are people who need to have an opportunity to be on their own... think about our clustered villages. If your neighbour lives too close to peep into your window, an Estonian plants a high hedge in between the houses. This is not that a neighbour is a bad person. Simply, one has to have a zone of privacy.
>
> **Mikk** (2006): All by ourselves /.../, here we are the owners /.../, we can decide ourselves what to do, what not to do, how are we going to decorate things. It's just... the privacy and, well...o the feeling of being the owner. In the past, every Estonian wanted his own farmhouse and now I want my own house.

A family house tends to stand for a symbolic value of individual freedom warranted on a scale that inherently encompasses the outdoor space of a garden, signifying the specific meaning organically attributed to a house of one's own – a salient expression of a preference for the private use of green space in an otherwise urban setting.

> **Marika** (2000): When I had arrived here and put my bags down, then I was filled with the feeling that this was the place where I would like to die. /.../ I have again a lilac blooming under my window, a fireplace in sauna and green grass, I throw the door open and walk into my home yard. Now, now I have arrived at home.
>
> **Birgit** (2006): I have dreamed about having my own garden all my life, being able to step outside my front door and be in a garden.

House owners' emphasis on privacy as a desired function of space, combining interior and exterior facilities and enabling various individual and shared activities for family members, bespeaks the daily residential practice having met their preferred lifestyle and understanding of home.

> **Rahel** (2000): Almost every evening when we come home from work we set a fire in the fireplace in wintertime, but also in cold spring and autumn times. On Saturdays and Sundays we have fire going all day long... Fire belongs with having your family together.
>
> **Tom** (2006): We have always wanted our own house. Privacy is the main thing. /.../ My wife, of course, liked gardening, so that was her reason. She always has to have her fingers in the soil. Then she's in a good mood.

8 Within the limits of local planning and construction regulations.

High appreciation of the opportunity for creative self-engagement in the (re)designing, (re)constructing or repairing of the house and, importantly, the garden is characteristic of both the male and female members of families of devoted house owners, for this is genuinely part of their perception of a way of creating a sense of home.

> **Toomas** (2000): Although I have very little time, it gives you such a great feeling because you do something for your family and yourself… We could have hired a gardener like we hired a lighting designer, but my wife and I both think that the garden is such an intimate place in your home, which you create forever and you want to be part of it…

Regardless of a house owner's social position or economic capacities, with the necessity or pleasure behind the perceived need for a personal touch, self-involvement seems to reflect shared cultural dispositions.

> **Kadri** (2006): That feeling of being at home is created when you do something yourself, right? When someone else does it for you, you just move in, then yes, it may be a very cool design and so on, but still, that's why we did our own design… picked out the colours for the walls and all that.

The meaning of a house of one's own is tightly interwoven with the pervasive norm of property ownership, not necessarily defining, but certainly strengthening a sense of home. While making quite a differentiated group of economic capacities, house owners – whether the heirs, earlier house purchasers from before and after the societal transformation or owners of recently purchased properties – share a strong sense of responsibility in maintaining their property. Even when occurring, for different reasons, in circumstances of low solvency or investment capacity the overwhelming cultural preference for residing in a family house seems to be in pursuit of the ability to adjust to and manage the complicated phases forming in their lives.

> **Inna** (2000): You see, it's an old house which needs constant care, work. You must have a big wallet and if you don't… it is difficult. We would like to let more things done by hired men, but /…/. We collect money and then get things done one after another, year by year…
>
> **Eve** (2006): For me, it's the fulfilment of a huge dream, yes. /…/ when it comes to a house, you are willing to spend all your earnings on and I don't know what else, time and all that. /…/ No matter how it turns out, it's not that important. Just the fact that you have your own little nest that you work on, little by little it builds, no matter how it shows.

As long as the experience of residing in a family house is conceived as a process of continuous home creation and part of a preferable lifestyle, the daily running of a house and garden, whilst with the load of occasional concerns, is considered a creative activity and fulfilling achievement.

Re-constructing identities and residential heritage culture

The house owners' representations of their current residential experiences in a family house tend to tell the stories of inherited cultural dispositions through evidence of inter-connections building between generations. This implies that today's owners share an inclination towards reconstructing their appreciated childhood experience of parental homes, grandparents' town or country houses or family's second homes, even if only of seasonal use, in the endowment of an experience of a house to their children whenever their overall individual capacity and structural circumstances allow.

> **Toomas** (2000): Before we moved to X (large-scale 1970s' housing area in Tallinn), we lived in the countryside at my grandparents' house. Ever since have I been wishing that my daughter had the same good and safe childhood home as I have had...and you live your childhood only once.
>
> **Kadri** (2006): I have lived in a house since I was a child and life in a flat has never been for me. Like when you know that there are people next to you, under you, above you, everywhere...

In Bourdieu's words (1994 [1990]) this attempt reveals a particular cultural 'feel for a game' reinforced also by the eventual disapproval of experiences of collective residing under the previous regime and the offers of the residential markets; albeit the market related rhetoric of property ownership is important in house owners' representations of their intentions or experiences but overshadowed by the symbolic, emotional and practical consumer values. Also, as concerns the reconstruction of dispositional heritage, the process assumes to be understood as a continuous evolvement of personal values, tastes and lifestyles reflected in distinct decisions on (re)designing family residences. As unattached from social, economic and cultural structural circumstances at a time there build both the inter-generational and intra-generational distinctions between individual house owners.

> **Inna** (2000): My mother-in-law's garden was something different. It was a cabbage garden. She has a different lifestyle. I had to re-make it in my own way /.../ We have a few herbs for summer cooking, but mainly there is lawn now and flowers /.../ It took quite some time, but now I feel this is my home.

However, the common feature that applies to house owners under observation, particularly concerns their perception of a single-family house as enabling a greater personality in home creation, the expression of personal taste manifested on spatial scales of a house and the garden and, hence, (re)invention of owner identity. In these terms, designing or redesigning a family residence follows the basic logic of conceptualising the aesthetics and functional quality of residence. The question of taste, often judged upon the visibility of the aesthetics is, however, a sort of intangible category. There appear to be two broadly distinguishable dispositions towards the aesthetics and usability of a detached house – the one, which stems from the historical heterogeneity of the Estonian residential architecture and the other one praising a more homogeneous design of new developments, especially, on the neighbourhood level.

> **Markus** (2000): You cannot expect everyone to have the same taste. Detached housing areas are suitable places for expressing oneself. Houses look like their owners /.../ in Canada /.../ their detached housing areas are depressingly boring, insensitive. But there should be some general rules for everyone as to the height, capacity of the buildings and fences, which no one should violate. On the other hand, these laws should be rather liberal to enable the creation of a sense of personality.

As concerns the pursuit of homogeneity or unity of architectural solutions, then this rather refers to interviewees' yearning for harmony together with personality missed in many a neighbourhood of either the exaggerated and contradicting built forms or, reversely, the monotonous new developments of single-family housing.

> **Tom** (2006): Having houses of functional style next to log houses... That was out of question for us from the beginning. If we were going to [pick a place to live], then we wanted to have a unity of style. A mixed mess was out of question.

The interviewees' criticism applies to the extreme cases of both the 1990s' top-market developments of detached housing where the non-functional or ignored planning regulations and uncontrolled construction practice of the time resulted in incomprehensible diversity of architectural styles and volumes in single neighbourhoods, and later development of identical family houses in sprawling areas. As a consequence of that anomic transition period of early capitalism, the first group of areas and houses, in particular, have already lost their high status value they had at the time of construction. One of the status markers, which continually delineates between different forms of new houses, is drawn between signature houses and 'catalogue-houses', identified as low quality[9].

The distinctions between house owners' preferences for particular architecture of family residences builds on the ways they rationalise their preference rather than

9 Upon expert estimations, in Estonia only ca 10% of new single-family houses are 'catalogue houses'; the rest arebuilt by custom projects (representing different architectural quality although sometimes reproduced in other developments – *authors' comment*) characterised by significantly different construction practice in comparison e.g. to Scandinavian countries. This finding suggeststhat residents' personalised ways of relating to their houses are characteristic of Estonian residential culture, and that the market for standardised houses is still developing in Estonia (Jagodin 2010; Lige 2010).

on differences in the duration of their personal experience as house owners. The more refined taste for traditions with considerable cultural or professional knowledge is expressed upon the experience of the possession of older buildings of heritage architecture, whereas house owners with more popular taste attribute high value to functional and technological qualities of a building. They also refer to the symbolic aspects signifying traditional family life, bespeaking their view on cultural identity.

Andres (2000): I wanted my house to be different, with personality… not like the ones in X and XX (the new detached homogeneous residential developments). I am also convinced that these old houses built in the Estonian time (pre-WWII) are much more durable than those contemporary cardboard boxes. My house has history, and, from the construction perspective, it's much stronger. /…/ We have fantastic window-frames. I did not have a heart to replace them with contemporary glass-pack windows. I am happy I didn't. I've got such a wonderful house now.

Mari (2006): We definitely wanted /…/ a gable roof. /…/ my husband, he thought that it is typical to an Estonian house, with the winters and the snow and all that. The second thing I liked was a mansard floor. /…/ I thought that, well, it would be lovely, this space right under the roof. You see them on photos. They're really cosy, aren't they?

By pointing at well-known examples of Estonian functionalist architecture in Tallinn and in a resort town, Pärnu, from the period of the first independent statehood of Estonia[10], the house owners, appreciating *neo-functionalism*[11], implicitly connect their preference with cultural identity consecrated in the symbolic images from the country's past. With generally greater knowledgeability in the field of architecture, the adherents of neo-functionalism also rationalise on spatial and functional qualities of a contemporary house and are conscious of current as well as the past fashion in architectural design.

Tom (2006): We have actually admired the functional style for years… Pärnu is an interesting place /…/ where you walk around and notice first one beautiful house, then another one /…/ I don't like those crude catalogue houses. /…/ That massively

10 The so-called white-modernism from 1920-1930s and its exploitation in contemporary housing construction as new modernism has been claimed appealing not only to residents but also producers of housing: architects as well as developers (Ojari 2010).

11 Bourdieu and his associates have commented on their study of the French housing market, the functionalist aesthetics as of a 'taste for modern ways', to be appealing to individuals of lower levels of income, educational and social status (2005: 31), which for specific cultural and historical reasons cannot be confirmed in the case of Estonia, where the (neo) functionalist buildings attain a distinct elitist image as is also confirmed elsewhere (*cf.*Lillemägi 2002; Kalm 2003; Ojari 2010).

> consumed style we see very often in Estonia. /.../ those bell-shaped lamps and sofas with dusters /.../ That was completely out of question. And this is why the functional style may have suited me more, I would say so.

Either the house owners are in favour of traditional mix or specific architectural solutions (*e.g.* gable-roof buildings of different style), or the re-emerging functionalist architecture, they draw on differentiated knowledge of the history and specifics of architectural design, whilst equally prioritising personality as a reflection of their taste for aesthetics and functionality.

This is quite obvious that residential identities are built on the lived experience with significant reference to the built structures of different architectural design, including the (re)established or newly invented iconic buildings, which symbolise particular cultural values as well as opportunities for preferred lifestyles and, eventually the ways of residing. In the circumstances of downright homeownership, the ownership of a family house is a 'taken-for-granted' aspect of constructing identities, unless the specific quality of houses and property value is to be considered in defining status-based identities. All in all, the contemporary house owners' occasional and somewhat romanticised images – the '*cosy mansard space*' and '*(neo)functionalist clean forms*'– representing the perceptions of *typical Estonian* houses are considered to carry an important message for conceiving of the construction of individual identities as deeply intertwined with collective identities on the level of a neighbourhood as well broadly, on the level of the nation.

Concluding remarks

The continually high single-family housing preference in Estonia tends to accrue from the image of a desired way of residing characteristic of a particular residential culture of symbolic value. As associated with the notions of freedom and privacy for creative action on a wider scale of the residential space of a house and garden, a detached house signifies a promise of opportunities for personal fulfilment and performance of lifestyle-driven expectations unattainable in any other type of residence.

While marginal in the urban residential scenes, the aspired way of residing in a single-family house bears upon cultural dispositions passed down in intergenerational exchanges in families as well as upon the visibility of the aesthetics, form and functional qualities of residential architecture. Single-family residing qualifies a heritage preference for its sustainability through the profound societal transformations in the previous century and up till today. Especially under the socialist regime, this preference was hardly realisable for specific ideology governing the system, as it is today, although for very different reasons, such as the intensive offers of other multiple alternatives in the markets and limited economic capital at the disposal of individuals and families. No concomitantly profound change in individual cultural dispositions has, nevertheless, appeared that enables permanent discontinuities at the level of preferences in different societal periods.

Single-family residences, appearing in varying quality as signature buildings or mass-produced products are becoming a more widely affordable investment, unless in the conditions of economic recession. Having attained a status of a home ideal of powerful emotional appeal as an authentic space, the meaning of single-family residence is being reconstructed into a consumption and status product along with other types of residences perceived as attractive. However, the consumption-based manifestation of status and lifestyle is only one dimension of the preference of the "house of one's own" because it is blurred with the aspiration to continue or re-create traditional residential identities conceived as part of the personal as well as social history of the country. Hence, the experience of single-family residing appears as a desired mode for home-creation enabling, through creative self-engagement in the designing and construction process on a wide scale of residential space the opportunity, used regardless of the social positions of house owners – (re)invention of cherished residential cultures and the continuous becoming of the individual and collective residential identities.

References

Ahas, R. and Silm, S. (2006). *Tallinna tagamaa uusasumite elanike ajalis-ruumilise käitumise analüüs*. [The analysis of the space-time behaviour of the residents of new suburban settlements in the Tallinn Metropolitan area] TÜ Geograafia Instituut. [Online]. Available: http://www.tallinn.ee/est/ehitus/g7016s45052. (2012, November 16).

Ærø, T. (2006).'Residential Choice from a Lifestyle Perspective.' *Housing, Theory and Society,* 23 (2): 109-130.

Bachelard, G. (1999 [1957]). *Ruumipoeetika*. [Poetics of Space] Tallinn: Avatud Eesti Fond, Vagabund.

Benjamin, D. N. (1995). 'Afterword, or Further Research Issues in Confronting the Home Concept' Benjamin, D. N. (ed.) *The Home: Words, Interpretations, Meanings and Environments*. Avebury: Aldershot, 293-307.

Borgegård, L.-E. and Kemeny, J. (2004). 'Sweden: high-rise housing in a low-density country' in Turkington, R., van Kempen, R., and Wassenberg F. (eds.) *High-rise housing in Europe: current trends and future prospects*. Delft: Delft University Press, 31-48.

Bourdieu, P. (2005). *The Social Structures of the Economy*. Cambridge: Polity Press.

Bourdieu, P. (1999 [1972]). *Outline of the Theory of Practice*. Cambridge: Cambridge University Press.

Bourdieu, P. (1998). *Practical Reason. On the Theory of Action*. Cambridge: Polity Press.

Bourdieu, P. (1994 [1990]). *In Other Words. Essays towards a Reflexive Sociology*. Stanford, CA: Stanford University Press.

Bourdieu, P (1993). *The Field of Cultural Production. Essays on Art and Literature*. Cambridge: Polity Press.

Bourdieu, P. (1989 [1979]). *Distinctions. A social analysis of the judgement of taste*. London: Routledge.

Bruns, D. (1993). *Tallinn. Linnaehituslik kujunemine.* [Urban development of Tallinn] Tallinn: Valgus.

Burnett, J. (1986). *A Social History of Housing 1815-1985*. London and New York: Methuen.

Chaney, D. (1996). *Lifestyles*. London: Routledge.

Clapham, D. (2006). 'Housing Policy and the Discourse of Globalization.' *European Journal of Housing Policy*, 6 (1): 55-76.

Clapham, D. (2005). *The Meaning of Housing. A pathways approach*. Bristol: Policy Press.

Cooper Marcus, C. (1995). *House as a Mirror of Self.* Berkley: Conari Press.

Dovey, K. (1999). *Framing Places. Mediating Power in Built Environment*. London: Routledge.

Eesti arvudes 1920-1935 (1937). [Estonia in Figures 1920-1935]. Tallinn: Riigi Statistika Keskbüroo.

Edensor, T. (1997). 'National identity and the politics of memory: remembering Bruce and Wallace in symbolic place.' *Environment and Planning D*, 29: 175-194.

Elamistingimused (2000). [Living conditions] Tallinn: Statistics Estonia.

Forrest, R. and Kearns, A. (2001). 'Social cohesion, social capital and the neighbourhood.' *Urban Studies*, 38 (12): 2125-2145.

Gentile, M. and Tammaru, T. (2006). 'Housing and Ethnicity in the Post-Soviet City: Ust'-Kamenogorsk, Kazakhstan.' *Urban Studies,* 43 (10): 1757-1778.

Gottdiener, M. (1995). *Postmodern Semiotics: Material Culture and the Forms of Postmodern Life*. Oxford, Cambridge: Blackwell.

Gullestad, M. (1984). *Kitchen-Table Society. A case study of the family and friendship of young working-class mothers in urban Norway*. Oslo-Bergen-Stavanger-Tromsø: Universitetsforlaget.

Hall, T. and Coffey, A. (1999). 'Self, Space and Place: Youth Identities and Citizenship.' *British Journal of Sociology of Education*, 20 (4): 501-513.

Harrison, M. and Davis, C. (2001). *Housing, Social Policy and Difference.* Bristol: The Policy Press.

Hauge, Å. L. and Kolstad, A. (2007). 'Dwelling as an Expression of Identity. A Comparative Study among Residents in High-Priced and Low-Priced Neighbourhoods in Norway.' *Housing, Theory and Society*, 24 (4): 272-292.

Ilmonen, M. (2007) Vetovoimainen kerrostalo. [The attractive block of flats] In: Arkkitehdit NRT Oy. Kerrostalojenkehittäminen. Helsingin kaupunkisuunnitteluviraston julkaisuja 2007, 10: 9-19.

Income and Living Conditions (2005). Tallinn: Statistics Estonia.

Jagodin, K. (2010). 'Foreword.'*100 Maja/Houses. Estonian National Exhibition at the 12th International Architecture Exhibition – La Biennale di Venezia.* Tallinn: Estonian Center of Architecture, 205-207.

Jenkins. R. (2008). *Social Identity*. 3rd edition. Oxon: Routledge.

Kalm, M. (2003). 'White Boxes – the Architecture of Prosperous Estonia.' *Maja*, 4: 30-31.

Kauko, T. (2006). 'Expressions of Housing Consumer Preferences: Proposition for a Research Agenda.' *Housing, Theory and Society*, 23 (2): 92-108.

Kalm, M. (2001). *Eesti 20. sajandi arhitektuur. Estonian 20th century architecture.* Tallinn: Prisma Prindi Kirjastus.

Kannike, A. (2005). 'Negotiating Privacy. Individual Strategies and Cultural Change in Soviet Estonia.' Kalm, M. and Ruudi, I. (eds.) *Constructed Happiness – Domestic Environment in the Cold War Era.* Tallinn: Estonian Academy of Arts Proceedings 16, 76-82.

Karsten, L. (2007). 'Housing as a Way of Life: Towards an Understanding of Middle-Class Families' Preference for an Urban Residential Location.' *Housing Studies*, 22 (1): 83-98.

Kemeny, J. (1992). *Housing and Social Theory.* London: Routledge.

Kemeny, J. (1995a). *From Public Housing to the Social Market. Rental policy strategies in comparative perspective.* London: Routledge.

Kemeny, J. (1995b). 'Informal allocation of housing wealth in Swedish social renting.' Forrest, R. and Murie, A. (eds.) *Housing and Family Wealth. Comparative International Perspectives.* London and New York: Routledge, 289-310.

Kristensen, H. (2007). *Housing in Denmark.* Centre for Housing and Welfare – Realdania Research.

Leetmaa, K., Brade, I., Anniste, K., Nuga, M. (2012). 'Socialist Summer-home Settlements in Post-socialist Suburbanisation.' *Urban Studies*, 49 (1): 3-21.

Lewin, F. A. (2001). 'The Meaning of Home among Elderly Immigrants: Directions for Future Research and Theoretical Development.' *Housing Studies*, 16 (3): 353-370.

Lige, C.-D. (2010). 'Standardized vs. Experimental: About Private Residential Architecture in Estonia and the Nordic Countries.' *100 Maja/Houses. Estonian National Exhibition at the 12th International Architecture Exhibition – La Biennale di Venezia.* Tallinn: Estonian Center of Architecture, 213-217.

Lillemägi, I. (2002). 'The Third Coming of White Houses.' *Maja*, 3: 20-21.

Mallett, S. (2004). 'Understanding Home: A Critical Review of the Literature.' *The Sociological Review*, 52 (1): 62-89.

Mandic, S. and Clapham, D. (1996). 'The Meaning of Home Ownership in the Transition From Socialism: The Example of Slovenia.' *Urban Studies,* 33 (1): 83-97.

Mazanti, B. (2007). 'Choosing Residence, Community and Neighbours – Theorizing Families' Motives for Moving.' *Geografiska Annaler B*, 89 (1): 53-68.

Nicolaides, B. M. and Wiese, A. (2006). *A Suburb Reader.* New York, London: Routledge.

O'Dwyer, L. (1999). 'Housing Inheritance and the Private Rental Sector in Australia', *Housing Studies*, 14 (6): 755-776.

Ojamäe, L. (2010). 'Making choices in the housing market: a social construction of housing values.' *Research in Economics and Business: Central and Eastern Europe*, 1 (2): 41-58.

Ojamäe, L. (2009). *Making Choices in the Housing Market: Social Construction of Housing Value.* Tallinn: TLU Press.

Ojamäe, L. and Paadam, K. (2009a). 'Eluase.' [Housing and home] L. Hansson (ed.) *Töö, kodu ja vaba aeg. Argielu Eestis 1985–2008.* [Work, Family, and Leisure. Everyday life in Estonia in 1985-2008]. Tallinn: TLU Press, 91-111.

Ojamäe, L. and Paadam, K. (2009b). 'Housing Conditions and Neighbourhood Satisfaction.' Vetik, R. and Helemäe, J. (eds.) *Segregated Disparity: the Russian Second Generation in Two Estonian Cities.* Amsterdam: Amsterdam University Press.

Ojari, T. (2010). 'Estonia's Private Residences: Three Views.' *100 Maja/Houses. Estonian National Exhibition at the 12th International Architecture Exhibition – La Biennale di Venezia.* Tallinn: Estonian Centre of Architecture, 208-212.

Paadam, K. (2007). 'Understanding Distinctions in Ways of Residing: The Socio-Physicality of Relations and Capacity.' Ilmonen, M., Lehtovuori, P., Pakarinen, T. (eds.) *Prospectûs. Kirjoituksia kaupungista ja suunnittelusta.* Espoo: Helsinki University of Technology, 255-267.

Paadam, K. (2004). 'Kuidas sünnib ja muutub eluviis?' [Origins and changes of a lifestyle.] *Ehituskunst [Estonian architectural review]*, 30-40.

Paadam, K. (2003). *Constructing Residence as Home: Homeowners and their Housing Histories.* Tallinn: TPU Press.

Paadam, K., Gromark, S. and Ojamäe, L. (2011). 'Consuming Quality – Residential Prospects in Interdisciplinary Focus. The Fahle Maja Case.' *The World Economy: Contemporary Challenges.* Congress of Political Economist International, Warsaw: Difin SA, 317-332.

Paadam, K. and Ojamäe, L. (2008).'Ideological shifts and shifting relations of actors in the field of housing.' *Social Aspects of Housing Redevelopment. Housing in Ideologies/ Ideologies in Housing.* Proceedings of CIB W069 21st and 22nd Housing Sociology Conference: 28 September - 2 October 2005, Maribor and 7-10 October 2004, Helsinki. Rotterdam: International Council for Research and Innovation in Building and Construction, 208-222.

Perkins, H. C., Thorns, D. C., Newton, B. M. (2008). 'Real Estate Advertising and Intraurban Place Meaning: Real Estate Sales Consultants at Work.' *Environment and Planning A*, 40: 2061-2079.

Perkins, H. C. and Thorns, D. C. (1999). 'House and home and their interaction with changes in New Zealand's urban system, households and family structures', *Housing, Theory and Society*, 16 (3): 124-133.

Rappoport, A. (2001). 'Theory, Culture and Housing.' *Housing, Theory and Society*, 17 (4): 145-165.

Roopalu, H. and Vesi, A. (1959). *Individuaalehitus Eesti NSVs.* [Private construction in Estonian Soviet Socialist Republic] Tallinn: Eesti Riiklik Kirjastus.

Rowlands, R. and Gurney, C. M. (2000). 'Young People's Perceptions of Housing Tenure: A Case Study in the Socialization of Tenure Prejudice', *Housing, Theory and Society,* 17 (3): 121-130.

Ruonavaara, H. (1996). 'The Home Ideology and Housing Discourse in Finland 1900-1950.' *Housing Studies*, 11 (1): 89-105.

Ruonavaara, H. (1998). *Theorising Housing Careers.*Paper presented for the ENHR Conference: Housing Futures: Renewal, Sustainability and Innovation. Cardiff University, 7-11 September.

Sirgy, M. J, Grzeskowiak, S., Su, C. (2005). 'Explaining housing preference and choice: The role of self-congruity and functional congruity.' *Journal of Housing and the Built Environment*, 20, 329-347.

Social Trends 4 (2007). Tallinn: Statistics Estonia.

Social Trends 2 (2001). Tallinn: Statistics Estonia.

Statistics Estonia. (2012) Households by place of residence and kind of dwelling 2011. [Online]. Available: http://pub.stat.ee/px-web.2001/Dialog/varval.asp?ma=HHR011&ti=HOUSEHOLDS+BY+PLACE+OF+RESIDENCE+AND+KIND+OF+DWELLING&pat

h=../I_Databas/Social_life/06Households/06Household_living_conditions/01Dwellings/&lang=1 (2012, November 24).

Støa, E. (1996). *Boliger og kultur. Åtti-tallet boligfelt sett i lys av beboernes boligidealer.* [Dwellings and Culture. Norwegian one-family housing areas from the 1980s viewed in the light of the inhabitants' notion of the ideal home]. Dr.ing. dissertation 1996: 4. Trondheim: Universiteteti Trondheim, Norges tekniske høgskole.

Tallinna linnaelanike osalus linna arengu kavandamisel (1995). [Participation of residents in planning the urban development of Tallinn] Tallinn: Tallinna Linnauuringute Instituut.

Tammaru, T., Leetmaa, K., Silm, S., Ahas, R. (2009). 'Temporal and Spatial Dynamics of the New Residential Areas around Tallinn.' *European Planning Studies,* 17 (3): 423-439.

Vestergaard, H. (2006). 'Single-family detached housing: a branch of paradise or a problem?' Doling, J., Elsinga, M. G. (eds.) *Home Ownership: Getting in, Getting from, Getting Out. Part II.* Amsterdam: IOS Press, 75-92.

Välja, L. (ed.) (2012). *Stalinistlik maja. Kortermaja tüübid ja säästev uuendamine [Stalinist house. The types of blocks and sustainable renovation]* Tallinn: Tallinna Kultuuriväärtuste amet.

Warde, A. (2005). 'Consumption and Theories of Practice.' *Journal of Consumer Culture,* 5 (2): 131-153.

Woodward, I. (2003). 'Divergent Narratives in the Imagining of the Home amongst Middle-class Consumers.' *Journal of Sociology*, 39 (4): 391-412.

Estonian men's lifestyle magazine 'Mees': a manual of masculine identity in a transition society

Barbi Pilvre

Introduction

In the contemporary mediatised society, both individual and group identities can be seen as mediated. Lifestyle journals are one of the places where gender identities in a particular culture and era are most intensely constructed. Instability of hegemonic masculinities – even crisis of traditional masculinity – following the development of technology, environmental issues, changes in the concept of work and emancipation of women in the global perspective makes the question of media's role in constructing masculinities actual. According to Craig (1992: 1) the analysis of men and masculinities provide valuable insight into social relationships, to lend a broader understanding to the social forces involved in patriarchy.

As Jackson, Stevenson and Brooks (2001) have shown, men's magazines have an interesting position in the media scene and also in the society in general, in discussing and promoting certain ways of being a man. The first men's lifestyle magazine in Estonia 'Mees' (1995-1997, 13 issues) was an attempt to offer male readers an opportunity to consciously contemplate, or construct, a gender identity through readership of a specialist men's magazine. Published in an era where masculine identity changed rapidly (since Estonia gained independence and entered market economy and consumer society in the 1990s), 'Mees' provides remarkable documentation, and can be seen as a milestone, representing a changing gender order in a transition society. 'Mees' is worth of analyse, as many of the trends of the following years in gender ideologies in Estonia are presented in this magazine in a concentrated form.

The transition from socialism to capitalism and reconstruction of a national state brought along changes in gender order in all of the former socialist countries (Watson 1993, Novikova 2000): neotraditionalism and masculinisation of the culture have been mentioned as main trends. Success, strength, harsh competition were glorified; while care and emotional spheres were marginalised. Neoliberal ideologies and U.S. corporate culture spread in post-socialist cultural space and according to Connell (2005/2007) became a main venue for constructing masculine identity in former socialist, postcolonial states. George Bush-spirited mixtures of masculine identities can be found everywhere in those countries, consisting of nationalist, religious, corporate interests that readily ignore alternative points of view. Despite controversies and intellectually interesting clashes from the point of view of Western gender researchers, masculinities in the postsocialist transition have only seldom been chosen as the object of social research by either Eastern or Central European academics (Kolga 2000, Gapova 2002, Zdravomyslova & Temkina 2002, Oushakin 2002; Novikova & Kambourov 2003; see also Hearn & Pringle 2006). In social studies, sex has been a variable in gathering social statistics and masculinity has been generally accepted as an invisible norm in the whole postsocialist culture-room, including Estonia. As gender studies as a discipline was missing in Soviet academy, gender ideologies weren't theoreticised in an academic sense. Developing gender research throughout the 1990s and first decade of the twenty first century, has tackled mostly issues related to women. Thus, men and masculine identities in a transition society is still an innovative choice of research objective today, which is also a justification for this analysis.

Despite the availability of factual information and sociological data that showed a crisis of Soviet and postsocialist masculinities, other ideals, including ideal gender order, found their place and blossomed in the cultural sphere. In Estonia, reconstruction of a national state in 1990s gave birth to the idealisation of gender order similar to that of the 1930s, accordingly promoting conservative values and neotraditional gender identities in the public debate. Hegemonic masculine identity, the ideal goal of male identity in the last severeal decades in Estonia, can be hence described as a hybrid of corporate masculinities and nationalist strives (Pilvre 2011).

The content of the magazine has to be seen as the presentation of ideal hegemonic masculinity of the time. By design, the male role models were portrayed within a particular lifestyle and instructions provided in relation to: knowledge of good old school habits, weapons, history, alcoholic drinks, women's psyhology, and so forth. Influenced by Anglo-American fashionable new men's magazines of the decade ('Arena', 'GQ' 'Men's Health', *etc.*), new themes such as health and fitness and other lifestyle choices can also be traced, making the journal 'Mees' an interesting and controversial lifestyle manual of an era that paved the way for other men's lifestyle magazines produced in Estonia later ('Meeste elu', 'EE Mees', different internet portals) and prepared the market for Estonian versions of foreign men's lifestyle magazines, 'Playboy' and 'FHM' among others.

In the chapter, content analysis and thematic analysis are used as a combined method. The chapter is aiming to outline main discourses of masculinities in a sample consisting of magazine texts (229) and advertisements (116) of all 13 issues 1995-1997 and to interpret the discourses discovered within the Estonian postsocialist transition context. No studies on consumption of the magazine texts (readership, auditorium analyses) have been made on the magazine, and questions of how the representations were read, negotiated or contested in their era, is not considered in the following analysis.

In relation to the researcher's point of view, it has to be mentioned that I have worked as a journalist in the mid-1990s, when 'Mees' was launched, and was also active as one of the first gender researchers with an interest in the construction of gender identity in the media, including men's and masculinities' representations. In the first half of 1990s, I had published several essays on masculinity in the literature journals 'Looming' ('Alistatud mees'/'The Supressed Man', 'Pehme mees'/ 'The Soft Man') and reflected on the appearing new corporate-style masculinities in the daily 'Hommikuleht' ('Uued mehed' – 'The New Men'). Problematising masculinities was not common in Estonian public discussion then. The emergence of the magazine 'Mees' on the market excited me as a gender researcher professionally.

Theoretical framework

Gender identity, masculinity and media

Media, including advertisements have been regarded one of the main tools for people which help to model their own identity (Goffman 1979, Gauntlett 2002) and they are among the key institutions in gender socialisation. According to Goffman (1979) the performance of gender in social situations is analogous to the gender in media texts (advertisements). Saco (1992: 27) interpreting Goffman concludes that as particular displays of – for instance men – become ritualised, we learn to read them as displays of masculinity.

In relation to the concept of masculinity, Craig (1992: 3) has put it briefly: 'Masculinity is what a culture expects of its men'. Masculinity seen as a social construction (Kimmel 1987, Connell 1995) means that biology determines whether we are male or female and culture determines what it means to be male or female, and what sorts of behaviours and personality attributes are appropriate for genders. It is obvious that masculine identity has never been one single hegemonic masculinity (Connell 1987, 2000) and we can speak of different masculinities. In the last decades of the twentieth century, along with changing fashion, musical movements and globalisation 'a more fluid, bricolage masculinity' (Beynon 2002: 6) has emerged.

The assumption that media help to consitute gender difference, rather than reflect or represent that difference, is a widely shared understanding of media's role in gender construction nowadays.

Gender representations in the media construct idealised visions of men and women or as Kimmel has put it: 'The media portray a wide variety of masculine images, informing us about the positive characteristics toward which we should aspire and warning against the negative facets of personality that we must avoid. Media representations tell us who we are, who we should be, and who we should avoid.' (Kimmel 1992: xii). Also in recent theoretical literature, the media is seen as presenting models of masculinity (Moss 2011).

Lifestyle magazines, especially through their visual imagery, present myths, which according to semiotical tradition (Barthes 1956/1972) are seen as uncontested and generally unconscious assumptions that are so widely shared in a culture that they are considered natural, instead of being recognised as products of unique historical circumstances. Following semiotical tradition, Saco (1992: 25) argues that masculinity in the media has to be seen as signs, masculinity is constructed in the media through sign systems and signs refer to the style of clothing, behavioural mannerisms, and so forth.

Strate (1992), analysing beer commercials, has argued that the myth of masculinity answers the question: 'What does it mean to be a man?' And that the question can be broken into five separate questions: 'What kind of things do men do?' 'What kind of settings do men prefer?' 'How do boys become men?' 'How do men relate to each other?' 'How do men relate to women?' (Strate 1992: 79). It can be assumed that those questions are relevant in problematising men's media representation not only in advertisements, but also other media texts of popular culture.

According to Hearn and Pringle (2006: 96-97) it could be important to examine, in which kinds of journalistic and other media contexts, men are given meaning as a gender or as gender. Those contexts could, according to the authors, change the typical man-woman segregation and apparent gender-neutrality, what is prevalent and taken for granted in mainstream journalism (dailies). In the following article, obviously, the magazine 'Mees' as a journal for men is regarded a context where men are given meaning as a gender, that men are presented as 'men', as gendered beings, not neutral, unquestioned norm for human beings, as in dailies.

Role of magazines in consumer society

Consumer society is definitely the context which has to be considered studying men's magazines (Jackson, Stevenson, Brooks 2001). Traditionally, male identity has been associated with production and female identity with consumption, but by the development of consumer society also relations between consuming and masculinity have progressively deepened over the twentieth century, and simultanously masculine identity has fragmented.

Glossy magazines do not emerge from the initiative of the newsrooms and journalist ambition but as collaborative initiatives of advertising departments and journalists; with the main purpose of the production of popular magazines to sell advertisements to an audience. Gill, in the overview of gender in magazines (Gill 2007) defines magazines as 'simultaneously cultural texts, parts of increasingly concentrated media empires and a means of selling highly specific blocks of consumers to advertisers' (*ibid.*: 181). Also Edwards (1997) has interpreted the emergence of British men's magazines in the 1980s and 1990s as overt legitimisation of consumption; they were not about sexual politics but had more to do with new markets for the constant reconstruction of masculinity through consumption.

Gill (2007: 204-217) describes the development of British men's magazines, which have set men's magazine trends for the following decades in the Western world. Since then, the main dilemma for men's magazines has been how to openly address men as gendered persons and not provoke suspicions of homosexuality. This question has been resolved firstly by abundant irony and secondly, through an almost hysterical emphasis on women's bodies and heterosexual sex. According to Gill (2007: 217) men's lifestyle magazines aimed at heterosexual men typically 'construct masculinity in terms of playfulness, flight from responsibility, detached and uninhibited pleasure-seeking and the consumption of women's bodies.' Although the language is ironic and the tone self-deprecating, the representations of men's magazines are profoundly ideological, designed to naturalise gender difference and male power. In the 1990s, Western glossy magazines were already available in Estonia, especially in the media circles who actively read and also eagerly copied formats of Western journalism. Coming from a very different but idealised world, influence of those on the journalists should not be underestimated.

The magazine is a specific journalist format with its own history and generic peculiarities. Analysing any media representation, genre as one of the main discoursive agent has to be always considered (Fairclough 1995) and hence direct conclusions based on media representations should not be drawn with society on the whole, without taking generic framing into accountance. It has to be kept in mind that popular culture, including popular media, often carries strong traditional values and and promotes stereotypical gender order and representations (Gill 2007). Popular cultural images are to be seen more as signs than simple depictions of reality, but they still appear in a certain social-cultural context and are not arbitrary.

Estonian post-socialist context - illusion of female supremacy

Gender researchers generally share Connell's idea that despite universalities in gender order there exists a 'vast diversity of gender patterns across cultures and down history' (Connell 2009: IX). Estonia, like all the countries in Central and Eastern Europe, has been shaped by a transition process that covers all areas of life and it has been viewed as a 'civilization shift' or process of Westernisation, where attitudes and values of a post-socialist country are transferred to new societal structures (Lauristin and Vihalemm 1997). Strömpl (2000) has described a conflict between the Western values, beliefs and ideologies and actual attitudes, habits, lifestyle and knowledge inherited from Soviet Union. Theorising gender in this context has been complicated as there existed a formal gender equality in work-life and formally also in public sphere in general in the Soviet Union, including Estonia. Both men and women were by law obliged to participate in the labour market and children were taken care by state-organised care facilities. Generally, at the same time, in the public discussions in Soviet cultural space at large, masculinity was perceived as a problem in connection with alcoholism and other self-destructive practices. Dependence of men on their wives and mothers who were supposed to take care of their grown-up sons and husbands were problematised (Gapova 2002: 652). Zdravomyslova and Temkina (2002: 53) claim that late Soviet liberal discourse considered men to be weaker than women biologically, psychologically, and demographically. They argue that Soviet emancipation of women was looked upon negatively both by women and men as the 'feminisation' of men and the 'masculinisation of women'. Novikova, Pringle *et al.* (2002: 92) show that 'victimisation' and 'infantilisation' of men has been a topic since the 1980s in the Soviet territories and following this, the public discourse has condemned women's occupying men's places.

In Estonia, weakness, alcoholism and self-destructive practices of men and over-emancipation of women at the same time, as described in post-socialist cultural space elsewhere, has been a theme in public discussion since the1970s. In the beginning, it was inspired by popular literature, by female authors like Aimeé Beekmann, who in her many books, wrote about emancipated and educated women who had problems finding an equal partner. Later, data on men dropping out of school, their lower education level, worse health and social exclusion have been constant points of departure in public and also policy discussions (Kolga 2000; Uljas and Raun 2000; Kutsar 2007). Estonian data on men's health, education, violence and social exclusion also have been included in European comparisons (Hearn and Pringle 2006). In a way, data about Estonian men's weak position, in regard to many indicators, is blocking public discussions about gender equality and women's weaker position in the society, as it is usually set forth in Western equal rights discussion. As Novikova, Pringle *et al.* (*ibid.*) have put it sharply, in Eastern Europe 'steady 'cannibalisation' of gender equality packaged as sexual transgression/perversion' can be found.

On the other hand, feminist or gender sensitive research has shown that despite the worrying data on men and the illusion of traditional female supremacy in Estonia, patriarchal ideology continued to influence life in different ways. The private sphere remained patriarchal in essence as men were not supposed to take part in domestic unpaid labour, and similarly, men sustained their power hierarchies in public sphere (Narusk 1994, 1996; Pilvre 2000, Kurvinen 2008, Kivimaa 2009, Pilvre 2011). After the new independance, conservative tendencies prevailed and there were pressures towards reinstituting a society with traditional gender roles, bringing along the masculinisation of the public sphere – the tendency described by many Western scholars in research upon postsocialist transition society from gender aspect (Watson 1993, Gal and Kligman 2000, Pascal and Kwak 2005).

According to Zdravomyslova and Temkina (2002: 54) postsoviet gender relations are described also by some Russian scholars as the trend of exclusion of women from the public sphere (the political sphere, highly paid jobs, most profitable business, *etc.*), or as discrimination against women. The emerging gender order and the process of Russian transition is named by the term 'male democracy' and also the term 'revival of the patriarchy' is often applied (*ibid.*). It might be interesting to mention here that Susan Faludi (1991) described a backlash in women's emancipation movement and rise of antifeminism and conservative values in USA during the same period, in her famous book 'Backlash. The Undeclared War Against Women'. Also Whitehead (2002) has described reactions towards feminism in the period in question, as women's emancipation has been accused of fostering male criminality and redundant and dysfunctional forms of masculinity. Perhaps there have been some simultaneous developments in gender orders in different societal and political contexts since the end of the 1980s in late modern era, despite the relative isolation of the East from the West.

In the beginning of 1990s, in Estonia, the male breadwinner model became popular in public discourse. Women were suggested both by public opinion and leading political forces to stay at home again, as women did in the idealised 1930s, before Estonia lost its independence in 1940. In the 1990s, the emancipation of the nation and emancipation of women did not match according to the general opinion, as writer Hasso Krull (1995) has expressed very precisely. Conservatism in social values and norms concerning gender roles since have been typical in Estonia (Soolise võrdõiguslikkuse monitooring 2009, 2010) and it has to been accentuated that men's and women's values differ to a great extent (Kalmus 2009). Men's identity in Estonian society has in recent period, according to Pajumets and Hearn (2012) largely been constructed in relation to work, in the context of survivalist values. It is interesting to notice how consumerism in 1990s was introduced by media, however, real life was mostly about making both ends meet for most of Estonians. In the 1990s the market economy and developing consumer society brought along new possiblities and also commercial pressures to accentuate gender difference by gendered consumption and homemaking (Pilvre 2000). Corporate American-style masculinity, along with the development of market economy, has set the norm of financial success as the essence of being a man, and this type of hegemonic masculinity favoured a certain, economically dependant type of woman. Changes in masculinity could seem remarkable on the surface: new career and consuming habits, but basically the patriarchal rule continued to structure the society as it had been before the new independance, during the Soviet regime.

Stemming from the 1990s, these tendencies still prevail and I dare to claim that they are hardly challenged by the gender equality discourse initiated mainly by European Union policies.

Heterogeneous spectre of Estonian masculinities

Along with the development of the capitalist regime, inequalities among men grew and now we can talk about different hegemonic and subordinated masculinities according to Connell's definitions (1995). Estonian businessmen emerged in the process of privatisation in the 1990s, often earlier members of Estonian Soviet *nomenklatura* who had access to management of industrial enterprises. In the redistribution process of state-owned industrial enterprises, the basis for further business development was created. Obviously, not all men had access to the redistributed state properties, but it depended on the previous position during the Soviet regime. At the same time, a generation of young ambitious men emerged, who were willing to take advantage of the unregulated entrepreneurship environment of Estonia in the 1990s.

Many men previously hired as a paid labour force by kolhoz and sovhoz-type large farms in the countryside lost their work as the state farming system was dismissed. Dropping out of the society was a typical fate for them as they did not have enough resources to start their own farms as was supposed by the dominant ideology of rebuilding flourishing private farms in the 1990s in Estonia. Also numerous factories in big cities were closed as they had been part of the Soviet industrial system and the workers, often Russian speaking men, did not find their place in the new system. Social exclusion of middle-aged men;

former skilled workers, who had dropped out of the society during economy reorganisations in former socialist Baltic states has been described and theoreticised in recent studies (Tereskinas 2009).

Many male fortune-seekers from the West came to Estonia to start their businesses and take advantage of the missing or just-emerging legislation in Estonia, as well as the cheap costs. As Western origin was an asset in itself during those times, those men often very smoothly joined the local business and political elites. As a result, a heterogenous spectre of masculinities developed in 1990s Estonia, including successful businessmen and political elite as carriers of hegemonic masculinity and several subordinated masculinities of the former industry workers, kolhoz and sovhoz workers in the countryside. Russian or other non-native Estonian men constituted one big group of emerging subordinated masculinities being formulated in the 1990s as they had lost – along losing their work in the closed factories – their position in the political system of the Soviet era (as Soviet Union's dominant nation was Russians). Russians were also labelled occupants in the context of the restored Estonian Republic's nation-state ideology as Estonian official history was rewrittern during late 1980s and early 1990s.[12] Dominant male actors in the nation- and state-building processes had almost unlimited freedom to create new institutions or shape old institutions according to their will, as this was also expected by the people. New state, political and judiciary systems, as well as a totally different economy, had to be established. The media was mostly reorganised and privatised. Social care and education were partly reorganised and cultural institutions were probably the most untouched area, as they remained in the margins of society during this turbulent era.

Most likely, since then, male domination in the workplace has been typical of the organisational culture in postsocialist Estonia; having its roots in the reorganisation of institutions in the 1990s. The labour market has been gender segregated horizontally and vertically since the Soviet period and the tendency continued during 1990s (Vöörmann 2000) and also later. Today there are gender differences among careers, not only measured by numbers, but also perceived by the employees (Masso 2010). However, male initiative in reforming the society has been seen since 1990s as natural dominance by both men and most women and it has only been questioned in recent years along with other gender equality discussions.

---

12 Especially the unification of Estonia and Soviet Union was reconceptualised and earlier 'deliberate process' was, according to the Molotov-Ribbentrop treaty from 1939 made public in the late 1980s, defined now as forced occupation.

There are some specific features in Estonian masculinities connected with new technologies that have to be mentioned. According to Bourdieu (1998) technology is universally one of the main culturally masculine fields and also one of the pillars of masculine identity and male domination. Traditional hegemonic masculinty is associated with production and convenience with means of production. Hence, universally in the media, technology, tool and car stories and advertisements in men's magazines foster the association of masculinity and production. Also in Estonia, orientation in, and knowledge of, cars and technological goods and also of emerging new technologies that appeared on the market in the 1990s were naturally included as desirable in the every-day and media constructed versions of the desired hegemonic masculine identity.[13]

Empirical study: Magazine 'Mees' 1995-1997 and its discourses

The advertising market and, accordingly, the magazine market were developing intensely in the 1990s in Estonia. The number of magazines increased 33% during 1990-1999 (Vihalemm 1997: 37-38). Continued commercialisation changed the media into a market-driven industry and led to the increasing importance of the entertainment function of the media (*ibid.*: 40). Popular women's magazines 'Eesti Naine', 'Anne', 'Stiil' were doing financially well and the first society journal 'Kroonika' was launched in 1996.

In that developing magazine market, the launch of a special lifestyle magazine for male readers was awaited, if only to look back to the past. Still, for the author as a gender-sensitive journalist and a starting gender researcher, it was a remarkable event when it happened.

The magazine 'Mees' was issued in 1995-1997, 13 issues altogether by publishing company AS Esmaspäev and AS Printall, as the initiative of restaurant entrepreneur Tõnu Hellam and chief editor, military historian, Hannes Walter. It reached a distribution of 10 000.[14] 'Mees' consists mainly of journalistic content, mostly text. The magazine does not look very attractive and photos are of poor quality. It can hardly be called a 'glossy', but we have to consider that it is a product of its era, when layout standards, design know-how and the print industry were only starting to develop in Estonia. Advertisements are few (a total

---

13 As Estonia has few remarkable traditional heavy industries, the only one worth mentioning is electricity production from local oil-shale, the economic priorities have been set in developing new technologies, such as ICT and biotechnologies. Top level of virtual services of Estonian state and in banking are subjects of national pride since 1990s as Estonia was the leading country of ICT development, the phenomenon was named Tiger Leap.

14 According to oral information from Tõnu Hellam in March 2012.

of only 116 in all 13 issues) and very unprofessional from today's point of view. The concept of the magazine was, however, very ambitious, despite the poor appearance. The slogan of 'Mees', articulated in a declaration in October issue 1995 by Walter was: 'To be a man, who breaks through in life, is able to create something, is respected and at the same time remains healthy and can enjoy being a man.' The aim of the journal was openly defined by him as pedagogical, not entertaining, and that successful men had to tell others their life-concepts. 'It is not important whether your tool is a wheel, a wallet or a weapon'. It is obvious that the role of the editor-in-chief has been decisive in compiling the ideology of the magazine. Within the first issue, he appeared in many pictures and wrote many of the interviews himself. The important role of editor-in-chief was not, however, an exclusive phenomenon in Estonian journalism in this era. Many journalist projects were actually one-man projects, as the whole field of journalism was reorganised and new initiatives emerged continuously. It can be assumed however that the special focus on arms, military and political history was Walter's taste and choice.

In order to have a better picture of the magazine, a rough content analysis has been made. The sample consists of 13 magazine numbers, altogether 116 advertisements and 229 magazine texts. In the following two tables, results of the content analysis by advertising and story themes are presented.

Table 1: Advertisements (N=116) by themes in 'Mees' 1995-1997.

Theme	Number of stories	Percentage
Goods, services	36	32
Fashion	21	18
Media	14	12
Tools, materials	11	9
Alcohol	9	8
Meubles, machines	8	7
Tobacco	6	5
Phones	6	5
Cars	5	4

As Tabel 1 shows, advertisements of different goods and services compose the biggest group, consisting of advertisements of restaurants, sport clubs, mobile phone operators, travel and office equipment sellers, security service, *etc.*

Regarding the profile of the magazine, as awaited, fashion advertisements make the second biggest group. Media advertisements (journals, TV programs), tools, cars, *etc*. make smaller thematic groups of advertisements.

It is obvious that, differently from Western glossy men's lifestyle magazines of the time, 'Mees' can be hardly named a monument to consumer culture. But it can however be considered as one of the first sites where men's gendered consumption is presented in a distinct form; men are a clear target group of advertisements in which it is discoursively articulated that masculinity can be constructed by consuming specific culturally masculine goods. Until 'Mees', advertisements had been presented as gendered only for women, in women's magazines, in women's sections in newspapers, or as universal and genderless in different magazines and newspapers.

Table 2 shows rough thematic analysis of the sample consisting of 229 stories.[15]

Table 2: Stories (N=229) by themes in 'Mees' 1995-1997

Theme	Number of stories	Percentage
Fashion	41	18
Personalities	34	15
Health, care, psychology	33	14
Food, drink, tobacco	25	11
Military, security	24	11
Cars, traffic	20	9
Games	18	8
History, political history	12	5
Women	12	5
Business	8	4
Phone	1	0

15 Some smaller technical text units such as cross-words, subscription cards, remarks have been not included in the sample, so the exact number of texts in the 13 magazine numbers is a bit larger.The lenght of the stories is not taken into accountance in the analysis, news and larger stories are counted as equal units. That makes the comparison problematic, but still gives some measurable empirical data to base the following qualitatve anaysis of the magazine content.

Fashion and style

Stories and advertisement on fashion make a remarkable part of the content of 'Mees'. There are altogether 41 stories (18% of the sample) and 21 advertisements (18% of the sample) on men's fashion and style, although many of the stories are short tips. Clothing and style are thus visible themes in 'Mees', largely present also in advertisements, many of them on local Estonian brands. It has to be noticed that the articles on men's clothing and style are mainly written by female fashion designers. Several of the advertisements show classical business suits and costly accessories: watches, jewelry, glasses. Style connoisseurs such as a famous Estonian fashion designer, Ivo Nikkolo, and also some society gentlemen, are interviewed. What and how to wear; how to choose accessories such as ties, shoes and men's jewelry, are discussed. In this discourse the traditon of the old-school gentleman who knows how to dress and how to wear a suit; someone with a cared-for appearance, is constructed.

Elsewhere, standards of male beauty over time, with pictures, are discussed by a female fashion designer. It is concluded in a light mocking way: 'By men women can regard beautiful scars, tattoos, pretty bottom, tight skin pants, big hands, golden heart, talent of presenting poetry, listening and ability to ask questions instead of talking about themselves all the time, kissing skills, skill to play some musical instrument, sun tan or also pale skin'. In the same article fatherhood is described as 'beautiful' and sexy fathers Robert De Niro, Anthony Hopkins and Robert Duvall are mentioned.

It is noticeable that longer stories on fashion and bodycare include historical insights and facts about culture or cultural figures and, besides being entertaining, are intended to spur ambition. In this way a man's care of his body is legitimised in 'Mees'. For example the cosmetic problem baldness is discussed presenting and interviewing some well-known bald cultural figures in Estonia. Baldness is named 'sexy', and a contemporary trend, but also a problem that could be solved and cured. In another story a specific masculine care ritual razoring is presented ('the whole truth about razoring') and the historical figure King Camp Gilette, inventor of gilette machine are written about.

In Soviet times men's appearance was not much discussed, although special issues for men appeared of the only Estonian fashion magazine 'Siluett'. New consumer possibilities and the developing business culture in the 1990s ushered in the demand for men to take care of their body. It is clear, however, that the Western beauty and health industries were not yet interested in Estonian market in the middle of the 1990s as there are almost no international advertisements of health and beauty products and services in 'Mees'.

State, nation and military discourses

Taking just a brief look at the magazine, the dominance of military stories is clearly visible, as these are long stories, concise and well illustrated, although the articles on weapons and military technologies do not make the biggest group (24 stories, 11% of the sample). Role of military discourse in nation building, going on in Estonia in the 1990s, is the broader context for such representations. New political forces such as the political party Isamaa (Fatherland) were openly military-minded. Interest in and knowledge of military technologies, hunting and personal weapons, including knives, is represented as obligatory in masculine identity in 'Mees'. Different weapons are introduced through several issues of the magazine by specialists.

The presence of military discourse is a remarkable difference when comparing this to Western men's life-style magazines of the 1990s. It is worth mentioning that at the same time trendy glossy magazines such as 'Arena' or 'Gentlemen's Quarterly' presented the new man's ideology. Weapons as an important theme in the magazine 'Mees' could be explained by the novelty of the issue. In the Soviet period, weapons – just weapons of Soviet origin, of course – were strictly in the possession of the army and only hunting weapons were allowed to be possessed by private persons under a special licence. Western weapons had been the object of desire and admiration by military-minded male during the whole Soviet period as far as information on these was available. Interest in historical weapons – mainly of the German army – was strictly forbidden by law in Soviet Union, but had cult-status in certain circles. This interest was considered an act of subversion, and can be explained by supressed strivings for independence. Now, as 'Mees' shows, there was a possiblity to see and know more of those weapons. The slogan of this whole discourse is explained in a statement by the editor-in-chief: 'A weapon decorates a man.' How to keep the weapon, how not to spoil it, how to handle it – those issues are covered extensively. It is intresting to mention that even cars were presented as weapons such as 'Land-Rover, the war-horse of XX century'.

Discourse on state and nation-building could not be missing in 'Mees' as a messenger of its time. Stories on espionage and political history can be seen as parts of the remarkable military discourse in the magazine. There are 12 stories (5% of the sample) on political history, but the length and the expertise level of the content of stories has to be taken into account. Nostalgia towards the 'real' or ideal Estonian Republic of the 1930s is pervasive in this discourse. Consistency of Estonian statehood is implicitly present in many theme-presentations. That is to say, the Estonian new currency 'kroon', introduced in 1992 is presented as historical, having a 70-year history since, for a period in the 1930s, the

Estonian republic also had the kroon as currency. Introduction of the etiquette of diplomacy is presented in several issues of the magazine, including also the history of Estonian diplomacy. As part of the romantic nation-building discourse actor Tõnu Lume is portrayed, as he played a film role of legendary Estonian wrestler of the beginning of XX century, Georg Lurich. The film is representing the nostalgie-driven cultural production which was trendy in the 1990s in Estonia.

In 'Mees', religion and church-life also are presented as themes in a couple of stories and portraits. Presentation of religious practices as part of gentlemen's obligatory knowledge is again a major difference, if to compare the magazine with the Western men's magazines of the time. Tips for visiting church are given as part of etiquette to be obtained by a gentleman. A priest has given an interview after coming back from USA, in a section 'Man, who came back'. Lutheran church bishop comments surprisingly on traffic. He refers to his professional expertise and is complaining about missing of charity in Estonian traffic. Presence of church and religion as themes in men's magazine can be understood in the context of statehood reconstruction discourse and of imagined lifestyle, inspired by the ideal 1930s. Lutheran church itself also had positioned itself in the new independant state as a main actor, being oppressed during Soviet regime.[16]

Security can be seen as a subdiscourse of state and nation building in the context of 'Mees'. Security companies legitimised the showing-off and usage of physical power in civic society as a new phenomenon emerging in the developing Estonian state of the 1990s. As criminality was blossoming as a result of value crisis and anomia, security business found its large market. A presentation of a well-known in Estonia, security man Urmas Sõõrumaa's businesses is an example of this discourse.

Emerging corporate culture

Obviously, personality stories include several themes and discourses and can not be categorised under one thematic label. In the interviews and portraits of different outstanding men in 'Mees' (34 stories, 15% of the sample), sometimes only professional issues such as building business or interior design are tackled,

---

16 Estonia has never had a state church and the Estonian nation is the most non-religious in the EU, as statistics show (Eurobarometer 2005). Typically, people in Estonia have not been attending church regularly, except during Christmas, and religion has never been a part of the compulsory school curriculum. However, during the whole Soviet period and especially during the independence movement of the second half of the 1980s, the church had a remarkable role as a carrier of anti-Soviet feelings.

sometimes lifestyle, hobbies and the norms of masculinity are included. As men are represented by their public activities, discourses of the emerging corporate culture and corporate masculinity are the most important feature in the personality stories.

As mentioned above, the new economy of the state was being built up by emerging capitalist entrepreneurs. Portraits and interviews of men who had created, or who were actively creating, something are included in most of the magazine issues. There are stories about well-known architects, building entrepreneurs and interior designers. Also advertisements in 'Mees' construct the discourse of rebuilding the country (11 advertisements, 15% of the sample, are categorised as Tools, materials). Creating a new urban physical environment was a real challenge in Estonia in the 1990s. Building entrepreneurs and architects could be seen also as very masculine in this context as building one's own house was seen as a feature of a 'real man' in public discussion. Professional standards are stressed by architects, as the emerging new environment of the first half of the 1990s was quite uneven, since literally every man was urged to start building. In the discourse of corporate culture, building is seen in the context of business. It is not just romantic home-making. A well-known Estonian architect declares that a house is also to be seen as a safe investment, 'different from a car that can be changed often'. Other emerging young star architects stress professionality and give advice to the imagined reader that before starting to build one's house, it is wise to consult architects. It is instigated to think big: 'If you want a castle, there should be also a park'. It also is advised to build winter-gardens instead of warm-houses and not to grow cabbage and potatoes in the city. There are also statements that the period of building over 300 m^2 houses in Estonia is over and potential clients are advised to think more practically. An idea – novel in Estonia – is launched that one can also change lodging during one's life-time, according to needs, as it is done in USA many times during one's lifetime.

At that time it was innovative new philosophy that private property is clearly seen as capital, not just a home. Just recently, in the end of 1980s and early 1990s in Estonia there had been a prevailing ideology in public discussions to return to father's farmhouse in the country, to get back land in the process of privatisation and bring life back to countryside. New, urban business-minded yuppie ideology can be seen as opposing peasant romanticism and some political forces or general attitudes of earlier years.

There are several stories with interior designers as it was also an emerging and trendy new business. Workplace and the cabinet interior are regarded very important. A journalist in an introduction to an interview with an interior designer writes: 'Now, as many men work until late hours, a cabinet could be named even more important than home'. Representations of traditional and creative physical power, as in the story about a young forger, can be seen as legitimising male physical power and craft to create something new and typical of traditionally masculine professions.

Although business in itself can be seen as innovative in the Estonian context, the main pathos of 'Mees' is inspired by history and returning to traditions, introducing old forgotten skills, crafts and values and traditional masculine professions. A portrait of a male dentist is one example of innovative changes in the labour market. Men became active in areas of society which had been female-dominated in the Soviet Estonia. As a dentist's business was seen as promising in the emerging capitalist market, male doctors moved into the field.

Health, care, well-being and hedonism

Generally, themes of health, care, well-being and hedonism in 'Mees' are presented as intellectual issues, framed by cultural and historical context. Thus these 'non-serious' themes are presented as suitable for 'noble' men to be interested in.

Probably in the discourse of health and care in 'Mees', the similarity to or influence of Western men's magazines is obvious, as several texts on men's health are translated from Western magazines. Altogether 33 texts (14% of the sample) are categorised under the thematic group health, care and psychology, including also stories on well-being and sex.

In men's magazines in general, constucting this discourse, according to Gill (2007) the key issue is how to avoid accusations of homosexuality; how a man can enjoy his manhood while caring for himself, his clothing and health without being labelled gay. It has to be stressed that homosexuality is a non-issue in 'Mees'. It was decriminalised in Estonia in 1992, but gay liberation only appeared into public discourse a decade later on.

Surprisingly, heterosexual sex isn't a dominant theme, but is represented in the context of cultural history and psychology. An ideal gentleman introduced by 'Mees' is probably supposed to know about buying sex, as history of brothels is covered in one article. Sexual revolution came in Estonia with delay, only arriving in the 1990s. Prostitution was a new and largely accepted field of entrepreneurship in Estonia in those times. It was not understood as sexual violence generally, and the job of the prostitute was even named, with a certain respect, 'the oldest profession of the world'. Legalisation of prostitution was an issue from time to time in public discussion and critical voices belonged only to marginal feminists then. There are also some other stories on sex: a story about having sex for the first time with a new partner and after the birth of a child, for instance.

There is one story on fatherhood in which a Finnish masculinity researcher Jouko Huttunen is referred to by an Estonian author. The ironic heading on the cover of the journal is 'Is child an investment of a stay-at home father?' The author concludes that in Estonia a classical, old-fashioned patriarchal father is the prevailing type of father, but in Finland and in other Nordic countries there has emerged a new type of father, willing to spend more time at home with children.

The issue of care is visible, also discursively, in different stories on other themes. In statements by men in an article on leaderhip, care is mainly associated with making money and giving family financial security. A managing director of a company says: 'I find myself thinking sometimes if our children get an impression that we only make efforts to cover material needs. In fact we keep in mind other things – I want a secure home for my family, human relations, which give mentally safe basement for life'. Another director says that earlier he was suffering when his wife was complaining to her friends about their poor living conditions. Now, after building the house he himself has changed and is more and more appreciating home and personal relations. He is coming home earlier now and has noticed with pleasure that also his wife has discovered a homemaker in herself and is making their life more cosier.

Regarding men only as breadwinners and not as emotional beings is thus questioned, but this discourse is not dominant as mostly men are represented by their professional life. Self-destructive behaviour is tackled also in 'Mees' as among Estonians, especially men, the number of suicides has been continuosly high. Psychotherapy is introduced, referring to Woody Allen's films – again a cultural framework – and men are called to seek help if life is too difficult. There are some random stories on medical issues concerning cardiovascular diseases and stress. Those were regarded as prestigious in 1990s Estonia and associated with the busy life-style of entrepreneurs. (Sudden death and the prestige of heart disease was an issue tackled in one of my own essays written that time, 'On sudden death'). Elsewhere, bad side-effects of different drugs are presented in an informative story.

What is remarkable is that even plastic surgery is covered in a couple of stories as a very specific, new field of medicine in Estonia in the 1990s. At that time, most people had never thought about plastic surgery, however, in the public discourse of the 1990s, it was associated with new possibilities and even luxury. Women's breast enlargement and facelifts were seen as part of an elite lifestyle, affordable to the chosen rich. Plastic surgery for men presented in the magazine 'Mees' could easily be interpreted as revolutionary in the context of the prevailing concept of dedicatedly work-oriented and military, nationalist minded masculinity. But those stories can be explained most likely as demonstrating the influence of advertisement within the content, as the borders of advertising and editorial content were really flexible in these days.

Novel in the 1990s, is the discourse of hedonism in 'Mees'. Hedonism in 'Mees' is vastly associated with enjoying life by means of masculine habits such as consuming alcohol, tobacco and good (not healthy) food, as well as playing games. Hedonist ideals are backed-up with concise cultural-historical materials, presenting enjoying life as an intellectual activity.

Tobacco and alchohol advertisements (13 texts altogether, 15% of the sample) are prevalent in the magazine. Although not many, they are often large and colourful, even with two-page pictures. Connoissance of wines and wine culture and other alcoholic drinks and different tobacco products is presented as an important part of gentleman's identity in texts on alcohol, tobacco and food (25 altogether, 11% of the sample). Hegemonic masculinity in the 1990s also included cooking, if meat was in question.[17] Hence, food in 'Mees' is mostly meat. There are instructions by different well-known men on how to prepare different meat and how to serve it in the best way. In addition, some recipes are available. Knowledge of games (18 texts, 8%) such as billiard, horse-racing and hunting skills are also introduced in detail, as part of desirable traditional gentleman's identity and possiblities to enjoy life in traditionally masculine ways remembered from good old Europe.

Feminism, women and representing gender difference

'What is your opinion of women, fighting for equal rights?' one society gentleman, an artist, is asked and the answer is: 'I am horrified.' Feminism is commented on critically in some other interviews with men and is mainly identified by sexual harassment and the strange, more gender-equal, etiquette that is seen abroad. Commenting on American society, one intevieweé says: 'Oh yes, it is very interesting that girls greet you first. It is taken as an offence when you open doors for women; it is out of question that you help women to put on a coat.'

Discourse on gender difference and normative femininity are intensely constructed by women portrayed in 'Mees'. There are only 12 stories on women (5% of the sample), so we can say that women are secondary in 'Mees'. Some

17 It has to be mentioned of course that meat as a product is universally symbolically masculine. This association is widely used in also Estonian advertising industry and it can probably refer to ancient hunting habits, when men really went into the forest to kill animals and bring back food.

magazine issues are without any stories and pictures on women. Even the special number of 'Mees', dedicated to women, named 'Naiste-Mees' ('Ladies-Man') does not portray many women.

Editors choose the women to be portrayed in an issue, according to their aims. The women's function in the magazine 'Mees' is to reflect upon men and maculinities and it is worth mentioning that those women are educated professionals. They appear mostly in the column 'Women on men', but they also discuss their personal gender identity and femininity. Women in 'Mees' are successful professional women, young or middle-aged, among them lawyers, designers, a journalist, artists, and even one of the most well-known feminist artists. There is no awaited exponation of female bodies, except some details in Western-originated advertisements. Visually, we find no nameless models' pictures as decoration in 'Mees', and only modest portraits of the fashion-designers and other experts, who are interviewed or write in 'Mees'.

In the special number 'Naiste-Mees' ('Ladies-Man') there are stories on female marine officers and a female priest, presenting women as exceptions in the traditional male and also very masculine professions. Future female helmsmens' gender identity is 'checked' by different framing questions by the journalist and the humourously presented conclusion is that they can not be reproached for anything but being too serious and efficient, they are 'not even demanding women's rights'. Surprisingly, normative femininity is constructed even in the interview with a woman priest as getting old is the main theme in the story and also the heading goes: 'A woman does not want to be old'.

In some cases, women compare Estonian and Western femininities, praise Estonian traditional femininity and gender order and criticise feminism. 'For me, the whole feminist movement is a struggle against the laws of nature... in European countries feminism is just a fight with wind-mills. Especially in Estonia, where, in fact, women have more rights than men', says one inteviewed journalist. 'Personally my position in the society is near to ideal. How could I even want to change things that are given me by nature.' She adds, joking, that if to think it over, she would change one thing that would be her bra size for a bigger one. A TV-star comments: 'Women are taken as decorative additional elements sometimes, belonging to men's games. On the other hand, I like to play such additional decoration from time to time.'

Women's identity talk stresses their traditional feminity, comparing Estonians to foreign women, who have become assumedly gender-neutral, and motherhood is stressed as important. One artist says in an interview: 'Men and women should have equal rights. But me, I want just to give birth and raise children in peace, without the tiring need to earn money. I want that the society would value raising children more than now.' Or elsewhere: 'Estonian women are feminine and should not lose it. They should give birth to more children and care for the home. Without children, women remain girls forever, unfortunately not young forever.'

Even the famous feminist artist is named 'man-eater' on the front cover of the issue and she is giving witty comments on men in her life and also motherhood. However, she argues for her feminist position. Asked about motherhood, she says 'I think that a child needs a mother who is alive. If I shall be taken away my ambitions and self-realisation, I would commit suicide.'

Discourse on gender difference and men's negative attitude to women's emancipation is also presented in stories on cars and traffic, by describing women's helplessness with cars, in a joking but sexist way. An interviewed car-seller says: 'Women's part /in buying a car/ is choosing colour.'

We can conclude that women in 'Mees' present dominant positions in the gender equality discussion of the 1990s. Defining and exposing themselves as desirable and desiring sexual persons was expected as a contrast to Soviet women in the context of the past, seemingly sexless, Soviet culture and the delayed, but stormy, sexual revolution in the 1990s. Estonian women, also successful, were then mainly opposing the ideas of feminism which were exported among other new Western ideologies to Estonia. Striving to show-off femininity, taking advantage of new gendered consumer possibilities that came with capitalism was dominant then (Pilvre 2000). Gender differences were generally seen as biological, natural, and worth maintaining or striving for.

Hegemonic masculinity presented by 'Mees' is thus backed-up by representations of strong, professional women who demonstrate their traditional femininity and claim not to strive for more emancipation and women's rights. 'Mees' is not openly sexist: masculinity is not confirmed by hysterical exposure of heterosexual sex and female bodies in a way we can think about typical men's magazines as 'Playboy' or newer Western formats as 'Loaded', 'FHM' or others, some of which emerged on the market in Estonian language in the 2000's. There is no direct objectification in the portrayal of women in 'Mees' by the editors. Maybe there was no need as, at the same time, women presented themselves as adjusted to the existing patriarchal order.

Conclusions and discussion

In this chapter , the first Estonian men's magazine 'Mees' (13 issues 1995-1997) is considered a remarkable site of representation of gender ideologies, especially of masculinities, of the postsoviet Estonian society in a concentrated form. 'Mees' is seen as a lifestyle manual of the era, presenting gender ideologies which have been sustained in Estonian public discourse in different developments until the present. In an easily readable format, this novel and popular men's magazine presented the normative statement of what was required to be a man at that time in Estonia. Military discourse is dominant in 'Mees', including military history and weapons as themes, mainly due to the personal interest of the editor-in-chief, historian Hannes Walter. This makes 'Mees' very different from Western men's magazines of the era. Discourse of nation-building is constructed in several texts, demonstrating consistency of Estonian political institutions: diplomacy, church, currency. Discourses of business-life and reconstruction of the country are constructed by representations of different male business professionals, among them several building entrepreneurs, architects and other men, who were creating the new physical environment of a capitalist, new Estonia.

A discourse on hedonism is presented by introducing new possibilities of 'knowing' to do with the consumption of alchohol, tobacco and the playing of traditional masculine games as well as paying attention to clothing and style. Hedonism is framed by rich cultural and historical material, presenting the consumption of alcohol and tobacco as intellectual activities. Health and personal care discourse are present, also framed by cultural-and historical context and introducing cultural figures; presenting the issues as appropriate to take interest in and in such a way legitimising men's care for their bodies and looks. Even plastic surgery for men is a random theme. Translated materials are used in many cases. Discourse of gender difference is presented mainly by the portrayal of women who mirror men's ideal and desired traits, but who also define feminity in their identity talk, according to the demands of hegemonic masculinity, as anti-feminist. It has to be pointed out, that women portrayed in 'Mees' are succesful professionals and not models or beauty-queens. What concerns gender difference and gender equality issues, 'Mees' represents ideas that are widespread even today, as many successful women still do not want to be associated with Western feminism. Interestingly 'Mees' is not openly sexist compared to Western men's magazines of the era as women themselves adjust to the subordinate role that hegemonic masculinity gives them.

There is a certain amount of irony and humour in some articles and columns of 'Mees' as it is typical to the Anglo-American men's magazine format. But within the discourses on militarism, state and nation-building and business-life, there is no irony according to my reading. Not surprisingly, the 'easiest' discourse is that of gender difference portrayed in stories on women. As those women's main task is to comment on men, fun and irony is present implicitly. Also articles on style and body care have been written with humour, as, according to Gill (2007) too serious representation of men taking care of their appearance can lead to accusations of homosexuality, which is excluded in 'Mees'.

To understand the gender order of contemporary Estonia, 'Mees' gives several keys. Gender idenitities are mediated today as media images influence or even dominate in our everyday practices. Legitimacy of military declination of Estonian cultural figures and politicians is visible in 'Mees'. It helps to understand the position of military discourse in relation to Estonian hegemonic masculinity today. Seeing the profound dedication to military issues in 'Mees', it is maybe easier to grasp, how it is possible that militarism is still so popular among male politicians and public figures, who join military games such as Erna trip, belong to Estonian Union of Defence (Kaitseliit) or serve as Estonian army reserve officers besides their civil profession.

There are some other minor, interesting facts to be mentioned. Concern with current politics is almost missing from 'Mees'. Probably as politics was one of the main themes in the dailies and television in the 1990s, 'Mees' has avoided it consciously. To stress this, one well-known leading academic figure and politician appears only as a car expert, presenting masculine hedonism. The choice of foreign guests and the men portrayed in that context is heterogeneous and random, typical of the journalism of the era, where easy availability of some materials or personal acquaintances could easily produce stories in papers or magazines. Among the few foreign men presented in 'Mees' are Polish politician Lech Walesa, boxer Mike Tyson, football player Pele, but also Finnish local lore historian Markku Tanner. The last is probably just a personal aquaintance of the editors.

Why, in the Estonia of the 1990s, was hegemonic ideal masculinity presented in 'Mees' like that?

Estonian people's national identity was in a very intense reconstruction phase in the 1990s and history was naturally a source of knowledge and inspiration. Political history, offered in a readable form, was probably also welcomed by readers. Militarism – being a peculiarity of 'Mees' – also could be something new and of interest to broad, especially male, audiences.

Coming out of the social deficit of communist times and early postsocialist years, consuming was just becoming part of a 'normal person' in 1990s Estonia. There was definitely a strong urge among Estonian men in the 1990s to become different from the Soviet-type man, who was typically known for lacking style, being badly dressed and, in the worst cases, being unkempt and stinky. Soviet men in those times were easily spotted abroad as being different from natives, which could become disturbing. They did not find their way in the rich variety of alcohol, tobacco and food that was available in free market countries. The lack of Western everyday knowledge could be a problem in normal communication and building business and political contacts abroad. At the same time, ambitions of Estonia's elite to 'return to Europe' were very strong. 'Mees' therefore filled in a gap, being a style-guide. There could be an enormous demand for such information in one's own language in the mid-1990s.

Gendered consumption for men, defining masculinities through consumption of different goods, is introduced by 'Mees' in a concentrated form. Emerging consumerist values in the Estonian society backed up such content-offering and today, obviously, consumerism has become a dominant ideology in mediated gender construction. A lifestyle-manual of its time, 'Mees' can thus be seen as a milestone of emerging consumer ideology in mediated form in a post-socialist culture.

The aim of entertainment media is of course to sell dreams and create illusions. Probably for most of male readers of the time, moral, intellectual and consumption ideals presented by 'Mees' were unobtainable. Although the magazine's content is based primarily on the individual choice and fabrication of editors, there has to be some relevance when compared to the real experiences of the readers in magazine content to gain their interest in it. 'Mees' circulation was comparably high, which shows that there was a readership, that found something in 'Mees', to entertain themselves, to build their own masculine identity, or to hook onto something in turbulent times.

References

Barthes, R. (1956/1972). *Mythologies*. London: Vintage Books.

Beynon, J. (2002). *Masculinities and Culture*. Philadelphia, Open University.

Bourdieu, P. (1998/2005). *Meeste domineerimine*. Tallinn: Varrak.

Connell, R.W (1987). *Gender and Power: Society, the Person and Sexual Politics*. Cambridge: Polity Press.

Connell, R. W. (1995). *Masculinities*. Cambridge: Polity.

Connell, R. W. (2000). *The Men and the Boys*. Sydney, Allen & Unwin; Cambridge, Polity Press; Berkeley: University of California Press.

Connell, R. W. (2002). *Gender*. Cambridge: Polity Press.

Connell, R. W. (2005/2007). 'Globaliseerumine, imperialism ja mehelikkused.' [Globalisation, imperialism and masculinities]. *Ariadne Lõng* VII, ½, 77-99.

Craig, S. (1992). Considering Men and the Media. S. Craig (ed.) *Men, Masculinity and the Media*. London: Sage, 1-7.

Edwards, T. (1997). *Men in the Mirror: Men's Fashion, Masculinity and Consumer Society*. London: Cassell.

Fairclough, N. (1995). *Media Discourse*. London, New York: Edward Arnold.

Faludi, S. (1992) *Backlash*. The Undeclared War Against Women. London: Vintage.

Gal, S. and Kligman, G. (2000). *Reproducing Gender: Politics, Publics, and Everyday Life after Socialism*. Princeton: Princeton University Press.

Gapova, E. (2002). 'On Nation, Gender, And Class Formation in Belarus... And Elsewhere in the Post-Soviet World.' *Nationalities Papers*. 30 (4), 639-661.

Gauntlett, D. (2002). *Media, Gender and Identity: an Introduction*. London, Routledge.

Goffman, E. (1979). *Gender Advertisements*. Cambridge, MA: Harvard University Press.

Gill, R. (2007). *Gender and the Media*. Cambridge, Malden: Polity.

Eurobarometer (2005). *Social Values, Science and Technology*. Special eurobarometer. European Comission. [Online]. Available: http://ec.europa.eu/public_opinion/archives/ebs/ebs_225_report_en.pdf (2012, July 19)

Hearn, J. and Pringle, K. (2006). *European Perspectives on Men and Masculinities. National and Transnational Approaches*. Houndmills Basingstoke Hampshire: Palgrave Macmillan.

Jackson, P., Stevenson, N., Brooks, K. (2001). *Making Sense of Men's Magazines*. Cambridge, Malden: Polity.

Kalmus, V. (2003). *School Textbooks in the Field of Socialisation*. Dissertationes Sociologicae Universitatis Tartuensis. Tartu: Tartu University Press.

Kalmus, V. (2009). 'Eesti elanike väärtusmustrid'. [Value Patterns of the Estonians]. *Inimarengu aruanne*. Tallinn: Eesti Koostöö Kogu, 114-116.

Kimmel, M. (1987). *Changing Men: New Directions in Research on Men and Masculinity*. Newbury Park, CA: Sage.

Kimmel, M. (1992). 'Foreword'. Craig, S. (ed). *Men, Masculinity and the Media*. London: Sage, xi-xii.

Kivimaa, K. (2009). *Rahvuslik ja modernne naiselikkus eesti kunstis 1850-2000*. Heuremata. Humanitaarteaduslikke Monograafiaid. Tartu: Tartu Ülikooli Kirjastus.

Kolga, V. (2000). *Estonia National Report on Men's Practices*. EU FPV Thematic Network: The Social Problem and Societal Problematisation of Men and Masculinities. [Online]. Available: http://www.cromenet.org/crome/crome.nsf/resources/2BDBA7F79D8159C7C 22569B300452739/ $file/Estonia.doc (2012, May 10).

Krull, H. (1995). *Feminism ja eesti kogukond*. Est.Fem, näituse kataloog. Tallinn.

Kurvinen, H. (.(2008). 'Reflecting a transition in the gender order – case of Nõukogude Naine/ Eesti Naine Magazine'. *Acta Historica Tallinnensia* 12, 87-102.

Kutsar, D. (2007). *Mees sotsiaaluuringu subjektina*. [The Man as a Subject for Social Research]. Sotsiaalministeeriumi toimetised nr.2. Tallinn: Sotsiaalministeerium.

Lauristin, M. and Vihalemm, P. (1997). *Return to the Western World. Cultural and Political Perspectives on the Estonian Post-Communist Transition*. Tartu: Tartu University Press.

Masso, M. (2010). 'Mehed ja naised tööelus'. [Men and Women in Work Life] *Teel tasakaalustatud ühiskonda II*. [On the Way to a Balanced Society II]. Tallinn: Sotsiaalministeerium, 26-39.

Moss, M. (2011). *The Media and the Models of Masculinity*. Lexington: Lexington Books.

Narusk, A. (1994). *Murrangulised 80-ndad ja 90-ndad Eestis: töö, kodu ja vaba aeg*. [The Breaking '80s and '90s in Estonia: Work, Home, and Leisure]. Eesti Teaduste Akadeemia Filosoofia, Sotsioloogia ja Õiguse Instituut, Tallinn-Helsinki.

Narusk, A. (1996). 'Gendered Outcomes of the Transition in Estonia'. *Idäntutkimus*. The Finnish Review of East European Studies (3-4). Special Issue: Women and Transition: The Case of Estonia, 12-39.

Novikova, I. (2000). 'Soviet and post-soviet masculinities: After men's wars in women's memories'. I. Breines et al. (eds.) *Male Roles, Masculinities and Violence: A culture of peace perspective*. Paris: UNESCO, 117-129.

Novikova, I. and Kambourov, D. (2003). *Men in the Global World. Integrating Post-Socialist Perspectives*. Helsinki: Kikimora Publications.

Novikova, I., Pringle, K. *et al.* (2003). ''Men', 'Europe', and Postsocialism.' I. Novikova and D. Kambourov (eds.) Men in the Global World. Integrating Post-Socialist Perspectives. Helsinki: Kikimora Publications.

Oushakin, S. (2002). 'Chelovek roda on: znaki otsustvija'. S. Oushakin (ed). *O muzhe(N)stvennosti: Sbornik statej*, Moskva: NLO, 7–42.

Pajumets, M. and Hearn, J. (2012). Post-Socialist Fathers 'At Home' and 'Away from Home' in 'Old Europe': Facing the Challenge through Masculine Identity Talk. *Studies of Transition States and Societies*, 4(1), 31-47.

Pascal, G. and Kwak A. (2005). *Gender Regimes in Transition in Central and Eastern Europe*. Bristol: Policy Press.

Pilvre, B. (2000). Taming the phantom of feminism in Estonia. In A. Dimitrakaki *et al.* (eds.) *Private Views. Spaces and gender in contemporary art from Britain and Estonia*. London: Women's Art Library, 60-71.

Pilvre, B. (2011). *Naiste meediarepresentatsioon Eesti ajakirjanduskultuuri ja ühiskonna kontekstis*. [Media Representation of Women in the Context of Estonian Journalist Culture and Society]. Dissertationes de Mediis et Communicationibus Universitatis Tartuensis 12. Tartu: Tartu Ülikooli Kirjastus.

Saco, D. (1992). 'Masculinity as Signs: Poststructuralist Feminist Approaches to the Study of Gender'. S. Craig (ed.) *Men, Masculinity and the Media*. London: Sage, 23-39.

Soolise võrdõiguslikkuse monitooring 2009. (2010). Sotsiaalministeeriumi toimetised, 1. Tallinn: Sotsiaalministeerium.

Strate, L. (1992). 'Beer Commercials: A Manual on Masculinity'. S. Craig (ed). Men, *Masculinity and the Media*. London: Sage, 78-92.

Strömpl, J. (2000). 'Changing rhetoric, changing institution: the process of democratization in an Estonian total institution'. *Estonian Social Science Online* 2, [Online]. Available: http:// www.psych.ut.ee/esta/online/2000/ (2012, May 10).

Tereskinas, A. (2009). 'Social Suffering, Post-soviet Masculinities and Working-class Men'. *Social Sciences/Socialiniai Mokslai*, 2 (64), 79-86.

Uljas, J. and Raun M. (2000). *Mees muutuvas maailmas*. [Man in the Changing World]. Tallinn.

Vöörmann, R. (2000). 'Men and Women On the Labour Market: Wage Ratios'. P. Maimik *et al.* (eds). *Towards A Balanced Society*. Tallinn: Ministry of Social Affairs of Estonia. United Nations Development Programme, 46-53.

Watson, P. (1993). Eastern Europe's Silent Revolution: Gender. *Sociology*, 27 (3): 471-487.

Zdravomyslova, E. and Temkina A. (2002). 'Krizis maskulinnosti v pozdnesovetskom diskurse'. S. Oushakin (ed). *O muzhe(N)stvennost: Sbornik statej*, Moskva: NLO, 432-451.

Whitehead, S. M. (2002). *Men and Masculinities: Key Themes and New Directions*. Cambridge: Polity.

PART II

LIFESTYLE CHOICES AND IDENTITIES IN TRANSFORMING SOCIETY

Social construction of identities in a cross-cultural experience of creating and designing homes

Katrin Paadam, Kristel Siilak, Liis Ojamäe

Introduction

The institutional changes in Estonia and joining the European Union, in particular, are clearly affecting individuals' perspectives in different fields of their conduct. On the account of multi-directional cross-cultural mobility enabled by this change, there is increasing internationalisation of all spheres of social life, with salient reflections also from individuals' intimate lives. Intensified mobility bound to the process of overall globalisation is affecting individual aspirations in education, work as well as enabling travelling opportunities. Hence, individual lives, no longer tied to one place, but wedded to several places at once become an endeavour of *globalising biographies* (Beck and Beck-Gernsheim 2009 [2001]).

These institutional and global changes have increased also possibilities for the formation of cross-cultural intimate relationships. Encountering of individuals from different societal and cultural backgrounds would potentially be reflected on transforming home cultures. This implies that individuals in cross-cultural relationships face a challenge of the entire (re)organisation of their lives within the web of multilayered relationships in different fields of their conduct and (re)construction of identities. This argumentation builds on the authors' contribution to the recent European biographical research project 'Euroidentities'[18] and has become a source of inspiration for the further study of the construction of identities on home site(s) of individuals engaged in cross-cultural intimate relations.

Historically, studies of the nature of cross-cultural relationships conducted, in particular, within the disciplinary perspectives of family sociology and migration studies centre round issues of race, ethnicity, cultural diversity and community, gendered dominance, discrimination, social security, sense of belonging, and identity (Beck and Beck-Gernsheim 2004 [1995]; Breger and Hill 1998; Crippe and Brew 2007; Seto and Cavallaro 2007; Stewart and Goldfarb 2007; Maehara 2010). In light of these issues, the analyses of the adaptation process into the new society and culture focus primarily on women's experiences. These studies have elucidated that family relations and traditions, policies as well as culturally shaped mentalities, stereotypical prejudiced dispositions and collec-

18 See also: http://www.euroidentities.org/

tive stigmatisation are of significance in supporting or weakening the position of individuals in the process of moving and adjusting to the new societal and cultural circumstances. (see also Breger and Hill 1998; Williams 2010; Schütze and Schröder-Wildhagen 2012). Williams alludes also to residential issues, mostly in the context of policy. By indicating on particular cases of Western-Asian cross-cultural relationships in the US, she asserts that the migrating partners 'often find themselves in dependent positions if their residency status in their country of settlement is contingent on their continuing marriage' (Williams 2010: 173).

With a number of problematic issues also present in inter-European mobility and formation of cross-cultural relationships, the situation in European countries is somewhat different in terms of free movement and changes in the institutionalisation of citizenship. Cross-cultural moving in Europe initially takes place for educational or employment purposes rather than for marrying into another country. Encounters at internationalised working and educational circumstances may eventually lead to cross-cultural marriages or cohabitations. Various studies have shown the increasing number of cross-cultural marriages (Molina *et al.* 2004; Sherif Trask and Hamon 2007; Bustamante *et al.* 2011; Bystydzienski 2011). For example, in Estonia, the number of cross-cultural registered marriages with one partner from a country of origin other than Estonia makes 7% of all registered marriages for the period 1994-2010 (Statistics Estonia 2012).[19] Registered marriages, however, do not show the actual patterns of intimate relationships. As has also been noted elsewhere, the declining marriage rates are substituted by increasing numbers of cohabitating partners (*cf.* Kasearu and Kutsar 2011; Hewitt and Baxter 2012). Families are forming on also the co-habiting cross-cultural partners.

The primary interest of this paper is to understand the process of the construction of identities in a cross-cultural home. More specifically, this is to enquire how the 'residential stories' informed by different socio-cultural experiences of individuals in cross-cultural intimate relationships become present in the process of creating 'international homes'. The paper seeks answers to the questions concerning the ways these experiences shaped within the encounter of cultures interfere with the perceptions of and actual ways of residing. The paper analyses how the experiences of (re)constructing identities reflect on cross-cultural practices of home creation conceived as a process of social construction of residence as home on differentiated capacities of individuals (Paadam 2003) involving residential choices as well as home design.

19 Databased on indication of partnersplace of residenceincross-culturalmarriages.

By applying the qualitative biographical approach, the study attempts an enquiry into the ways that the partners adapt to and (re)create their homes in new socio-cultural circumstances with a focus on home designing with tastes, habits, preferences informed by current lifestyles as well as distinct previous cultural experiences. The analysis draws on biographical interviews of couples of Estonian and Nordic or Southern European origin residing in Estonia.

Theoretical framework

Creating cross-cultural homes at the encounter of different tastes

Cross-cultural situations of home creation are considered complex as well as complicated where, on the backdrop of different cultural contexts, the perceptions of spatial organisation and designing of homes are brought together in the endeavour of an intimate relationship. Assuming that every modern marriage comes across the habits and rituals familiar from partners' unique experiences of daily routines in previous phases of their lives (*cf.* Beck and Beck-Gernsheim 2009 [2001]), the culturally mixed couples might face more profound distinctions of cultural worlds of men and women (Refsing 1998). Refsing also asserts that in cross-cultural marriages, partners 'may be required to adjust their concepts of selfhood and identity, and the question of which spouse will have to make the largest concession is not only influenced by the gender or the personal characteristics of the spouses, but also to a large extent by the demands made and the options offered by the socio-cultural environment in which the couple has chosen to live' (Refsing 1998: 193). Intimacy is not merely a function of private/public contrast but is linked to ways in which the self is available as a topic for dialogue with others (Chaney 1996: 121), which in the context of the present paper of cross-cultural intimate relationships highlights on the nexus of adaptation into a wider field of social relationships and the partner as a significant other, in particular.

This observation largely applies to cross-cultural home creation practices – the choice of residence and home design - with distinct preferences for home creation to be communicative not only of individual tastes and lifestyle preferences but reflective of the partners' intimate interactions on their home site, as well as of wider, possibly distinct, value systems. It should be noted that choices for home creation strategies are forming upon multiple dualities of structural opportunities and individual capacities. They may reflect compromises made between ideals and actual decisions (Dieleman 2001) as well losing or abandoning control of the presentation of self (Chaney 1996), more so during cross-cultural adjustment or the (re)invention of identities of intimate partners (*cf.*

Paadam *et al.* 2012). Therefore, individual tastes, while intimately related to personal preferences are not necessarily expressed or easily read in choices made for a residence or decisions taken on home decoration.

Nevertheless, tastes, as they appear in home design, form a judgemental category of perception. As is asserted, tastes are most commonly distinguished by categories of 'good' and 'bad' taste (Woodward and Emmison 2001), whereas, the negative judgements are considered particularly useful for self-identification on the scale of tastes (Douglas 2000 [1996]). These externally given judgements evoke self-consciousness and may inform individual strategies for home creation; furthermore, as in Chaney on Lury (2002), they are forming the background of the contemporary stylisation process and self-conscious creation of lifestyle.

It is considered, however, that the creation of a cross-cultural home is characterised by a particular complexity, where the negations of tastes between partners of distinct *habitus* are in the heart of the process, raising issues of symbolic manifestation of individual and collective identities. The notion of *habitus*, conceived by Bourdieu 'as a system of acquired dispositions functioning in a practical level as categories of perception and assessment or as classificatory principles as well as being organising principles of action meant constituting the social agent in his true role as the practical operator of the construction of objects' (Bourdieu 1990: 13), enables us to reveal differences and potential inconsistencies in the partners' experience of home creation. Related to habitus and, therefore, social positioning, Bourdieu avows that 'taste, the propensity and capacity to appropriate (materially or symbolically) a given class of classified, classifying objects or practices, is the generative formula of lifestyle, a unitary set of distinctive preferences which express the same expressive intention in the specific logic of each of the symbolic sub-spaces, furniture, clothing, language or body hexis' (Bourdieu 1984: 173).

Taste as a function and reflection of lifestyle is, however, considered to have the capacity to evolve in the practice of home creation. This implies that tastes for cross-cultural home creation are shaped within the inter-personal exchange as well as the socio-cultural circumstances forming in a given society with collective past experiences present at any phase of the process of home creation. The formation and expression of preferences for taste in home creation may, therefore, be viewed simultaneously, as cultural norms re-visited and as the dynamic process of learning and adaptation on a wider scale of social conduct.

There is, though, more to this advancement and possible alteration of tastes and their application in home creation practices – one cannot overlook the implications of fashion markets facilitating or even promoting cross-cultural exchange and opportunities for identity construction through the material world.

As fast and fragmented as the changing, increasingly internationalising fashion markets become accessible to a wider circle of consumers for home design, they do not evidence clear strategies of class differentiations (Rocamora 2002; *cf.* Warde 2005; Sassatelli 2007). When observed on the genesis of tastes and life-styles as in Featherstone (2007), the cultural capital at the disposal of individuals operates independently of income, amounting to the convertibility of social power. Whilst economic capital is essential to create a home to meet individual preferences then cultural capital is of special relevance, moreover, in a cross-cultural relationship, an extraordinary situation compared to situations in which individuals can rely on familiar cultural categories. Sensitivity towards cultural signs presented in a home environment is a reflection of identities and partner's recognition of each other's endeavours.

Constructing and manifesting identities on home design

The symbolic effect of the choice of residence and home design manifesting individual partners' or a couple's taste is considered equally bespeaking partner's cultural and economic capacities, as well as their social capacity to negotiate the construction or reconstruction of their identities in the incarnated nature of cross-cultural intimate relationships.

The studies of material culture are particularly eloquent in regard to the meaning of objects displayed in homes of individual households to be the embodiment of significant connections building between family members and self-identity (Hurdley 2006; Money 2007; Woodward 2010 [2007]; Miller 2012 [2008]). Miller (2012 [2008]) suggests that closer insight into ways people decorate their homes and present material objects in their interior enables understanding individuals' positions in family relationships as well as their intentions and actions individually. Woodward (2010 [2007]: 6) broadens this view by asserting that, 'the object is given meaning through the narrativisation of the broader discussion of self, identity and biography, which link aesthetics to ethics of self, and social identity'. This linkage between the object and self can be observed upon the ways the stories are told. In other words, the ways individuals tell their stories about objects they possess at home simultaneously tell the stories of storytellers (*cf.* Hurdley 2006: 729). In this sense, the biographical approach to the study of cross-cultural home-creation practices, incorporating distinct pre-relationships and shared experiences, allows a closer look into the dynamic of the meanings attached to objects – the biographical companions – and their symbolic significance as to the perception of self. Furthermore, apart from the economic value of things, once a part of the home experience, the objects are to make sense on a different level of perception (*cf.* Sassatelli 2007 on Kopytoff

1986; Appadurai 1986). Kopytoff (1986) goes so far as to personify things through their own biographies, attributing things the status of agency: 'A culturally informed biography of an object would look at it as a culturally constructed entity, endowed with culturally specific meanings, and classified and reclassified into culturally constituted categories'. Craig's (2011) interpretation of this approach states that a cultural biography focuses specifically on the chain of events through which an object becomes culturally marked and unmarked as a particular type of thing. Nevertheless, it is suggested that specific objects appropriated into home design render cultural significance as a 'means of representation,that is making the everyday into symbolic display of tastes and social affiliation' (Chaney 2002: 65). They may be a part of stylisation (as in Chaney 2002 on Lury 1996) or they may not be an expression of this intention, but possibly be subject to re-interpretations in the course of home practice. As argued by Woodward and Miller (2010 [2007], 2012 [2008]), the objects individuals present in their homes are in the interplay with the construction of self-identity as they are attributed the meanings.

Miller also refers to the relevance of the biographical dimension in the understanding of the meanings of things, by pertinently noting the absence or non-presence of objects in homes. Having studied the homes of London households from an anthropological disciplinary perspective, Miller shows how the emptiness of a home may relate to earlier development of self in the experience of a childhood home where the children were denied creativity by authoritative parents. Miller asserts that this experience can lead to adult home creation and design practices with occupants of home space having 'no independent capacity to place something decorative or ornamental within it' (Miller 2012 [2008]: 13). As for cross-cultural home design practices, the emptiness of home may be discussed in terms of either of the partners' possibly limited opportunities to express their individual identities through objects of cultural value in a gendered relationship of dominance by one or the other of the partners; or the dominating socio-cultural context de-capacitating individuals of the opportunity of presentation of self-identity.

As a reflexive process (Giddens 2009 [1991]) the construction of identities is bound to external categorisations (Jenkins 2000) from beyond the relationship, through other social interactions with implications for self-identification; the more so in cross-cultural situations of home creation where the partners are engaged in identity work, and adjustment to new social and cultural circumstances, as well as in search for the acceptance (Paadam *et al.* 2012) and a sense of belonging in the community (Williams 2010). Therefore, Hauge's and Kolstad's assertion that home creation and designing processes, seen as an expression of identity for oneself and others, is most relevant for the study of cross-cultural experience of home creation: 'location, exterior and interior have something to say about the social group one belongs to, and provide information about one's lifestyle and personal taste.' (Hauge and Kolstad 2007: 273).

Taste and aesthetics of objects chosen for home design are considered important sources of the understanding of construction and manifestation of identities (Woodward 2001; Miller 2012 [2008]). Miller conceives of the significance of the notion of aesthetics in individual narratives of home decoration not to implicate the arts but rather to refer to patterns of a 'sometimes overall organisational principle that may include balance, contradiction and the repetition of certain themes in entirely different genres and settings' (*ibid.* 293). It is argued that objects of home design are considered central in cross-cultural home creation. This implies that the meanings and symbolic value of objects displayed at home are important to both partners, individually and together, as they enable the maintenance of genuine relatedness to one's cultural roots in support of the continuous re-construction of identities.

On research and analysis

The social constructivist epistemological approach applied in this essentially biographical research explicates 'how different practices and mental structures are shaped by structural conditions and how these structures are simultaneously shaped by agency' (Domecka *et al.* 2012: 37). The main assumptions behind the attempt of a biographical study of cross-cultural home creation is 'to understand the changing experiences and outlooks of individuals in their daily lives, what they see as important, and to provide interpretations of the accounts they give of their past, present and future' (Roberts 2002: 1). Or as has been noted by Holstein and Gubrium, biographical research enables a focus on a life story, which is constructed in individual narratives upon everyday experiences (Holstein and Gubrium 2000). At the same time, 'if stories in society reflect inner lives and social worlds, society has a way of shaping, reshaping, or otherwise influencing stories on its own terms' (Gubrium and Holstein 2009: 15). The way people talk about their lives can 'give insight into and draw attention to the *silences* in biographical accounts, and thus make visible the 'taken-for-granted' aspects of people's lives that are more often than not structurally founded and thus important for understanding the informant in the context that the life unfolds within' (Nielsen 2008: 18-19). The biographical interviews in this study are conducted with a specific interest in individuals' housing histories, which, following the established approach in residential research in Estonia (see Paadam 2003; Ojamäe 2009), aims at gaining comprehensive data on the dynamic and interconnectivities forming between different experiences of home and construction of identities and the new emerging realities of cross-cultural home creation. Self-narration of biographical experiences or, as put elsewhere, the oral expression of individuals' experiences of feelings and events enables people to 'discover deeper meaning in their lives' (Atkinson 1998: 2).

The empirical analysis relies on 12 individually conducted biographical interviews (from August, 2011 to March, 2012) with partners from 6 cross-cultural couples residing in Estonia. With one partner of Estonian origin, the selection of couples by the origin of the other partner, coming from either Northern or Southern Europe is defined upon a broader assumption of social and cultural differences what the partners might bring into the new shared life (*e.g.* family traditions, welfare systems, *cf.* Allen *et al.* 2004). All interviewees share the residential experience in the city of Tallinn; two couples have moved to the suburbs.

We reached the interviewees through snowballing, by making use of social networks, information provided by the interviewed couples and what has been available in Estonian media channels. The interviewees aged 26 to 47 are professionally active in different fields including art, education and science, economics and business, engineering and international relations. Four of the couples have children between the ages 1 and 11 years. The couples are at different family phases from 2 to 13 years together. Partners/spouses are of the same age.

Interviews were conducted at the interviewees' homes in most cases, allowing the researcher to also explore the authentic sites for cross-cultural home experience and later interpretation of the interview data. As was apparent, the interview situation at home was also convenient for the interviewees. Conducting interviews at people's homes is a procedure often used in the study of material objects and home creation strategies (*cf.* Paadam 2003; Woodward 2003; Hurdley 2006; Money 2007; Miller 2012 [2008]; Ojamäe 2009). By covering the interviewees' entire residential experiences from childhood onwards, the interviews focused on current practices of creating and designing homes of partners/spouses in cross-cultural relationship.

Thematic narrative analysis, focusing on the communicated content rather than precise description of the structure of the narrative, has been applied to the analysis of the interview data. This implies that the analysis was centred on interpreting how and 'what has been said' and less on 'how a story unfolds in a conversational exchange' (Riessman 2008: 58). In the process of analysis, common thematic elements are defined and theorised across a number of cases (*ibid.* 74).

Residential choices of cross-cultural couples

The residential choices concern the type of residence as well as location with a potential for the organisation of space, which would, nowadays, meet the often lifestyle-driven preferences for residing. Residential choices are considered as part of home creation strategies together with decisions taken on home design. The individually analysed stories of people intimately related in cross-cultural marriages or partnerships demonstrate how the choice of a residence is being constructed in anticipation of creating a home as a dynamic process of identity construction. With unique personal experiences shaped in past collective cultural circumstances, and intertwined with adjustment to new cultural and social situations, the individuals in the process of cross-cultural home creation face a multitude of challenges. In the following, the challenges of home creation are displayed in representations of different couples' experiences of residential choices by indicating how their former residential and social experiences on a wider scale interfere with their current decisions and actions. The analysis reveals similarities of main instances of couples' experiences and each of the specific analytical categories are presented here through a story in which they appear most explicitly.

Earlier cultural experiences and shared residential preference

The way individuals come to negotiate their choices of residence relates to the value and meaning of home constructed within all earlier experiences as well as the later shared residential experiences alongside the evolving cross-cultural, intimate relationship. The analysis of the stories suggests that the experience of a childhood home, including a family's second home, is one of the most significant residential experiences, which triggers adult housing choices. The childhood experiences of homes, if they are positive, inform individual dispositions and make a strong argument for partners in a cross-cultural relationship to find a common ground with which to embark on their earlier experiences, when designing their shared strategy of home creation. This occurs regardless of different societal circumstances and, therefore, the distinct personal experience of residential conditions in the pre-relationship past.

The story of home creation of an Estonian/Northern-European couple, Sirje (37) and Mikael (39), started with a common housing career as cohabiting students, first, in a 'third' country, and then in Estonia. Their several moves in the city in search for a larger space, as well as greener residential neighbourhood, have been motivated by the growth of their family, but also been, significantly, informed by positive childhood memories in the background.

Mikael, who grew up in a small Nordic town, is eloquent about his daily life in his parental house and the neighbourhood, with a clear indication that this experience plays an important role in the formation of his adult preferences for a family house.

> **Mikael**: It was a house in a newly built area. All people who lived there were quite young and had children. In the morning children could go out and play. When the food was ready for lunch the parents were screaming out from the window that now the food is ready, please come and eat. Actually, the atmosphere, generally, in that area... the atmosphere was very good /.../ Ideal home would be a house. In that sense I probably paint a similar picture as I described my childhood home.

For Sirje the childhood experience denotes summers spent with the family in the countryside, which in contrast to her daily residential experience in an urban large-scale housing district from the socialist period of the country's history, has grown into a strong and lasting sense of emotional affiliation.

Both partners' narrations are salient, regarding a wish to restore their childhood experiences through the current choice for their own family residence. Representations of their individual stories of shared preference simultaneously reflect the persistence of a home ideal of 'a house of one's own', characteristic of the residential culture of their countries of origin (see also Paadam 2003; Ojamäe 2009; Paadam and Ojamäe in the present book).

Individuals' capacities and management of the process of decision-making

Building up a common housing career in the endeavour of creating a home takes more than the acknowledgement of shared preferences of partners with different cultural backgrounds, which is nevertheless an important platform for further decision-making. The experience of acquisition of a family residence brings forward a specific aspect of capacity, a problem that cross-cultural couples potentially face both on the interpersonal level and more widely in the society. More specifically, insufficient endowment with capacities, as language skills and knowledge of specific cultural and institutional situations, revealed in the cross-cultural adaptation process, might result in unanticipated compromises between residential preferences and actual choices.

With shared preference for a family house, also familiar from their past experiences, Annika (34) and Paul (41), another couple of Estonian/Northern-European origin, had to give up their idea of obtaining an original project of their own taste and, instead, decided on a purchase of a completed suburban family house. The reasons behind the decision, which neither of the partners fully approves of, are related to Paul's low knowledge of the local language, indispensable for the control of the designing and construction processes. Annika, on the other hand, having no knowledge of house construction lacked willingness and interest in taking over the responsibility.

> **Annika**: Well, let's say all things like... connected with the care of the building /.../ I need first to learn about them myself and then translate, so to say, the main message for him into English. This means that when I hire workers /.../ then actually I become /.../ also the project manager. I need to arrange everything, be present and as well push around the whole business.

Consequently, the couple is experiencing some dissatisfaction with the location and the opportunities to organise and design their home space.

Their story evidences language skills as one of the primary attributes – the cultural capital – that needs to be obtained and, if possible, maximised (in Bourdieusian terms) when moving across cultures and settling down in distinct societal circumstances. The representations of management of the decisions taken on residential choices also support the argument that low capacities of partners, accompanied with mistrust of a given field of professional performance, enforces reconsideration of home creation strategies.

Trust in one another and abstract systems

Trust in expert systems (*cf.* Giddens 1990) would be a normative basis for individuals making their residential choices. It is however, observed that trust in the professional performance of construction institutions, which builds on previous cultural experience, may lead to overlooking the potential encumbrances present in another culture. Together with partners' full trust in one another's professional expertise, as well as concomitant division of roles in the practice of home creation, may turn out to be an altogether unfortunate experience, demanding readjustment of originally designed strategies. Incapacities of individuals' to adapt to unfamiliar cultural and institutional contexts may remain latent until particular circumstances of decision-making occur, and become conducive to inadequate residential choices.

This is what happened to Triin (41) and Peter (47), an Estonian/Northern-European couple of house buyers. Sharing a similar preference for lifestyle, their choice for a house with a garden to be purchased came easily. This is more due to their trust in each other's professional qualifications, which also defined the order of their appearance in the process of home creation. Triin, for example, regarding her husband's earlier experience in the field, did not interfere with her husband's decision in the matter of choosing a new house, rather than an old house, as he had considered the newly built houses of higher quality. She, in her turn, was to apply her creative talent on designing the garden, which she is actually practicing, although not in overly satisfactory circumstances within the whole context of their residence. The purchase of a new building was, admittedly, a miscalculation in terms of the quality, which demanded adjustment to meet their expectations.

> **Triin:** Peter did not want an old house, he wanted a new one. But afterwards he understood that, in Estonia, this old house is of much better quality, actually, than a new house. /…/ Peter's father has also built and sold houses and they have to give about 12 years of warranty /…/ In short they have such a long warranty and they take responsibility for everything. So they do not even dare selling low quality houses.

The experiences of couples having encountered problems, in terms that they misrecognise the differences between normative categories of perception, which appear when moving between societies, evidence the complicated nature of adaptation, in particular, its cultural dimensions, bespeaking the need for the advancement of individual capacities to enable adequate engagement in the society. On all levels of interactions, trust is an essential component in the endeavour of creating a cross-cultural home. Albeit, the overwhelmingly trustful dispositions, or equally, the mistrust, seem to refer to the taken-for-granted perceptions of easy moving between close cultures with some historical similarities (Estonia/Northern Europe), as well as the rootedness of the awareness of potential cultural differences in the experience, in terms that it encumbers successful adaptation.

Economic capacity and professional self-fulfilment

The professional performance and economic capacities of partners are of direct affect on their home creation strategies, as concerns the major decisions on the choice and purchase of a residence. The stories of Estonian/Southern-European couples hardly tend to be unequivocal about the adaptation process interconnected with individuals' cultural dispositions towards professional performance and home creation practices. As the absence of sufficient economic capital makes entering the residential markets fairly impossible, the couple's home creation strategies are also postponed or adjusted to circumstances available at a particular phase of their housing career. The analysis of the interviews, however, suggests that the emerging difficulties for an 'in-moving' partner to engage in professional activities, tend to be related to earlier problems already encountered in the culture of origin. This also concerns the inability to advance personal cultural capital (knowledge and language) to enable smoother adaptation on a wide scale of human conduct.

The stories of Helen (33) and Marco (39) are particularly evident of the economic constraints to their choices of residence, and thus, the temporal solution, with which neither of them is satisfied. While Helen is having a professional career, Marco is unable to engage in working life. Although he reasons that cultural differences, as well as sort of 'closed community's' prejudiced attitudes towards strangers, are obstacles to his self-fulfilment in Estonia, it seems to be a long-term problem since his adult years back in his home country in Southern Europe.

> **Marco**: This (field of art) was one of my passions that became work for a while /.../ I think it is not possible anyway (in Estonia) because I'm not connected with people. I'm a foreigner /.../. And then there is no money /.../ This is a small place /.../ since I finished school I have done a lot of casual work /.../ And I had no regular job, I was mainly doing a lot of work for different companies /.../ when I tried some work I was quitting, mainly I was doing cleaning offices, this kind of stuff.

At the phase of their relationship, where Helen is being the only serious breadwinner, is not only encumbering their home creation process, but is also complicating the relations with Helen's Estonian family – an important potential support-group of significant others – as they grant no recognition to Marco as a full family member. The couple is currently incapable of discussing or negotiating their preferences for their future residence, as they are absorbed in solving professional and, consequently, existential problems, which have brought them to a standstill in finding ways out of uncertainties, towards re-inventing their personal and cross-cultural family identities. So far, they have managed to create a sense of a common home, mainly due to Helen's efforts and her encouraging offer to Marco to apply his artistic talents, with which he is gifted, in redesigning their flat.

The story, which represents a female spouse's almost sole-effort in making a cross-cultural home function, particularly, on the backdrop of a male partner's (potential) failure in a new culture, also alludes to uncongenial perceptions of gender relations, and a kind of latent male dominance, which neither of them consciously acknowledges.

Social capital and gender relations

The representations of cross-cultural relationships give evidence of contested perceptions of successful adaptation in new cultural spaces, with ways the partners shape their social networks at the core of home creation practices. A notable inter-field affect is observed bridging the boundaries of public and private spheres, which concerns the seemingly paradoxical experience of an in-moving male partner's professional success and economic security, and his simultaneous incapability to engage in local community relations. The consequential denegation, or cultural secession, framing the nature of the entire home-creation practice, seems to be lying in a complex of constitutive dimensions of the presence of an in-moving partner's ethnic community of origin, overt disinterest in the local society, or acquiring skills to communicate with this new society on different levels. In addition, strong cultural identity and hegemonic dispositions as to gender relations, supported by the other partner's incapacity, or possible unwillingness, to facilitate adaptation of a different nature, also function for secluded individual and family strategies.

Carlos' (42) and Piret's (31) story represents a mode of cross-cultural home creation practice dominated by the male partner. Carlos, a successful South-European businessman, while having adapted to the new societal context only in instrumental terms which concern his professional activities, fully controls his family life. While taking the responsibility for providing for his family in all respects, including the choice and financing of the purchase of a family residence, he also seeks his wife's approval, though the decisions are already made by him, solely. What is significant about Carlos' strategy is that there is primarily 'his strategy', which he believes to be 'theirs'. Carlos' wife, Piret, does not take a stand, rather, remains a passive partner accepting her husband's choice of a family house. Both their stories bespeak, though in distinctive ways, about the traditional norms dominating their relationship and home creation practice.

> **Piret**: Well, this was mainly Carlos' decision /.../ First this place felt a bit strange to me, as well as the house, with its weird structure /.../ But, well, by now I am used to the idea of a house. We will see how it works out.
>
> **Carlos**: The property – I found it myself./.../so I took care of it, but Piret also likes to live in X [name of the area]. I mean if we talked about it and I said I want to buy a house in X, then she agreed.

While devoted to his family and professional work, Carlos is disintegrating himself from the local community relations by delimiting his social circles onto the very private level of his home space, as well as his locally settled ethnic circles, with full confidence, which apparently emanates from his experience of disappointment in his own inability to adapt to the new culture.

> **Carlos**: I am making my own little world. I am living in Estonia... as I could be living in Latvia or Finland. Estonian society – I don't care anymore. I care about my work, I care about Piret /.../ but if you mean about attachment to the country, then – zero.

Unorthodox devotedness and open prospects

This is the observation of the study that successful professional engagement and economic security, provided independently by both partners, may facilitate cross-cultural adaptation, equally as do the dispositions towards learning about one another's culture. The individuals' experience introduced below seems to have bearing upon what has been claimed by Beck and Beck-Gernsheim (2009 [2001]) on globalising biographies characteristic of the young, highly educated, career-oriented generation of mobile lifestyles.

The youngest interviewed couple, Letizia (26) and Margus (29), represent an entirely different experience of cross-cultural relationships and home creation practices. Quite contrary to her Southern countrymen, Letizia has had a smooth adaptation to the new culture and society. She expresses her sense of belonging into two cultures with pride (*e.g.* she hosts and gives Estonian gifts to her native family and friends). Letizia's and Margus' cross-cultural intimate experience shows how an egalitarian relationship, supported also by both parental families in two different countries, favours adaptation as well as re-invention of double identities. At the present phase of their relationship they have made their home in a rented flat. As they perceive their career prospects to be open, which they tie their further home creation strategies with, they see no need for housing purchase.

> **Letizia**: I don´t want to go away from Estonia now. I really like it and I see like 3 years here. But, if for instance, for work or for some other reason we would have to move to South- America or China, or wherever, I pack my stuff and I go.

> **Margus**: Although I have travelled a lot and lived in different places then // I don't know, sometimes I think that I would like to live somewhere else again. /.../ If I think about buying a flat or a future home for my retiring age it does not necessarily have to be in Estonia. /.../ I just don't know where I would like to work or live after three or four years.

Letizia and Margus represent a match of cosmopolitan dispositions with no cultural inhibitions; they are open to professional challenges and easily adaptive to any new circumstances.

It is, however, observed that adaptation to cultural differences on the private level of an intimate relationship, as well as on levels of community relations, or societal structural conditions, with a considerable effect of childhood experiences having shaped individual cultural dispositions, tends to favour or complicate the process of residential choices. Except for a young Estonian/Southern-European couple representing a different type of disposition towards home creation, the study of the experiences of cross-cultural homes, as they appear in individual stories, evidence geographically identified differences. This implies that upon historically formed cultural closeness, there is a greater propensity for the Estonian/Northern-European partners to adapt more easily to a cross-cultural relationship, as well to the conduct on a wider scale of cultural and social relations.

Choices for home design

Preferences and tastes for home design are like preferences for a particular residence, shaped within the experiences in earlier homes, as well as in a wide range of cross- culture encounters. These encounters include a multitude of, more or less, conscious observations of different native and cross-cultural relations forming within the context of home and residence. It has to be noted that while the experiences of home design from individuals' parental homes are of remarkable importance, they do not necessarily, exclusively, or infinitely, define the tastes for adult choices. Quite the reverse, for example, the Estonians having been brought up in their parents' limited opportunities for the expression of their personal tastes in their home design (under the Soviet socialist regime), tend not to be disposed to reproducing their childhood experience in their adult strategies. Rather, they explore and choose between a diversity of designs, once in the phase of designing their homes, induced by the choice of a residence.

It is characteristic of interviewees in cross-cultural relationships that their cross-cultural conduct, having started already in their teenage years when travelling and visiting relatives or friends in other countries, as well as studying or working abroad, has also been a resource, as well as an inspiration, for the advancement of knowledge and formation of their tastes. This concludes that individuals' preferences and tastes are in continuous evolvement, in particular, in today's ubiquitous offer of opportunities for home design.

Symbolic tokens and changing meaning of objects

Coming from historically, and culturally close, countries tends to predispose individuals in cross-cultural relationships towards easier adaptation to each other's preferences and tastes for home design, as well as acceptance of differences and coming to an agreement. This is particularly characteristic of the Estonian/ Nordic couples, sharing somewhat similar tastes due to earlier cultural interactions.

Sirje and Mikael, for example, admit having grown into their similar adult preferences, facilitated by Sirje's repeated visits to Mikael's country of origin, which already occurred before they met and became a couple.

> **Sirje**: My contact with X has probably been so long – before I met Mikael, I had already been to X several times because we have relatives there. If it has developed during fifteen years, I actually think that quite a few things are very similar, in a way that I am not able to say what is his and what is mine, they have somehow mingled.

Combining different elements of home design, amongst them the gifts from parents, inherited objects, and pieces of local Estonian design purchased together, makes the daily practice of home creation for all Estonian/Nordic couples. While particular objects are of continuous symbolic meaning, having special emotional value to individual partners, other objects may have distinct and changing significance at different periods of a relationship, and the dynamic process of home design. The meaning and value attributed to objects of home design is informed by the needs, as well as the altering tastes throughout the personal histories as well as the history of a couple.

At the beginning phase of a common home creation Sirje and Mikael gratefully accepted the pieces of furniture from the Mikael's side of the family, as the couple had limited economic capacity at that time. Currently, when in an economically sound position, the relative's help is no longer needed but the couple is keeping the pieces that are of important meaning, as cherished memories and symbolic identifications of cultural origin.

> **Mikael**: I have one cupboard which has been made by my grandmother's father, must be like from the nineteenth centuries /.../ He was a sort of wooden art teacher /.../ in our children´s room we have also cupboard from my mother's childhood home /.../ Then /.../ a carpet which is from my grandmother and I remember when I was small...

In a similar vein, Paul, Annika's husband, recognises their more pragmatic disposition at the mature phase of a common home experience, allows viewing particular objects as commutable. This, however, does not concern objects of deep emotional and symbolic value.

> **Paul**: But I don't have anything that I couldn't replace with something new. Perhaps not something that is connected with the memories.

Annika's and Paul's experience, which is relatively similar to that of Sirje's and Mikael's, adds however, a relevant nuance to the understanding of the sensitive nature of making a home in a cross-cultural relationship, as a process of deep self-reflexivity. Annika's account of her experience reflects the perception that the objects given to them by her husband's side of the family when they first started to design their home as symbolic tokens of recognition of their relationship, and of her as a family member. This experience has had a positive effect on the development of her self-identity in this cross-cultural union.

> **Annika**: I have been present when these things have been given to him (Annika's husband). I mean they have been given, so to say, during our life together /.../ And I think, well, we match quite well with his parents /.../ Since the time that we have been really, really properly together, you know, and that they have seen that we share a common home, it's since then that they have started giving us /.../ some pictures and paintings.

What makes the designing of a home specific for individuals having moved across cultures is their somewhat emphasised need to manifest their identity through the ways they organise the space by displaying objects which are simultaneously meaningful for their owners, as well as offsetting the others. As visually tangible, objects presented in home space might appear as means of accommodating the differences and gaining recognition in strange cultural relationships, or eventually, re-invent identities on the level of the couple's conduct. It is also quite apparent that the Estonian/Nordic partners, Sirje and Mikael, as well as Annika and Paul, are creating a sort of hybrid home, where the couple's cultures of origin are merging in a reflection of a new level of the couple's taste.

Egalitarian choices and dominated decisions

The analysis allows the assertion that different practices of designing cross-cultural homes also bespeak equal, as well as unequal, opportunities for partners to express their identities defined by the partners' cultural perceptions of gender relations, shaped in distinct earlier experiences of social structural conditions. Again, the Estonian/Nordic couples' representations render salient inclination towards constructing home design strategies, based on mutual respect of individual partners' identities. These balanced intentions of home creation are realised by choosing things for their home that are of significance, if not symbolic value, to both partners, yet signifying their culture of origins. This is clearly a conscious strategy revealed throughout the narrations. This is perhaps less explicit, but such a tribute to partners' cultural identities, made observable through the presentation of particular objects of significance to either of the partners, becomes the means of increasing the social capital, forming on a widening international circle of friends, and their recognition of this type of practice.

Triin, who tends to be the professionally inclined, more active, and trusted partner in designing her common home with Peter, has been trying to arrange the objects in their home in ways that credit both partners. This is to the degree that directs them towards the exchange of identities and the formation of a particular couple identity, as salient in Triin's story of her 'husband's bed'.

> **Triin**: So here is the bedroom. This (bed) is from Peter. It is from Peter's home. /.../ I liked it a lot. /.../ I have also noticed it in a number of X (a Nordic country) homes /.../ my relative's husband is also X (a Nordic nation) and when he visited us he exclaimed: Oh it's from X (special region in a Nordic country) /.../ a typical bed... such a traditional bed that has been in their homes in the North /.../ when Peter saw that bed he bought it /.../ this is a must for every X (a Nordic nation), so it's good.

The experiences of egalitarian relationships bespeak the potential exchange of preferential dispositions, as well as tastes and fulfilment on the level of the reinvention of identities. This observation equally concerns the cross-cultural couples with more established home creation strategies, as well as those in the phase of a relationship where the priorities are clearly different. The lifestyle preferences are, however, represented in both experiences of shared homes, manifested in the ways the home is organised and designed, even only as temporary places.

Letizia and Margus, having not permanently settled down yet, design their home with different objects bought from various travels representing their mobile lifestyle; the majority of small objects presented in their home are gifts made to each other, and as such, the symbolic tokens of recognition of their shared home, and themselves as a couple.

> **Letizia**: So basically all these little things /.../ like everything has /.../ like particular meaning. he started to bring from abroad stuff //before I got more presents for myself, but now, when he is coming back (from the trip), it´s more like something little for the house.

Gendered relations with unmistakable dominance of one, usually, the male partner, represent different experiences of more explicit as well as of implicit nature. In the case of explicit domination of one of the partners, the decisions taken on the organisation of the home space, as well as the presentation of objects, are regimented to the taste of the dominating partner. This implies that there is no sign of cross-cultural intimate partnership, or symbolic emphasis of distinct cultures, displayed upon objects in semi-private rooms open to guests, that make sense in terms of intimates' self-identification, or external categorisation. In extreme cases, one of the partners' identity disappears into the material invisibility of objects of cultural indications in the home design.

Carlos' and Piret's home is dominated by Carlos' choice and his own cultural taste, to be displayed on almost all objects and the entire home design. Significantly, his design project entails a strong symbolic emphasis on all design elements, exclusively related to his culture, which apparently insures him with a sense of (ontological) security. Regarding his generally negative dispositions to the local culture, it is not quite clear whether his choice of objects genuinely represents his taste, or is an attempt of explicit demonstration of denegation, or even a sort of protest, or perhaps, a mode of protecting his identity. A perspicuously emotional element in his narration, concerning the gifts donated to him by his close relatives back from his native home, seems to confirm that he cherishes these objects for their symbolic significance.

> **Carlos**: I have already the whole dormitory waiting for me in Spain; that is coming. It is art nouveau style. /…/ kept right now in one of the apartments of my aunty. She has different apartments and, well, it is mine because it was a present from my grandmother, so I need a place to put it. Until I don't have the place I am not taking it here.

With a strong inclination towards explicating his culture in his private sphere of their home, it is becoming a sort of visual expression of identity of only one of the partners. His wife, however, while generally accepting Carlos' approach towards home making, is determined to apply her personal taste in the design of her private space in a room of the large family house, alluding to the differences of their tastes and her need for self-expression.

> **Piret**: I said it right at the beginning, that as there is sufficient space/.../ that I would have my place/.../well, like office where I can do my own things, and, and where I can decorate the whole room in such a way that I do not need to take anyone else into account. That I could have my own room, or, or well, let's say my own corner or a more private place.

The implicit case of domination, as has already been alluded to in the previous section of this chapter, might occur, circumstantially, in the case of weak adaptability into the new cultural and societal relations. This implies that the partner with a socially and economically weaker position in a relationship is found to be discriminating against the other partner's potential to take the decisions on home design and, what is supposed to be the common endeavour, the entire cross-cultural home creation process. Interpretation of Marco's and Helen's experiences, allows us to suggest that Marco's passive disposition towards engaging into working life has not only put the sole responsibility for home creation on Helen but has made her neglect her own preferences for home design. Marco and Helen are not negotiating their actual tastes for home design, as there is no economic capacity to realise any of their ideas. Rather, Helen is making an effort to evoke her husband's creative capacity by inviting him to contribute to the design of their temporary residence provided by Helen (*e.g.* some interior decoration, styling the furniture).

> **Helen**: It was when he was here for the first winter. I was in such a work stress /.../ Then he realised that all the walls were beige, all the flat was of such light beige colour, very hyper tasteful...that he won't survive another awful sludgy Estonian winter in this flat, that he needs colour in his life /.../ But, well, I would be also pleased with entirely white /.../ very neutral environment.

Their story shows that at particular phases of cross-cultural home creation, designing might not be a prioritised activity and tastes are simply overlooked.

The analysis of home design practices of more or less established relationships, in a phase where partners have or are to define their common strategy for home creation (having purchased a house, a flat or are negotiating the options), the home design issues clearly come into focus. However, the ways homes are designed, and how particular objects are presented, are reflective of the nature of the partners' relationship, and of how the partners have negotiated and adjusted to each other's cultural differences. The home design might reveal in what ways the partners in a cross-cultural relationship have given each other opportunities to manifest, as well as support, through the symbolic cultural value expressed on materiality of objects, or any design element or idea, the (re)invention of their personal, and possibly the shared, identities.

Conclusion

Cross-cultural home creation practices are part of the European, and worldwide, internationalisation of social relations affecting the transformation of all spheres of human conduct and becoming new realities of everyday life. This process of cross-cultural home creation is a consequence of multi-directional cross-cultural mobility. The encounter of cultures, as on the level of intimate relationship of partners of different origin, as well as on community level home creation, assumes adjustment and learning ways to communicate individual and collective identities. Creating a home on a cross-cultural basis is therefore considered a complicated endeavour of individuals, the more that moving across cultures inevitably purports adaptation and engagements in other fields of human conduct, let alone professional activity, which is indispensable for self-fulfilment as well building economic capacity to access the desired way of residing as an essential dimension of lifestyle.

With a qualitative biographical narrative focus on the creation of the home of individuals in an intimate cross-cultural relationship, this chapter, by exploring the representations of the experiences of Estonian/Nordic and Estonian/Southern European couples, has been seeking an understanding of the meaning of this experience in regards to the construction of identities. In-depth enquiries, specifically into the practice of residential choices and home design, allow the observation that the ways partners negotiate their preferences in the process of common home creation provide salient evidence of their previous unique residential experiences, as well as perceptions and imagery, shaped within the wider context of collective and dynamic social practices.

The appreciated experience of a parental home in childhood comes explicitly to the fore in discussions of adult strategies of creating a home for the family. With a particular regard to children's well-being, but with equal import placed on adult family members' lifestyle preferences, a family house with a garden appears, knowing no broad-scale cultural boundaries as a universally acknowledged ideal in stories of individuals with a positive earlier memory in the background of this aspiration (*cf.* Bhatti 2006; Bhatti and Church 2001; Hondagneu-Sotelo 2010; Paadam and Ojamäe in this book). However, it is noted that partners coming from historically and culturally closer societies, e. g. Estonian-Nordic couples, show relatively easier situations in the negotiation of any residential preferences. There is also a suggestion that the cultural differences along the North-South axes across Europe are less unequivocal between cross-cultural couples of the young mobile generation, having been socialised into the internationalised interactions.

The realisation of the negotiated residential, often lifestyle-driven, preferences for home creation in a cross-cultural relationship, therefore relates to the phase in the relationship and family life, individuals' and couple's cultural, social and economic capacities to act in circumstances of their private life and societal conditions in a country they have chosen as the place of their home. However, representations of individual lives under scrutiny in this study, urge stating that cultural capital in the form of knowledge of a particular society, the ways it functions in individual and institutional levels of relations in its different fields (in the context of home creation in the residential markets and construction field) is indispensable, and to be obtained through the development of language skills, in order to achieve the desired results.

The distinct cultural perceptions of family life, home and gender relations shaped in previous social experiences, however, tend to be projected on the nature of cross-cultural relationships and ways the home creation practices are shaped within the negotiations on partners' preferences. Negotiation of preferences in a cross-cultural relationship is considered to be part of the process of the (re)construction of identities, viewed as a continuous reflexive process through compromises or dominance of one of the partners, leaving the other partner with no opportunity for self-expression in home creation. As the analysis shows, the dominant partner should not necessarily be of local origin, with supporting relations provided by the community. In the internationalised modern societies, the newly forming ethnic networks, together with individuals' strong cultural dispositions, may lend support to distinct patterns of constructing identities of dominance.

Partners may, however, also find themselves in a phase where they account difficulties in compromising their preferences or coming to an agreement, in particular, when discussing the details of their home design, which is, perhaps, of the greatest relevance in the process of constructing identities in a cross-cultural home. The analysis of cross-cultural couples' experiences discloses the nature of intimate relationships, as well as the ability of partners and, especially, of a partner entering the new society to adapt to the newly forming circumstances in their lives as important functions of successful home creation practices. The ways partners adjust to each other's differences are also a crucial part of the overall adaptation process into the other fields of their conduct.

Home design, which is a complex process of organising the residential space, where the ways, the use, and presented objects bespeak identities of individual partners', as well as the couple's identity, or their individual positions and opportunities for expressing their identities, in a cross-cultural relationship. The objects symbolising cultural identities of partners of different origins are as significant as the objects chosen, because their common decision along the cross-cultural relationship reflect the evolvement of their values and tastes. Home design, with objects displaying taste and cultural belonging, are a significant function of constructing individual identities, as well as categorisations or external recognition from the part of the community or social circles, revealing the complexity of the process with present, and past, collective and individual expectations coupling in the endeavour of cross-cultural home creation.

References

Allen, J., Barlow, J., Leal, J., Maloutas, T., Padovani, L. (2004). *Housing and Welfare in Southern Europe*. Oxford; Malden; Carlton: Blackwell Publishing Ltd.

Atkinson, R. (1998). *The Life Story Interview*. Los Angeles; London; New Delhi; Singapore: SAGE Publications.

Beck, U. and Beck-Gernsheim, E. (2009 [2001]). *Individualization: Institutionalized Individualism and its Social and Political Consequences*. London; Thousand Oaks; New Delhi; Singapore: SAGE Publications.

Beck. U. and Beck-Gernsheim, E. (2004 [1995]). *The Normal Chaos of Love*. Cambridge: Polity Press.

Bhatti, M. (2006). 'When I'm in the garden I can create my own paradise: Homes and gardens in later life.' *The Sociological Review*, 54(2): 318-341.

Bhatti, M. and Church, A. (2001). 'Cultivating Natures: Homes and Gardens in Late Modernity.' *Sociology*, 35(2): 365-383.

Bourdieu, P. (1990). *The Logic of Practice*. Cambridge: Polity Press.

Bourdieu, P. (1984). *Distinction: A Social Critique of the Judgement of Taste*. Cambridge; Massachusetts: Harvard University Press.

Breger, R. and Hill, R. (1998). *Cross-Cultural Marriage.Identity and Choice*. Oxford: Berg Publishers.

Bustamante, R. M., Nelson, J. A., Henriksen Jr., R. C. and Monakes, S. (2011). 'Intercultural Couples: Coping With Culture-Related Stressors.' *The Family Journal: Counselling and Therapy for Couples and Families*, 19(2): 154-164.

Bystydzienski, J. M. (2011). *Intercultural Couples.Crossing Boundaries, Negotiating Difference*. New York; London: New York University Press.

Chaney, D. (2002). *Cultural Change and Everyday Life*. Basingstoke; New York: Palgrave.

Chaney, D. (1996). *Lifestyles*. London; New York: Routledge.

Craig, A. (2011). 'When a book is not a book: objects as 'players' in identity and community formation'. *Journal of Material Culture*, 16 (1): 47-63.

Crippe, C. and Brew, L. (2007). 'Intercultural Parenting and the Transcultural Family: A Literature Review.' *The Family Journal*, 15 (2): 107-115.

Dieleman, F. M (2001). 'Modelling Residential Mobility: A Review of Recent Trends in Research.'*Journal of Housing and the Built Environment*, 16: 249-265.

Domecka, M., Eichsteller, M., Karakusheva, S., Musella, P., Ojamäe, L., Perone, E., Pickard, D., Schröder-Wildhagen, A., Siilak, K. and Waniek, K. (2012). 'Method in Practice: Autobiographical Narrative Interviews in Search for European Phenomena'. Miller, R. (ed.) *The Evolution of European Identities: Biographical approaches*. London: Palgrave Macmillan Ltd. 21-45.

Douglas, M. (2000 [1996]). *Thought Styles: Critical Essays on Good Taste*. London; Thousand Oaks; New Delhi; Singapore: SAGE Publications.

Featherstone, M. (2007). *Consumer Culture and Postmodernism*. Los Angeles; London; New Deli; Singapore: SAGE Publications.

Giddens, A. (1990). *The Consequences of Modernity*. Cambridge: Polity Press.

Giddens, A. (2009 [1991]). *Modernity and Self-Identity: Self and Society in the Late Modern Age*. Cambridge: Polity Press.

Gubrium, J. F., and Holstein, J. A. (2009). *Analyzing Narrative Reality*. Los Angeles; London; New Delhi; Singapore: SAGE Publications.

Hauge, Å. L. and Kolstad, A. (2007). 'Dwelling as an Expression of Identity. A Comparative Study Among Residents in High-Priced and Low-Priced Neighbourhoods in Norway' *Housing, Theory and Society*, 24 (4): 272-292.

Hewitt, B. and Baxter, J. (2012). 'Who Gets Married in Australia? The Characteristics Associated with a Transition into First Marriage 2001-6.' *Journal of Sociology*, 48(1): 43-63.

Holstein, J. A., and Gubrium, J. F. (2000). *Constructing the Life Course*. New York: General Hall.

Hondagneu-Sotelo, P. (2010). 'Cultivating Questions for a Sociology of Gardens.' *Journal of Contemporary Ethnography*, 39(5): 498-516.

Hurdley, R. (2006). 'Dismantling Mantelpieces: Narrating Identities and Materializing Culture in the Home.' *Sociology*, 40(4): 717-733.

Jenkins, R. (2000). 'Categorization: Identity, Social Process and Epistemology.' *Current Sociology*, 48(7): 7-25.

Kasearu, K. and Kutsar, D. (2011). 'Patterns Behind Unmarried Cohabitation Trends in Europe.' *European Societies*, 13(2): 307-325.

Kopytoff, I. (1986). The cultural biography of things: commoditization as process. Appadurai, A. (ed.) *The Social Life of Things: Commodities in Cultural Perspective*. New York: Cambridge University Press, 64-91.

Maehara, N. (2010). 'Emotional Ambiguity: Japanese Migrant Women in Mixed Families and their Life Transition.' *Journal of Ethnic and Migration Studies*, 36(6): 953-966.

Miller, D. (2012 [2008]). *The Comfort of Things*. Cambridge: Polity Press.

Molina, B., Estrada, D. and Burnett, J. A. (2004). 'Cultural Communities: Challenges and Opportunities in the Creation of 'Happily Ever After' Stories of Intercultural Couplehood.' *The Family Journal,* 12: 139-147.

Money, A. (2007). 'Material Culture and the Living Room. The Appropriation and Use of Goods in Everyday Life.' *Journal of Consumer Culture*, 7: 355-377.

Nielsen, A. (2008). 'From Questions of Methods to Epistemological Issues: The Case of Biographical Research.' Alasuutari, P., Bickman, L. and Brannen,J. (eds.) *The SAGE Handbook of Social Research Methods*. Los Angeles; London; New Delhi; Singapore: SAGE Publications, 81-94.

Ojamäe, L. (2009). *Making Choices in the Housing Market: Social Construction of Housing Value: The Case of New Suburban Housing*. Tallinn: Tallinn University, Institute of International and Social Studies.

Paadam, K. (2003). *Constructing Residence as Home: Homeowners and their Housing Histories*. Tallinn: TPU Press.

Paadam, K., Ojamäe, L. and Siilak, K. (2012). 'Cross-cultural Exchanges: Intimate Relationships and Transforming Societies.' Miller, R. (ed.) *The Evolution of European Identities: Biographical approaches*. London: Palgrave Macmillan Ltd, 211-232.

Refsing, K. (1998). 'Gender Identity and Gender Role Patterns in Cross-cultural Marriages: the Japanese-Danish Case.' Breger, R. and Hill, R. (eds.) *Cross-Cultural Marriage. Identity and Choice*, Oxford: Berg Publishers, 193-208.

Riessman, C. K. (2008). *Narrative Methods for the Human Sciences*. Los Angeles; London; New Delhi; Singapore: SAGE Publications.

Rocamora, A. (2002). 'Fields of Fashion: Critical Insights into Bourdieu's Sociology of Culture.' *Journal of Consumer Culture*, 2: 341-362.

Roberts, B. (2002). *Biographical Research*. Buckingham: Open University Press.

Sassatelli, R. (2007). *Consumer Culture. History, Theory and Politics*. London: SAGE Publications.

Schütze, F. and Schröder-Wildhagen, A. (2012). 'European Mental Space and its Biographical Relevance.' Miller, R. (ed.) *The Evolution of European Identities: Biographical approaches*. London: Palgrave Macmillan Ltd., 255-279.

Sherif Trask, B. and Hamon, R. R. (2007).*Cultural Diversity and Families. Expanding Perspective*. London; Thousand Oaks; New Delhi; Singapore: SAGE Publications.

Seto, A. and Cavallaro, M. (2007). 'Cross-National Couples in the Mainland United States.' *The Family Journal*, 15: 258-264.

Stewart, P. and Goldfarb, K. P. (2007). 'History and Trends in the Study of Culturally Diverse Families.'Sherif Trask, B. and Hamon R. R. (eds.) *Cultural Diversity and Families. Expanding Perspective*. London; Thousand Oaks; New Delhi; Singapore: SAGE Publications, 3-20.

Williams, L. (2010). *Cross-border Marriage Migration in Global Context*. Basingstoke: Palgrave Macmillan.

Woodward, I. (2010 [2007]). *Understanding Material Culture*. London; Thousand Oaks; New Delhi; Singapore: SAGE Publications.

Woodward, I. (2003). 'Divergent Narratives in the Imagining of the Home Amongst Middle-class Consumers. Aesthetics, Comfort and the Symbolic Boundaries of Self and Home.' *Journal of Sociology*, 39(4): 391-412.

Woodward, I. (2001). 'Domestic Objects and the Taste Epiphany. A Resource for Consumption Methodology.' *Journal of Material Culture*, 6(2): 115-136.

Woodward, I. and Emmison, M. (2001). 'From Aesthetic Principles to Collective Sentiments: The Logics of Everyday Judgments of Taste.' *Poetics*, 29(6): 295-316.

Migrant career women's discursive (re)constructions of their domestic partners' masculine identities

Marion Pajumets, Jeff Hearn

Introduction

Cross-border migration from 'New Europe' to the welfare democracies of 'Old Europe' has often been studied as an economic, or demographic, issue that does not appear to have significant gender dimensions. This analysis complements the supposedly gender neutral macro-perspective view, by seeing gendered well-being as a constitutive element of migration, permeating migrants' acculturation in the host country and their decision to stay, or move on, to a third country or return to their country of origin, either as a family, or individually.

Indeed, masculinities and femininities may challenge migration decisions, just as they are often challenged by migration experiences. It becomes complicated to construct one's gender identity if the host country's gender system differs considerably from that which one originates, and is used to. And even if the gender system is not so dissimilar, one might, in the new context, command less status and reduced resources to feel an 'adequate' man or woman, mother or father. On the other hand, and importantly, people may also, even simultaneously, see migration as an opportunity in terms of gender identity and gendered well-being. A new and changed gender environment may facilitate reconsideration of the content of masculinity and femininity, and this process might be positively embraced by some migrants (for example, some gay migrants who expatriate to sexually more liberal countries).

This chapter focuses on what we see as a theoretically fascinating case of masculine identity (re)constructions, of men who have migrated following their highly skilled female partners, and the latter's new employment opportunities. While those women advanced their careers transnationally, as diplomats, or medical doctors, their male partners became hardly engaged with the host countries' labour market, instead focusing on being supportive partners and caring parents. While this kind of home-centred lifestyle is rather typical for many female tied-migrants, it is less common for male migrants, even though educated or professionally qualified male migrants often become unemployed, or work in less skilled, or lower income jobs, in their host countries (see, for example, Little and Hisnanick 2007). Indeed, in many such cases the men concerned had been breadwinners back at home. Thus, these couples can be seen as not only migrating, but also enacting 'reversed gender roles'. This combination of circumstances sets up the material conditions for some complex and contradictory identity processes. Indeed, while our main analysis is on this intersection of migration and gender change, the results might also be of relevance for the consideration of the effects of 'reversed gender roles', even when there is no migration involved.

To complicate the situation of the migrated couples even further, they moved to 'Old Europe', from post-socialist 'New Europe'[20], where masculinity is hardly separable from employed work and income-earning. In other words, the rather private lifestyles of these Estonian men are highly feminised in their culture of origin, and thus most probably somewhat feminising to the men practising them. Hence, the masculine identities of these rather private post-socialist men were likely to become challenged in some respects.

As a reaction to this changed situation, not only did the men enact reaffirmations of their masculinities in their talk (see Pajumets and Hearn 2012), but also their female spouses positively supported the men's identity pursuits, thereby increasing the likelihood of the men's willingness to stay in the host country. This article elucidates the discursive strategies women creatively employed, in order to boost their spouses' gender identities in the context of the couples' current living arrangements and lifestyles, and their cultural implications on masculinity, as stemming from their home country.

We emphasise that the success of the couples' joint discursive efforts has effects beyond men's immediate personal gendered well-being; it also affects the acculturalisation and well-being of the whole migrated family, including young children; moreover, it is hard to imagine that most of the highly skilled female professionals would be able to fully contribute to the new foreign labour market had they been experiencing major emotional turmoil at home. Having said that, we suggest that macro-level migration processes, such as the regional economic growth and decline, brain drains / brain gains, national demographic trends, as well as physical resettlement, and migratory circulations themselves, are indirectly promoted and restrained by the migrants' well-being as gendered persons.

In this analysis, we conceptualise identity as *processual*, that is to say, continuously constructed in discourse and interaction, rather than determined by the social roles men enact. We would like to point out that the focus of this article is the construction of *masculine* identity, since what is at stake for those men is not

20 By 'Old Europe' we refer to those European states that had parliametary democratic systems and market economies prior to 1989. Most, but not all, such as Norway and Switzerland, belonged to the European Union before the 2004 enlargement. In this paper 'New Europe' refers to those CEE countries that had socialist regimes prior to 1989. Many, but not all, have joined the EU since 1989.

simply their sense of personal significance and dignity, but also a positive masculinity that is rather unthinkable for someone of Estonian background to achieve without the status often grounded in engagement with the public realm.

The chapter draws on semi-structured, open-ended interviews with Estonian female migrants making their careers in Finland, Germany, Belgium, Switzerland, France, and Luxemburg, that have been followed by their families. These interviews were generally rich in depictions of their partners, the rather domestic men migrants, as important, valuable, active, in control, and indeed masculine. As an analytic framework, the notion of 'positioning in discourse' (Davies and Harré 1990) is applied in this paper. While drawing on poststructuralist approaches, suggesting that language is a central means of creating 'masculinity', the analysis is located within a broad historical framing of transnationalisation of work, and the transnational changes in gendered power relations.

Gendering global migration

Cross-border migration has often been studied as an economic or demographic issue that does not appear to have significant gender dimensions. The focus of such macro-level research has typically regarded the economic effects of foreign labour on the labour market and macro-economic performance of the receiving country; push and pull factors when moving for work in another country; attitudes towards foreign-born workforce from the host population; and various so-called 'brain drains'. In recent decades, however, there has been significant growth of research on gender as a 'constitutive element of immigration' (Hondagneu-Sotelo 2003: 9), examining how gender permeates a variety of practices, identities, and institutions implicated in migration. This research strand has typically scrutinised the micro-processes in migrant families, communities and networks, often using open-ended interviews and ethnographic methods rather than broad surveys alone.

Such studies of the gendered processes of migration have predominantly elucidated the intersectional gendered lives of women migrants, for example, domestic workers (Hondagneu-Sotelo and Avila 1997; Salazar Parreñas 2000; Sousa Ribeiro 2008; Hochschild 2003), nurses (Widding Isaksen 2012), 'mail order' brides, (Narayan 1995), and prostituted women, including those from Central and Eastern European countries (Morokvasic 1991); however, the research focus has rather rarely been on how men's experience of migration is affected by their 'being men' or 'maleness', and how masculinities are reformulated in the context of different forms of migration, within changing global relations (Nawyn 2010). Pyle and Ward (2003) state that as economic activities become more global, some countries and groups benefit, but the hardships of many others increase. And this also certainly applies to certain men, as globalisation creates the potential for extensions of power for some men, and loss of power for other men (Hearn 2009).

Having said that, one arena of gendered research on migrant men is emphasised by Mike Donaldson and colleagues (2009) in their examinations of the renegotiations of masculinity of men who have moved to Australia from diverse regional and cultural backgrounds. They emphasised that migrant men generally consider their authority and power, both 'at home' and 'overseas', to be based upon the work they are paid to do. As such, work is a 'key element' in the reproduction of their manhood. Hence, men feel reduced, used, and taken-for-granted when performing work beneath their skill level, not to mention the disempowerment and emasculation that unemployment may bring. Men migrants' conceptions of themselves were also affected by women's greater opportunities in Australia to work and be more economically and socially independent of men. Migration to Australia also changed the household division of labour and subverted the type of masculinity based on being the head of the family and breadwinner of the house (Donaldson & Howson 2009).

Another strand of research on migrating men focuses on their fathering practices. Hearn and Niemistö (2012), for example, have analysed the relationship of fathering and working as managers in Finnish transnational corporations. They point to the strengthening of the ideology of separate public and private spheres: 'The more time the father/managers had spent in expatriate work, the greater the probability that their female partners stayed as housewives.' (*ibid.*: 10) (also see Hearn *et al.* 2009; cf. Haas and Hwang 2007). Taken that large transnational business and governmental organisations are prominent engines of cross-border migration, and given the barriers that women face in striving for international career opportunities, the typical skilled and well-paid expatriate still tends to be male. Not surprisingly, the importance attached to the support of the spouse and the family in various phases of expatriate assignments often rests on the assumption that the spouse is female and will not work abroad in a career-related position (Schuler *et al.* 2004). However, in this study the assumption is challenged. Thus, the men whose masculinity is the focus of this study are a relatively unusual group, as they are partners of professional women whose careers have led to migration as a consequence of their employment abroad.

The reversal of gender roles in the context of migration has rarely been studied up to now. However, more cautious gendered reorganisations of couples' (power) relations such as those in Brazilian families in the US (Debiaggi 2001), and in families with diverse geographical, racial, and religious backgrounds now living in Australia (Donaldson *et al.* 2009) have enjoyed some academic attention. At the centre of much of this gender change has been women's unprecedented pursuit to the destination country's labour market. Consequently, in the context of migration, being a professional, economically independent, indeed, a breadwinner, as well as not being the one who is always accessible to other family members' needs, ceases to be the privilege of men, and exclusively associated with masculinity. Regardless of the significance of those changes to the couples in question, those studies do not entail women making a career and men picking up the bulk of 'women's work' as in our study on Estonian migrant families in 'Old Europe'. Indeed the reversal of (heterosexual) gender roles has rarely been studied in non-migrant couples and families either. This makes our paper among the pioneers in this research field of reversed (heterosexual) gender roles, a field that probably has a growing resonance in the lifestyles of more and more couples in this globalising world.

To conclude, the Estonian men migrants in question enjoy many gendered, sexual, national, and ethnic privileges: they are not sent back from the Schengen border, as, for example, gay Mexican men would most likely be; neither do they suffer from the degrading sexualisation that young women from the 'New Europe' are still likely to confront in 'Old Europe'; nor indeed are they living on social welfare. Yet, those husbands in cooperation with their wives have to make a considerable discursive effort to reaffirm their gender identity more explicitly, and, at the same time, women also perhaps shift their gender identity, if more implicitly. Unable to feel an 'adequate' man and woman, and living in countries which are among the highest quality of life in the contemporary world, they may gain significantly less compared with similarly qualified locals.

Identity as a process, and subject positioning in discourse

While structurally based roles and role relationships function as an important springboard for personal identities, they are neither automatic indicators nor determinants of the latter (Snow and Anderson 1987). In other words, one's personal identities do not have to respond to one's social positions, and, therefore, can not be considered as given or fixed. Therefore, while the male partners of women interviewed for this study might not perform as a professional, a main breadwinner, and even perhaps a taxpayer – all of which are culturally considered normative for the male gender – they still have discursive means to achieve a positive view of themselves as men.

We argue here that language has a central place in constructing identity, including masculine identity. Language is the carrier of meanings; discourses of 'the masculine' define the meanings of masculinity in a given social context. Men, as well as women, act in the material sphere based on those mental meanings. Thus, masculinities do not have an essential, independent existence outside discourse, understood as founded in people's material circumstances. Or as Foucault would probably put it – discourses on masculinity are practices that systematically form the subjects of which they speak.

Importantly, any meanings based on language and interactions are subject to ongoing reformulations in discourse. Thus, this article adopts a *processual* perspective (Snow and Anderson 1987) on identity formation. Hence, the focus of identity research should not be on who someone *is* in any fixed sense, but rather on what is someone *doing* about identity (Rounds 2006: 135). We have earlier demonstrated that men (see Pajumets and Hearn 2012) engage discursively in re-affirming their masculine identity when going through large-scale and multiple changes. In this article we seek to show that wives and female partners support their men in it. In that sense, the women concerned could be said to be doing both direct identity work for themselves, and indirect identity work in relation to the men concerned.

We assume that a man's sense of being an 'adequate man' is likely to depend on his partner's verbal affirmations of his gender identity, that is, his heterosexual gender identity. It is likely to be rather challenging to see oneself as masculine if one's beloved spouse subverts this view. Her perspective may appear to originate from *inside* the couple relation rather than from the outside world, and is likely to be taken personally. Her views may act as a shortcut to a man's gender identity. Perhaps her opinions count for even more in those migrated couples where the women are more powerful than their husbands, including financially, in the public sphere.

In developing these arguments, we adopt the subject positioning in discourse approach (Davies and Harré 1990), suggesting that conversations have storylines and the positions people take in a conversation will be linked to these storylines (van Langenhove and Harré 1999: 17). In taking up a subject position in a storyline or a discourse, or being unable to resist one, a subject commits him or herself to a particular, limited set of concepts, images, metaphors, ways of speaking, self-narratives and so on that (s)he takes up as his/her own, and that (s)he gets emotionally tied to (Burr 2003: 199). One gets also locked into a system of rights, speaking rights and obligations that are carried with that position (*ibid.*: 111).

On the other hand, and not to be forgotten, people in interaction might accept the position offered to them by a storyline or, alternatively, try to *resist* it by changing the discourse. The process of negotiating identities through claiming, accepting and resisting subject positions often takes place in interactive situations that are not intended as arenas for power struggles. However personally these ways of speaking may be experienced, they are likely to be closely aligned with wider social and societal forms of discourse and, indeed, material-discursive practices. The analysis of these micro-processes thus helps us understand how macro structures are being formed and reproduced (Gálvez and Tirado 2006). As we said earlier, a male migrants' identity and well-being as a gendered person can be reassured or alternatively undermined through positioning, and being positioned in conversations has implications on varied structural phenomena including the acculturalisation of migrant families, their possible geographical and social relocations, and the norms of gendered divisions of labour in couple relations.

Estonian gender context and migration experience

Although the couples of this study reside most of the time in 'Old Europe', the social structuring and cultural patterns of Estonian society most probably remain an important frame of reference for them, therefore, these need to be considered in order to grasp the nature of the challenges to gender identity for the Estonian migrant men with rather domestic lifestyles in this study.

Estonia regained its independence from the Soviet Union as late as 1991. As part of the heritage from the Soviet period, Estonian women participate in the labour market almost as actively as men do; however, women are over-represented in the educational and care-related sectors, while they are generally marginal in the top managerial ranks, as well as in the country's political leadership. Indeed, only 38% of Estonian men think that companies would benefit from more female managers (Vainu *et al.* 2010: 34). Resulting from the combined horizontal and vertical gender segregation in the labour market, as well as women's disproportionate burden at home, which we will discuss shortly, the country's average hourly gender pay gap is 30% and thereby the largest among the European Union member states (Eurostat 2009). As for the division of labour at home, women are typically responsible for numerous daily, time consuming chores (Vainu *et al.* 2010), as well as the care of children, especially younger children (Pajumets 2010).

This differentiation of women's and men's work is reconstructed by Estonian parents' through their principles of upbringing their children. While parents prioritise IT skills, an enterprising spirit, and adventurousness for boys, girls are prepared for adulthood by being taught the art of manners, keeping house, and embellishing their appearance. However, both boys and girls in Estonia are taught how to think in relation to economics by their parents (Vainu *et al.* 2010: 45-48). Curiously, the valued gender traits in Estonia correspond closely to those assessed in the sex role scales derived from social psychological investigations in the U.S. in the 1960s and 1970s (for example, Bem 1974; see also Eichler 1980).

As for Estonian migration, low pay remains a problem for even relatively well-paid men in Estonia[21]. The differences in incomes compared to neighbouring Nordic countries, for example, are very large indeed, on the order of 300% and more. It is not a surprise, therefore, that seeking a higher salary has been the most important reason Estonians seek work abroad (Krusell 2009: 67). The largest numbers of recent Estonian migrants have been those who have emigrated to work in Finland, Sweden, Norway, and the UK (*ibid.*: 68), which are among the more affluent countries in 'Old Europe'.

Overall, estimations of Estonians living abroad range up to 130,000 (Kõre 2011). This is a considerable amount, with the total population of Estonia being roughly 1.3 million people. As in many CEE countries, many people optimised the risks of the rather unpredictable transformations by pursuing various transnational strategies and movements (Morokvasic 2004).

To conclude this background discussion to our analysis, it may be useful to consider our study in relation to Inglehart and Weltzel's (2005) 'world values map'. In this study, they positioned Estonia as a country that had not yet gone through cultural shifts from so-called materialist values to so-called post-materialist values. The former entails prioritising economic survival, i.e. working, earning and spending money, over post-materialist self-expression. Self-expressionist values, such as broader political participation, less authoritarian leadership, more active participation in organised culture and community life, general trust in people and institutions, social tolerance, and, last but not least, more equal gender relations, are not so prominent in Soviet successor states (*ibid.*).

While this kind of contrast that Inglehart and Weltzel (*ibid.*) describe can obscure many issues of difference, complexity, and economic deprivation, it can be seen as a framework presenting broad ideal-types. In 'Old Europe' there are, even with the more recent financial crisis, many people who have grown up in relative prosperity, take material welfare much for granted, and put energy on self-expression through community building, civil society engagements, and so on. On the other hand, paid work and breadwinning are certainly still central to many men's identity construction in Western European states, and self-expressionist masculinities, such as the 'nurturing father' and 'new men', are often cultural ideals rather than commonplace practices. Following this broad framework, Saar (2010) analysed Estonian data from the World Values Surveys of 1990, 1999, and 2008, and concluded that over this period Estonia came closer to the 'Old Europe' countries, but is still far less tolerant, and with less

---

21 GDP in current price per inhabitant is €10,700 in Estonia, €33,600 in Finland, €32,600 in Belgium, and €79,500 in Luxembourg (Eurostat, 2012).

valuation of self-expression. Thus, for our present purposes, Estonia can still be characterised as a country where 'survivalist' values persist, where labour migration is an important issue, where scant attention is paid to gender equality, and where there is relatively little tolerance towards alternative lifestyles.

Research methods

This analysis is a part of a larger project on varied gendered aspects of migration[22]. Interviews with ten couples, altogether 19[23] interviewees, were conducted at the end of 2010 and in 2011. The article, however, draws predominantly on interviews with women, all in their thirties or early forties[24]. The women concerned were either physicians or worked for different EU institutions such as the European Commission. The men were also generally highly educated. Before migrating they had worked as: owners or managers of different companies, IT specialists, journalists, researchers, teachers, engineers, military officers. All couples had young children, between one and three in number, living with them abroad.

The open-ended interview design facilitated the discussion of topics that the participants themselves raised; we also dedicated as much time to each topic as each interviewee needed. The participants decided the location of the interview conversation, and those decisions were perhaps somewhat restricted by their living in different regions of Europe. About half of the conversations were conducted via Skype, which participants had on their home computers, the other half were face-to-face. The average length of the interview was around two hours. Interviews were recorded and transcribed verbatim. The interview extracts presented in the analysis section represent patterns of identity talk that frequently occur in the interview material. They were selected from many similar extracts on the basis of their clarity and conciseness. Interviews were analysed using the positioning in discourse approach outlined earlier.

---

22 The interview plan included a wide range of topics, such as: how is masculinity / femininity reconceptualised; negotiations between family members before leaving Estonia; the implications of migration on children; future ideals and plans; and constructions of national / European identities.
The research team includes one doctoral student, the first author of this paper, and two master students – Kaisa Kaha and Lee Maripuu as well as their supervisors. All are from Tallinn University except the second author of this paper.

23 One woman exercised her freedom to withdraw from the project after initial agreement to participate. She refused to be interviewed.

24 Please see Pajumets and Hearn 2012 on those men's identity talk.

Male and female partners were interviewed separately. This is an important issue in research on couples, married or otherwise (Mansfield and Collard 1988; Duncombe and Marsden 1993). For example, it seemed possible that some men might have a less powerful position in the couple relation after migration, and might also want to reduce possible social c ontrol by their spouse during an interview. We also wanted to make it easier for women to express their own concerns regarding their own thoughts, possibly troubled, about their femininity and quality of mothering. We were aware of the high rates of marital problems including separations in the target group of our study; indeed, about half of the informants in our sample said they had visited marriage consultants or various psychological counsellors or advisers during their stay abroad.

Prior to the interview, all the participants were introduced to the project by means of an information sheet, with the topics of primary interest to the research group, the practical process of the project, and last but not least, the research team's ethical principles of working[25].

As a rule, women gained considerably in their personal income due to working abroad; on the contrary, men generally lost a large part of their previous (and what they perceived as their 'normal') income, and thus their financial independence. Men's connectedness to paid work and income-generating opportunities varied considerably[26]. No men worked at the time of the interview, for a company registered in their country of destination. Hence, if the men did have a personal income it was on an Estonian scale, and thus rather moderate for someone living in such expensive locations as Finland, Germany, Belgium, France, Switzerland and Luxemburg.

Constructing masculine identity

This study's male participants' lifestyles are in obvious opposition to the strong cultural linkages in post-socialist Estonia between paid work and masculinity. The couples' friends and relatives, from Estonia, often emphasised this discrepancy and criticised migrated couples' gendered lifestyles. The female interview-

---

25 The latter included the principle of confidentiality, and willingness from the part of the research team to discuss our interpretations with participants and to include the participants' interpretations if they differ considerably from those of the researchers'.

26 Three of the men kept their jobs in Estonia with reduced workloads and commuted between two countries on a weekly or monthly basis. Two men stayed in their country of destination while continuing remote work on some minor projects back in Estonia. Four married partners of Estonian female diplomats received a rather moderate subsidy from the Estonian state providing that they were not employed. Some owned real estate back in their homeland which gave them some income.

ees reacted to this challenge to their men partners' masculinity by employing two types of empowering discourses: they may either downplay the atypical nature of men's lifestyles by (over-)emphasising the men's work-orientation that is generally unquestioned in former socialist countries (even if far from absent among some men in 'Old Europe'); or they may discursively subvert the work and pay-oriented cultural assumptions as outdated, and strive to reformulate the contents of what might be called an alternative masculinity. The latter formulations are broadly post-materialist in character, and refer to the couples' valuation of 'self-expression' rather than their valuation of economic 'survival' (Inglehart and Weltzel 2005).

The two types of responses by women are alternatives, and discrete, only at an analytical level. In practice they are used in parallel by the same women during one single interview. This is in itself a finding of interest. We now consider these responses in more detail.

Claiming conservative masculinity

Women may reinforce a work and income-centred masculinity in their men by positioning them as *professional men,* and as *well off.* A frequent use of those depictions in the interviews indicates that the relatively equality-orientated gender environments couples faced in their destination countries (for example, Finland or Belgium), were not embraced as valuable triggers to reconsider or reformulate masculinity (and indeed femininity). These migrated Estonian couples have not quit striving towards normalcy and social acceptance, as defined in their conservative culture of origin. Hence, the women's two sub-discourses outlined below contribute to the *status quo* of a materialist, and indeed malestream, gender system. Interestingly, that very gender system is not especially supportive towards women.

The professional man

Migrant men were positioned as professional men in the interviews either by emphasising: their professional dedication and success back in Estonia; by overstating their current professional engagements abroad; or by anticipating men's future work and career prospects. Some women invested in all three (see Hollway 1984). They typically depicted the current slower period in their spouses' professional lives and careers as a temporary break to the men's full time, well paid, and socially highly valued occupational work and status, ranging in temporal terms from the distant past to the far future. Hence, the present moment was presented as an exception to the rule, and therefore not to be considered significant or damaging to their spouses' encompassing professional identity.

Next, we would like to present an example of such an investment in this discourse in a little more detail. Laura is a diplomat working for a European Union institution and living in 'Old Europe' with her two children and husband. Her husband should be considered rather domestic since he has rarely done any paid work since leaving Estonia, where he used to work in a school. In order to highlight his *professional achievements and position* Laura contrasts them with her own former job, managing a small business, which she characterises in generally modest and unflattering terms.

> **Laura:** I have to say, I did try to run the business, not that I had considerable success in it, but it remained so limited and small. My husband, to the contrary, has always pushed to develop himself, and he had colleagues of higher education predominanltly, while I was quarreling with workers who had about eight grades of schooling.

Laura's devaluing of her own past job and assigning much higher worth to her partner's makes sense in the backdrop of the Estonian dominant gender system. Generally speaking, men's work is expected to be worth more than women's (as crystallised in the country's gender pay gap). Her talk in the excerpt shows her own overshadowing of her present successful transnational career, which might be seen as almost too good to be true for a woman, and even perhaps as not fully deserved. Indeed, men as well as women participants in this study pointed out that in Estonia, women's professional contributions were rather poorly valued and that men, on the other hand, tended to be in better jobs or in a successful career track.

In talking about the present situation and future times, women continue to position their spouses as professionals. Some women point out that their husbands or life companions stay in touch with the developments of their area of work throughout their expatriate life, indeed, that the men's former colleagues have contacted them to ask their valuable opinions before making some major decisions for their company. The latter function to position men as essentially valued professionals who are enjoying a prolonged holiday.

Laura is typical for branding her husband in terms of an encompassing professional status. Note also that performing private sphere unpaid tasks such as childcare becomes equated with 'sitting at home' and 'doing nothing' in the following extract.

> **Laura:** You see he has been involved with some minor construction works; he's been helping people out, helped people with changing lodgings. And now that we have some connections with the couples of Estonian women married to the Belgian men, they started launching a business recently, and it might be that my husband can

> start working for them in some way, perhaps not on a full time basis and with full workload, but simply to go and help them out now and then. He's been doing that already. So it wouldn't be fair to say he is sitting at home doing nothing; it's not true.

While a few women like Laura positioned their husbands as soon returning to the labour market in their new homelands, that is in 'Old Europe', most female interviewees focus on their husbands resuming work in Estonia at some, often undefined, time in the future.

We should also make it clear that we are not at all excluding the migrant men's return to work on a more full basis; rather, our aim here has been to stress their women partners' considerable discursive effort to claim their rather domestic spouses' professional status, and work-centred masculinity characteristic to Estonia and most likely post-socialist societies more generally.

The well off

Economic well-being, being the breadwinner in the house, earning more than women, is an integral component of masculinity in the still relatively poor Estonia, but perhaps also more widely in the contemporary world. Losing one's economic autonomy in migration and becoming dependent on one's partner might be rather demanding on many men, as well as the participants in this study. However, their partners most eagerly and creatively continued to position their men as breadwinners, as financially autonomous, and in control regarding the sustenance of the family. Women thereby preserve the conservative and survivalist cultural enfolding of economic power and masculinity.

To begin with, all women depict their spouses as the *primary breadwinners* for the bulk of the couple's years together. Again, women play down their own past and their current financial contribution to the sustenance of the family, so positioning their spouses as having done more. For example, Maria, a diplomat, with two children, puts it in this way:

> **Maria:** Basically, from the start, and up to recently, he was the one supporting the whole family. My jobs were kind of ... rather marginal compared to his. I've always earned less, it's only now upside down.
>
> ***Interviewer:*** *How is the distribution of incomes now?*
>
> **M:** Now I'm earning considerably more, but it used to be the other way around.

Indeed, no women boasted about their own earnings despite the latter being immense, in some cases, compared to the average salary in Estonia, as well as being higher than the salary of the President of the Estonian Republic, as one husband humorously pointed out.

Some women, such as Sandra, a mother of two and a diplomat, stressed their husbands being *financially autonomous*, not only in the past and following the family's possible return to Estonia, but also during the time the interviews were conducted. Her husband received a moderate pay (that was diminished further during the economic downturn), that the Estonian state granted to its diplomats' married partners. In this quotation Sandra pampers her husband by contrasting his alleged financial autonomy to the far sadder status of some other men who are *economically dependent on their wives.*

> ***I**: You mentioned at some point that some men experience a deep fall after migration?*
>
> **Sandra:** To my mind it must be [hard] for most men to adapt to the fact that you are a dependant now. You see, these days, since the institution of the spouses' salary, it's a bit easier /…/ You do not get the feeling that your wife supports you in the diplomat families anymore. The system grants him his own social and pension funds; he remains an independent person, no matter the smaller income.

The concept of 'family income' was also widely used in the interviews. Women presented it as a salary earned technically by them, but that their spouses were assigned an equal right to spend. This idea was in some couples materialised by sharing a common bank account that was accessible by the two credit cards owned by women and man.

Finally, we would like to delineate one more discursive (and perhaps practiced) strategy some women employed to attribute their spouses *control over family maintenance*. The women positioned themselves as rather hopelessly dependent on their men's paperwork and ICT competences that in turn protected the families from potential financial (and further) disasters.

> **Sandra:** I consider myself an embodied helplessness. /…/ It's rather bizarre you know, I have not done any bank transfers for the last four years. I don't even know how the bank works where we live now. He is fully responsible for stuff like that. I was thinking recently what would happen in case something happened to him, I'd be totally lost. For example, I have no idea where to look for … in a nutshell, almost everything besides work is his responsibility; this includes paying the bills, and everything, you know, checking the water indicators, registering the car etc. /…/ To my mind he doesn't complain, because then he is the one to keep the household whole and running.

Some women quite eagerly positioned themselves as dependent on their husbands and grateful for their wide-ranging contributions. Indeed, there was a rather general feeling in women's interview material that they owe their spouses a great deal: materially, because they left their good jobs; practically, for running the households; and emotionally for endorsing their wife's dreams to work internationally and live far from the familiar surroundings of Estonia.

Claiming an alternative masculinity

Women also praised their male spouses for their dedication to their families, as well as for developing themselves through unpaid hobbies and community activities. The discourses of *modern family man* and *the active one* were emphasised in the data.

We anticipated that women might challenge the work and income-centred male norm. This was, firstly, because the study participants did not have to worry so much about material survival after migration; all but one family gained considerably financially by expatriating; indeed, life in the 'Old Europe' was conceptualised by one woman as 'living in a golden cage' – too prosperous to give it up and return to Estonia. Secondly, couples resided now in a somewhat different environment not only in economic terms but also regarding the dominant gender system. In many 'Old Europe' societies less work-centred, and more culture-, family-, community-, and care-oriented lifestyles are rather more accepted, although not widely prevalent, for men compared to post-socialist 'New Europe'.

The modern family man

Generally speaking, in Estonia mothers are seen as the primary parents, especially when children are young (Pajumets 2010); women are also attributed the main responsibility for daily household chores. The couples interviewed perceived their departure from a typical Estonian gender division of labour as less problematic when they were in their destination countries, where there are more other couples consisting of a more domestic man and a career woman; however, it becomes rather stressful 'at home', that is in their country of origin. Several women recalled that their partners get constantly asked by other Estonians, 'So, when will you return to work?' From this quarter, men have also been reported to have been seen as 'total losers', and 'victims of their wives'. Furthermore, some other Estonians have challenged some of the men participants' gender identity, by naming them as 'hens', and 'ladies of the house'[27] (and thus in both cases referring to the female gender). Hence, the participants themselves recognised and pointed out cultural clashes they have to deal with in their transnational emotional lives (Hearn 2007).

---

27 In Estonian 'kodukana', 'perenaine'.

Derogatory positionings of Estonian origin demean both men and their wives. Our interviews demonstrate that migrant career women are highly defensive in relation to their more domestic men's dignity and masculinity. In the excerpt below, Helen, a diplomat with three children, and a husband who used to be a sales manager, refuses for her husband to be positioned in a way that might slight him, and picks up a *modern father* discourse that presents him in a positive light.

> **Helen:** to my mind, it's no one else's business to tell us how we should live our life. /.../ It's up to us to choose and decide the way we please. Indeed, we've got three boys at home whom it really suits to be with their father. They do everything together, go bicycling and so on. You see, most children grow up barely having met their fathers because they are at work all the time; my husband too grew up with his father at sea. So, I am in the opinion that it's of such a great value he's at home with them. And he is a more stable person than me. I tend to become nervous and stressed out; he is the one now providing children with the steadiness.

Helen here differentiates fathers who are present and who are rarities from the more common *absent fathers*, a choice of discourse that gives her a chance to acknowledge the value of him as the father of her children. Sandra, whom we introduced in the previous section where she was presenting her husband in conformity with Estonian mainstream as a financially autonomous individual is even more explicit than Helen in positioning her spouse as an up-to-date, modern father, who becomes admirable for (not in spite of) his focus on family and care.

> **Sandra:** I find my husband quite a modern father that took it [the new more home-centred lifestyle] as an opportunity. /.../ We prolonged our stay in Luxembourg because I can really trust him as a father; perhaps even more than myself as a mother [laughingly]. /.../ I've always known he'd make an excellent father, and valued him for it. And becoming one has raised him even higher in my eyes.

Interestingly, Helen and Sandra, as well as Laura above, devalue their own skills and characteristics in order to put their partners on a pedestal - a discursive move that proves to be most widely used by women as a way to empower their spouses. The contrasting of one's husband's relatively good situation to that of male counterparts' rather worse state of affairs, and lesser luck appears to carry a similar function (see Sandra above and Maria in the next section). Hence, comparing, and contrasting groups and individuals, identifying with some people and distancing from others prove to be a highly popular discursive means to affirm gender identities under threat or challenge.

Secondly, we would like to point out (and illustrate with the cases of Sandra and Maria), that women tend to invest in different masculinity discourses in the different parts of a single interview. Women may argue that their husbands in fact do not differ so significantly from what is expected of them as men in work-centred Estonia, therefore claiming them the conservative masculinity. Then, later in the interview the women may identify their partners as the modern family men or as focused on other unpaid spheres such as community work, culture or hobbies, thus claiming alternative and self-expressionist masculinity.

In a nutshell, migrant career women, in search of dignity for their domestic men, embrace discourses of very different forms in terms of masculinity. This mixture of positioning those men can be placed in the context of more general, ongoing transformations in Estonia and among Estonians. Those couples can indeed be said to be both within, and outside, a post-socialist 'transitional society'. We will return to this topic in the discussion section.

The active one

A striking result from the interviews was that the female interviewees proved to be really afraid that friends or relatives, or society more generally, might position their spouses as *the passive ones*, which might be equated with 'inadequately masculine'. While a view of oneself as being active and masculine is most commonly acquired by working for pay outside home, migrant Estonian men who do not leave the private sphere to work outside home, also crave those positive characteristics. Their female partners usually also assist men in carrying out this extra element of identity work.

Women position their partners as *socially active* by emphasising that they are 'not entrapped within the walls of their house', that they do leave the house; and secondly, that they don't suffer of social isolation, and that they 'associate with other people'.

> **Maria:** My husband is socially rather active though, he plays soccer for example, he's made some relations, takes French lessons in the language school, *etc*. In that sense he's been active outside home, he's not sat inside the house. You see, there are rather many men in Brussels that hardly leave the room, especially among Estonians, that are introvert by nature. Basically, he's been doing all right there, despite not having found a job yet.

Here, Maria is positioning her husband as an active kind or person, by discursively contrasting and distancing him from other, less vigorous, and allegedly passive and introvert migrant Estonian men. We introduced Maria earlier in relation to her claiming her husband the position of the primary breadwinner. Hence, a parallel investment in conservative, as well as more post-materialist, masculinities is illustrated by Maria, as well as Sandra and other women.

To conclude, women typically presented their spouses as actively *engaged in personal development* of various kinds. The positive initiatives mentioned included: explicitly masculine activities that demand bodily coordination and control, such as 'soccer' or 'conquering the mountains', engagements in the local Estonian community, as well as more intellectual and cultural hobbies, such as 'reading widely', 'visiting museums', and 'travelling across Europe and beyond'. Those activities positioned men rather as *lifestyle migrants*, looking for a more fulfilling way of life, rather than *tied migrants* from families in search of better work and income opportunities. Such forms of personal development can be seen as more compatible with self-expressionist values. When contextualised within the general development of countries from more survivalist to more self-expressionist in their values (Inglehart and Weltzel 2005), these domestically located Estonian men are, in these respects at least, (re)presented as men of the future.

Discussion

Migration has predominantly been viewed in terms of macro-economic push and pull factors, demographic trends, and so-called brain drains/brain gains. Such perspectives have often failed to include significant gender dimensions. In this paper, we have sought to complement this line of research by scrutinising more micro-level processes, namely the struggle over migrants' gender identities in a changed and changing context. Moreover, we focus on men, masculinity, and migration, a topic even less studied in an explicitly gendered way than women's experiences and coping processes when abroad. According to Hondagneu-Sotelo, scholars addressing the relations of gender and migration must move away from 'women-only' studies on migration, because 'by focusing solely on women, we might ghettoise the study of gender and suggest that gender is only pertinent to the experiences of women. We should not inadvertently suggest that men are without a gender.' (Hondagneu-Sotelo 1999: 556, cited in Salazar Parreñas 2009: 4). Our study has taken this suggestion one step further, by considering women partners' construction of their men partners who have migrated with them, and who are living and working primarily in the private domestic domain rather than pursuing their own work career. Both 'masculine identity talk' by men (see Pajumets and Hearn 2012) and women's talk about men can be seen as responses to this gender challenge.

The career women in this study employed two main types of discourses, which could be interpreted as contributing to the empowerment of their spouses. First, they downplayed the atypical nature of men's lifestyle by stressing, even overstating, their conformity to more conservative expectations of men. Secondly, women discursively subverted employment, career-based, and pay-oriented cultural assumptions, as outdated, and strived to reformulate the contents of an alternative masculinity, as representing what might appear as *men of the future*.

Interestingly, the two types of talk are alternates, and discrete, only in an analytical sense; in practice the same women often used them in parallel within one single interview. This mixing of discourses suggests that migrants from CEE countries or 'New Europe' to the 'Old Europe' are influenced by two somewhat different sets of cultural norms around masculinities. On the one hand, they have spent most of their lives in countries that have, not so long ago, survived a total restructuring of the economy, and indeed, the related poverty. According to Inglehart and Weltzel (2005), those countries have been, and still are, too poor, and unstable, to have developed post-materialist values. On the other hand, the couples have now migrated to the richer and relatively stable democracies of 'Old Europe', where self-expression through participation in community life, civil society or organised culture may be considered as important as work, career and income. In many of those welfare states 'culturally softer', less work-centred, and more family, community, and care-oriented masculinities are more visible and more fully accepted compared to in the more survivalist 'New Europe'. We understand the Estonian women migrant interviewees' in-between and have-it-all discursive practices as reflecting personally experienced contradictions, that they and their male partners face. These are likely to stem from the experience of living between two cultures, 'two Europes', with somewhat different values, priorities, opportunities, and barriers.

This mixture of discursive pursuits by interviewees might also reflect post-socialist Estonia's transition from a survivalist society, towards a more self-expressionist, post-materialist society. The society from which the men and women concerned come from, are in transition. This dimension of difference is not to be understood as any kind of simple unified continuum, but rather as a process of great variation, unevenness and contradiction. Indeed, it might be argued that these kinds of contradictions are rather likely to be in evidence among the identity work of migrants from other 'New Europe' countries to the democracies of 'Old Europe'.

Similarly, identity constructions following 'reversals' of '(heterosexual) gender roles' might also be expected to involve contradictions between both re-affirmations of conservative, elements, and the assertion of new elements, even when transnational migration does not occur.

There are further transitions involved in this picture; the host countries in 'Old Europe' might appear to be relatively stable from some perspectives, but they too are experiencing massive economic, political and cultural upheavals, for example, through the economic crisis and austerity, the instability of governments in Belgium, the Netherlands, Italy, and so on, the rise of the far right in France and elsewhere, as well as cultural instabilities associated with new media, technologies and other cultural changes. Specifically, gender constructions, including masculinity, are likely to be in processes of change between more materialist and more post-materialist forms. Furthermore, the migrated men and women, both as individuals and as couples, are themselves likely to be in a transition of a more personal kind. Finally, constructions of past and present are the product of both memories and constructions of the past, and prognoses of the future, whether continuing in the host or returning to the home country.

This analysis also suggests that personal identities are not necessarily perfect reflections of social identities and structurally based roles (see Snow and Anderson 1987). The men interviewees in this study were constructed by their partners as powerful, even as public men (Hearn 1992), in spite of the rather domestic realities, as might be assessed by an outsider. This confirms that identity is not strictly determined by the social roles in a narrow sense that are performed; as noted, rather it is *processual* – an effect of ongoing identity work and identity talk (Rounds 2006), albeit within material contexts and grounded in the material realities of social life.

A final practical, and policy issue and implication of this article is that the 'private' well-being of family members is clearly important with regard to family decisions to stay in the host country, move on to a third country, or to return to the home country. Moreover, the construction of domestic men's masculine self-esteem, or the lack thereof, is also of more general demographic, and economic, significance for the countries involved. Constructions of the private and the domestic are thus intensely related to processes in the public domain (Bose 1987; Hearn 1992). As Gálvez and Tirado (2006) put it, the analysis of private micro-positioning in interaction helps us understand how macro structures are being formed and reproduced. Hence, studying the 'private' gendered well-being of migrants is one possible avenue of understanding the flows of migration and migrants' experiences in a globalising world.

References

Allen, S. M. and Hawkins, A. (1999). 'Maternal gatekeeping: mothers' beliefs and behaviors that inhibit greater father involvement in family work.' *Journal of Marriage and the Family,* 61: 199-212.

Bem S. L. (1974). 'The measure of psychological androgyny.' *Journal of Consulting and Clinical Psychology,* 42 (2): 155-162.

Bose, C. (1987). 'Dual Spheres.' Hess, B. B. & Ferre, M. M. (eds.). *Analyzing Gender.* Newbury Park, CA: Sage, 267-285.

Burr, V. (2003). *Social Constructionism* (2nd edn). East Sussex: Routledge.

Davies, B. and Harré, R. (1990). 'Positioning: the discursive production of selves.' *Journal for the Theory of Social Behaviour,* 20(1): 43-63.

Debiaggi Dantas Duarte, S. (2001). *Changing Gender Roles: Brazilian Immigrant Families in the U.S.* (Illustrated edition). New York: LFB Scholarly Publishing.

Donaldson, M. and Howson, R. (2009). 'Men, Migration and Hegemonic Masculinity.' in M. Donaldson, M., Hibbins, R., Howson, R. & Pease, B. (eds.). *Migrant Men: Critical Studies of Masculinities and the Migration Experience.* New York: Routledge, 210-218.

Donaldson, M., Hibbins, R., Howson, R. and Pease, B. (eds.) (2009). *Migrant Men: Critical Studies of Masculinities and the Migration Experience.* New York: Routledge.

Duncombe, J. and Marsden, D. (1993). 'Love and intimacy: the gender division of emotion and 'emotion work'.' *Sociology,* 27(2): 221-241.

Eichler, M. (1980). *The Double Standard: A Feminist Critique of Feminist Social Science.* London: Croom Helm.

Eurostat (2009). *The unadjusted gender pay gap 2009.* [Online]. Available: http://epp.eurostat.ec.europa.eu/statistics_explained/index.php?title=File:The_unadjusted_gender_pay_gap_2009.png&filetimestamp=20110704080244 (2012, November 26).

Eurostat (2012). Basic Figures on the EU, Spring 2012. *Eurostat Compact Guides.*

Gálvez, F. and Tirado, A. (2007). 'Positioning theory and discourse analysis: some tools for social interaction analysis.' *Forum Qualitative Social Research,* 8 (2).

Hearn, J. (1992). *Men in the Public Eye: The Construction and Deconstruction of Public Men and Public Patriarchies.* London: Routledge.

Hearn, J. (2007).'Feeling out of place? Towards the Transnationalizations of Emotions.' Fineman, S. (ed.). *The Emotional Organization: Passion and Power.* Oxford: Blackwell, 184-201.

Hearn, J. (2009). 'Patriarchies, Transpatriarchies and Intersectionalities.' Oleksy, E. (ed.). *Intimate Citizenships: Gender, Sexualities.* London: Routledge, 177-192.

Hearn, J. and Niemistö, C. (2012). 'Men, 'Father Managers', and Home-Work Relations: Complexities and Contradictions in National Policy, Corporations, and Individual Lives.' McDonald, P. & Jeanes, E. (eds.). *Men's Wage and Family Work.* London: Routledge.

Hochschild, A. R. (2003). 'The Nanny Chain.' Ely, R. J., Foldy, E. G., Scully, M. (eds.). *Reader in Gender, Work, and Organization.* Oxford: Blackwell Publishing, 401-408.

Hollway, W. (1984). 'Gender Difference and the Production of Subjectivity.' Henriques, J., Hollway, W., Irwin, C., Venn, C. & Walkerdine, V. (eds.). *Changing the Subject: Psychology, Social Regulation and Subjectivity.* London: Metheun, 227-263.

Hondagneu-Sotelo, P. (2003). 'Gender and Immigration: A Retrospective and Introduction.' Hondagneu-Sotelo, P. (ed.). *Gender and U.S. Immigration: Contemporary Trends.* Berkeley, CA: University of California Press, 3-19.

Hondagneu-Sotelo, P. (1999). 'Introduction: Gender and Contemporary U.S. Immigration.' *American Behavioral Scientist,* 42(4): 565-576.

Hondagneu-Sotelo, P. and Avila, E. (1997). 'I'm Here, but I'm There': The Meanings of Latina Transnational Motherhood.' *Gender & Society* 11 (5): 548-571.

Inglehart, R. and Welzel, C. (2005). *Modernization, Cultural Change and Democracy.* New York: Cambridge University Press.

Krusell, S. (2009). 'Employment of Estonian Residents Abroad.' Haugas, L. (ed.). *Quarterly Bulletin of Statistics Estonia 2/2009.* Tallinn: Statistics Estonia, 63-84.

Kõre, J. (2011). Tööränne – See On Imetore [Labour Migration – It's Wonderful]. *Postimees,* 19 January.

Little, R. D. and Hisnanick, J. C. (2007). 'The earnings of tied-migrant military husbands.' *Armed Forces & Society,* 33 (4): 547-570.

Ludgen-Sandvik. P. (2008). 'Intensive identity work: responses to workplace bullying trauma and stigmatization.' *Organization* 15 (1): 97-119.

Mansfield, P. and Collard, J. (1988). *The Beginning of the Rest of Your Life: a Portrait of Newly-Wed Marriage.* London: Macmillan.

Morokvasic, M. (2004). ''Settled in mobility': engendering post-wall migration in Europe.' *Feminist Review,* 77: 7-25.

Morokvasic, M. (1991). 'Fortress Europe and migrant women.' *Feminist Review,* 39 (winter): 69-84.

Narayan, U. (1995). ''Male-order' brides: immigrant women, domestic violence and immigration law.' *Hypatia,* 10 (1): 104-119.

Nawyn, S.J. (2010). 'Gender and migration: integrating feminist theory into migration studies.' *Sociology Compass,* 4/9: 749-765.

Pajumets, M. (2010). 'Estonian couples' rationalizations for fathers' rejection of parental leave.' *Fathering: A Journal of Theory, Research, and Practice about Men as Fathers,* 8 (2): 226-243.

Pajumets, M. and Hearn, J. (2012). 'Post-socialist fathers 'at home' and 'away from home' in 'Old Europe': facing the challenge through masculine identity talk.' *Studies of Transition States and Societies,* 4 (1): 31-47.

Pyle, J. L. and Ward, K. B. (2003). 'Recasting our understanding of gender and work during global restructuring.' *International Sociology,* 18 (3): 461-486.

Rounds, J. (2006). 'Doing identity work in museums.' *Curator,* 49 (2): 133-150.

Saar, A. (2009). 'Changes in Estonia's Value System in 1990-2008.' Estonian Cooperation Assembly (ed.). *Estonian Human Development Report 2009.* Tallinn: Estonian Cooperation Assembly, 108-113.

Salazar, Parreñas, R. (2000). 'Migrant Filipina domestic workers and the international division of reproductive labor.' *Gender & Society,* 14 (4): 560-580.

Salazar, Parreñas, R. (2009). Inserting Feminism in Transnational Migration Studies. *Migrationonline.cz* [Online]. Available: http://www.migrationonline.cz/e-library/?x=2183800 (2012, November 26).

Schuler, R. S., Pawan S. and Florkowski, G. W. (2004). 'International Human Resource Management.' Punnett, B. J. & Shenkar, O. (eds.). *Handbook for International Management Research (2nd edn.).*' Ann Arbor: University of Michigan Press, 356-414.

Snow, D. and Anderson, L. (1987). 'Identity work among the homeless: the verbal construction and avowal of personal identities.' *American Journal of Sociology,* 92 (6): 1336-1371.

Sousa Ribeiro, J. (2008). 'Gendering migration flows: physicians and nurses in Portugal.' *Equal Opportunities International,* 27 (1):77-87.

van Langenhove, L. and Harré, R. (1999). 'Introducing Positioning Theory.' Harré, R. & van Langenhove, L. (eds.). Positioning Theory. Oxford: Blackwell, 14-31.

Vainu, V., Järviste, L. and Biin, H. (eds.) (2010). 'Soolise Võrdõiguslikkuse Monitooring 2009' [Gender Equaility Monitoring]. *Sotsiaalministeeriumi Toimetised,* 1/2010.

Veidemann, B. (2010). 'Eesti tööealise elanikkonna väljarändepotentsiaal aastal 2010.' [Migration Potential of Estonian Labour Force at 2010]. *Sotsiaalministeeriumi Toimetised* 8/2010: 1-31.

Widding, Isaksen, L. (2012). 'Transnational spaces of care: migrant nurses in Norway.' *Social Politics,* 19 (1): 58-77.

How does online experience inform our sense of self? NSFW blogger identity narratives

Katrin Tiidenberg

Introduction

'Nowadays, one of the most exciting social, as well as romantic, sites to visit is cyberspace,' Ben-Ze'ev (2004) writes in his book 'Love Online'. Based on in-depth interviews with witty, creative professionals (and not at all the furry-palmed and beady-eyed sex addicts stereotypically depicted as internet porn and erotica producers/ prosumers (Bruns 2006)), who emerged from behind NSFW[28] blogs, this chapter will illustrate the participants' narrative identities and their formation. I will outline how the bloggers' identity work constructs them as different from others, as responsible (or not) agents, and which events are constructed as formative or transformative in past time and space. This chapter will contribute to understanding internet as a social space for identity work and social reality construction, and belonging to online communities as a lifestyle choice.

Many of the former socialist countries are doing extremely well in terms of internet penetration, and the general population's internet agility. According to the data from Statistics Estonia, 90% of all Estonian households with children had a broadband connection in the first quarter of 2012. Estonia is also the first in the world in terms of digital freedom according to Freedom House's 'Freedom on the Net 2012' report. Banking, tax paying and voting have moved online (71% of users in Estonia had completed tax returns online and 62% gotten digital prescriptions, 2012, Statistics Estonia) and various online cultures and communities play an important role in people's everyday life. The bloggers included in this chapter are not from former socialist countries, but there is every reason to assume that internet-savvy people in transforming societies use online spaces for self-, and sexual-exploration and community related practices as much as anyone else. In the globalising, internet-connected world, struggling with the continuing occurrence of moral panics, it is important to understand how and whether 'virtual' online experiences inform our identities. This would mean that an aspect of our lives often considered playful (online communication, flirting, cybering[29]) could inform our choices in areas commonly considered serious (career, family values, monetary decisions, child-rearing or sexuality).

---

28 Not suitable for work – NSFW.

29 To cyber – to have cybersex.

Individuals are not fixed, but constantly constituted, and reconstituted, through the discursive practices they have access to in their daily lives (Davies 2003). With the line between being online and offline blurring (Orgad 2009), and the increasing popularity of SNS's[30], we can be fairly certain, that at least some of those discursive practices are accessed online. **tumblr**., the SNS where the participants of this research have their blogs, is a microblogging environment launched in 2007[31]. The platform is easy to use and incorporates social networking functions much more than previous blogging environments did. A user can post text, photos, video and audio files, links and quotes, but in addition, there is an opportunity to build a community by following other users and monitoring who follows you. From a researcher's point of view, blogs have some benefits over SNS's with less text (Facebook *etc.*), as they allow us, via the unabbreviated textual content, a clearer access to narratives of self.

There is a lot of sex-talk in ***NSFW*** content, and sex is commonly still hidden in our societies. Online, however, it can be explored without fear (or with lesser fear) of social repercussions (see Ross 2005; Daneback 2006). Deaux' (1993) social identity model suggests that members of stigmatised-identity internet-groups are more likely to incorporate their virtual-group membership into their self-concepts because it is important to them (cited in Bargh and McKenna 2004) and because of a lack of an offline equivalent for the group (Bargh and McKenna 2004). An online group built around discussions unavailable elsewhere (*e.g.* who talks about sex), is, therefore, a good place to start looking for what online participation does to our self-identity. Based on her analysis of an online soap-opera fan-forum, Baym (2000) emphasises that people in online communities define themselves not just in relation to their offline selves, and the medium, but also in relation to one another, and the group as a whole. Hence, instead of just looking at a person and the 'secret' content they prosume online, we need to look at whom these secrets are shared with.

Theoretical Context

Identity and Communicative Context

According to seminal works of Giddens (2010 [1991]), Beck (1998 [1992]), Bauman (2001) and others, *self-identity* is becoming an unavoidable topic in

30 Social networking site – SNS.

31 75 000 bloggers switched to it immediately after the launch and by now there are approximately 50 million blogs and 20 billion posts on Tumblr. (March 2012).The environment allows communication via exchange of public or private messages, commenting on other people's content, submitting content to other bloggers, liking other blogger's content and reblogging it, with or without added captions.

(late/liquid) modern societies. We all make daily identity-based choices about our looks, habits, health, values, *etc*. In this chapter, I am adopting the constructivist and practical-hermeneutic approach to identity, viewing it as a *reflexive project* (Giddens 2010 [1991]), a saturated self or a 'pastiche personality /…/ constantly borrowing bits and pieces /…/ from whatever sources are available' (Gergen 2000 [1991]: 150). It is patched together 'from the overwhelming expanses of mediated messages in our environments' (Baym and Markham 2009: x), or as Aberton (2010) puts it, demonstrates the characteristics of an assemblage in which the elements are not fixed, nor do they belong to a larger pre-given list, but are constructed, as they are entangled together. Identity has become a 'product of reflexively inscribed lifestyle projects that draw upon physical and symbolic resources of the media and cultural industries' (Allaste and Bennet, this book), yet that lifestyle too, is a product of choice, and can be either a form of social integration, or disintegration (Giddens [2010] 1991).

Social interactions raise the 'who am I?' question, and according to Alvesson *et al*. (2008) the attempt to answer it prompts *identity work*[32] – the mental activity an individual undertakes to construct and understand their self as coherent, distinct and positively valued. People craft their identities through interaction, in concert with others and out of the diverse contextual resources within their reach. According to Knights and Willmott (1989) and Sveningsson and Alvesson (2003) self-narrative is created by drawing on cultural resources as well as memories and desires to reproduce or transform one's sense of self (cited in Alvesson *et al*. 2008). Mallan and Giardina (2009) offer the concept of wiki to understand the identity constructed and narrated online. They use the term *wikidentity*to describe the identity work in SNSs, and argue that wiki-like behaviour has consequences for re-conceptualising identity, as something that is mediated by (rather than at odds with) technology. '…this 'wikidentity' becomes a particular, collaborative process that changes according to purpose, context, and form.' (Mallan and Giardina 2009)

Exploring identity online warrants including the concepts of self-presentation or *impression management* (Goffman 1959; Leary and Kowalski 1990; Trammell 2005). While some studies support the claim that online constructions of the self are idealised and do not reflect actual personalities (Manago *et al*. 2008), there are others that show the opposite. Vazire and Gosling (2004) used Festinger's Social Comparison Model to explore, among other things, impression management on personal websites. They found that identity claims there convey substantial amounts of information about their authors (high

32 A term originally coined by Howard, J. A. (2000). Social Psychology of Identities. *Annual Review of Sociology*, 26: 367-393.

levels of inter-observer consensus were noted and people were generally accurate in their assessments of website authors' personalities). Haferkamp and Krämer (2011) also conducted interviews and experiments that indicated the social comparison model at work in social media. Back *et al.* (2010) (relying on works of Ambady and Skowronski 2008; Funder 1999; Hall and Bernieri 2001; Kenny 1994) claim that self-presentation online integrates various kinds of personal information – private thoughts, facial images, and social behaviour, all of which contain valid information about personality.

Thus, trying to untangle what online experience does to identity and lifestyle construction, means following the people to the spaces where the reflexive choices are made; where identity work and impression management may happen.

Self- and Sexual Identity in Online Communities

One's identity creation involves others, both directly and indirectly (via the co-constructed social reality). Online relationships are highly similar to those developed in person, in terms of their breadth, depth, quality and longevity (Bargh and McKenna 2004). People whose initial meeting takes place online like each other more than those who first meet face to face (McKenna, Green and Gleason, 2002), and it is easier for people to show their 'real self' online (Bargh, McKenna and Fitszimons 2002). Joinson (2008) lists self-enhancement; finding meaning in your life; increased self-knowledge from social comparison; pleasure (from mental stimulation); heightened self-esteem from praise; and social support among the main motivators for internet use. Belonging to an online group is, hence, pleasurable in many ways. Pleasure inspires individuals to accept group messages and incorporate group meanings and attitudes into their own constructions of reality (Fulk 1993). In addition to the pleasure received from being online and interacting with other people, in case of an online experience that incorporates the sexual, there are additional hedonistic practices and therapeutic discourses (Attwood 2010) involved.

What about identity construction in specific subsections of social media? Pluempavarn and Panteli (2007) showed that social identity created in blogging communities has an effect on members, as well as on the community in general. Blogging offers people a unique opportunity to work on their self-identity via self-expression and social interaction (McCullagh 2008), and blogs serve as a form of self-therapy (Tan 2008). One could look at blogosphere as a figured world – 'a socially produced, culturally constituted activity' (Holland *et al.* 1998: 40-41) where people produce and perform new self-identities. Muise's (2011) research on women's sex blogs shows that they can be seen as a 'safe space' for discussion of (active and embodied) desire, and Wood (2008) introduces the notion of commons, when describing how women's sex blogs help develop vocabularies of desire, reduce shame, build community, and enable women to continue the process of regaining control over information about sexuality. This chapter is based on interviews with male, female, and transgender 'sex-bloggers', but the notions of safe space and commons are useful beyond just the gendered experience of blogging. Blogs allow for collecting substantial amounts of 'relatively un-self-conscious' naturalistic data (Hookway 2008), and it is my working assumption that a sex blog allows people to type themselves into being in a more open and layered way than, perhaps, some other form of non-sexualised social media participation.

SNSs and online communities are places where one can present and construct a self or 'type oneself into being' (Sundén 2003: 3) a phenomenon well-researched (boyd 2007, boyd and Heer 2006; Lampe, Ellison and Steinfield 2006; Siibak 2011). Ross (2005) has applied this thinking specifically to sexuality on internet, and called it 'typing, doing and being' sexual. The internet has been a cosy home for sex-related and pornographic content from the get-go, but as Attwood (2010: 7) writes: 'in porn's transition from material to online spaces, /.../ its consumption becomes part of a multitasking mode as users move between 'socialising, buying commodities and searching information /.../ chatting, peeping, cruising, masturbating and maintaining friendships' (Jacobs 2004: 73)'. The use of the internet for online sexual activities has been researched since the beginning of the 2000s, including work on searching for sexual partners, cybersex; issues of addiction, gender variances, *etc.* (see Griffiths 2001; Leiblum 2001; Binik 2001; Ferree 2003; Cooper *et al.* 2003, Daneback, Cooper and Mansson 2005; Daneback 2006; Ross *et al.* 2007; Daneback, Mansson and Ross, 2007; Albright 2008; Whitty 2008; Döring 2009; Attwood 2010; Sevickova and Daneback 2011; Brand *et al.* 2011). It is important to point out that this chapter's focus is not explicitly on sexuality and sexual identity, but on participants' narrative identity in a wider sense. Sex-related online experience just might, as illustrated in the literature cited here, provide a clearer view of it.

Methods and Data

Narrative identity (Ricoeur 1991 [1984], 1985, 1988, 1992) is a concept used by many narrative researchers (Holstein and Gubrium 1995; Bamberg 2003; Georgakopoulou 2006, 2007; Gubrium and Holstein 2008; Bamberg and Georgakopoulou 2008; Bamberg 2010). Ricoeur (1992) viewed identity as a matter of culturally and socially mediated self-interpretations, and saw narrative identity as a central form of that self-interpretation. McAdams (2003) argues that identity is an ***integrative configuration*** of self (integrated synchronically by assimilating the range of different and possibly conflicting roles and relationships; and in diachronically – that is, in time) (cited in Smith and Sparkes 2008). Introducing the concepts of synchronic and diachronic into the discussion of narrative identity, swiftly takes us to Bamberg's (2010) approach, which utilises both, and is the methodical beacon for this work.

Bamberg (2010) outlines three practical challenges that the self is facing. He explicates these in terms of ***dilemmatic spaces*** within which identity activities, and narrating, are navigated. These are: (a) successful diachronic navigation between constancy and change, (b) the establishment of a synchronic connection between sameness and difference (self and others), and (c) the management of agency between the double-arrow of a person-to-world versus a world-to-person fit (internal/ psychological agency versus external/ social agency). Explained in simpler terms, it means that the narrative analysis of interview data shows how the blogger accounts for how he or she has emerged over time as different from (but the same as) others, and simultaneously as someone who considers oneself to be a responsible agent (or not).

Interview data was gathered via in-depth interviews, conducted with the NSFW bloggers in November and December of 2011, via Skype video, voice and, in some cases, typed chat. 12 interviews[33] were included in this analysis, among those, 5 bloggers were female, one transgender and 6 male. Their ages ranged from 26 – 60, with most participants being in their mid to late 30s. Most of the participants had a university degree or equivalent, with some college students, one PhD, and a couple of graduate degrees. More detailed information on participants' background can be accessed in Table 1 in the Appendix.

Because of the sensitivity of the blog content and the interview questions[34], and to increase comfort and rapport, participants were given a choice of the medium. Typed-chat interviews took on average an hour longer (3 hours versus 2 hours), but produced more or less the same amount of data. No significant differences in terms of disclosure, thoroughness of account, *etc.* were found in audio, audio-video and text-based interviews. The fact that the interviewees and the interviewer either had a previously existing online relationship or had estab-

33 24 interviews in total were conducted, 12 of them were selected to be analysed for this chapter, following the same typical case / maximum variation principles.

34 An asynchronic email interview of 5 preliminary questions was conducted about 3 days prior to the scheduled synchronic interview. An interview plan consisting of 18 umbrella-questions and approximately 7-10 probes per each was prepared in advance. The questions focused on the participant's descriptions of their blogs and their blog content, their blogging experience, the level and intensity of interactions, relationships, emotional investments, types of OSA (online sexual activities) they participated in, their views on tumblr as a community, their offline context and their own interpretations of why they do it.

lished contact in the NSFW tumblrverse, (hence a mutual understanding of the cultural context in a text-based community), probably reduced the potential brittleness of the typed interviews.

The sampling strategy combined Weiss' (1994) rather ambitious claims of representability of the maximum rage with Cresswell's (1998) maximum variation and typical case strategies. Practically speaking, the snowball mechanism of identifying cases of interest from people who know people and who know what cases are information-rich (Cresswell, 1998) was used[35].

Results and discussion – Bloggers identity formation and sense of self

The results and discussion will be presented in three narratives. First, the speakers *sense of self* in terms of how it is seen as *different, yet similar to others*; second, in terms of whether it is seen as *externally influenced or internally driven*; and finally the speaker's *identity formation* through *time and space*. Concepts of identity work (Alvesson *et al.* 2008), impression management (Goffman 1959), online social comparison (Haferkamp and Krämer 2011, Vazire and Gosling 2004, Baym 2000), online self-presentation (Back *et al.* 2010), relationship development online (Bargh and McKenna 2004, McKenna, Green and Gleason 2002, Barg, McKenna and Fitzsimons 2002) the role of pleasure in integrating group values (Fulk 1993); and, in general, the reflexivity of the identity project (Giddens [2010] 1991) are used to contextualise the narratives of identity construction.

There will be multiple contradictions in each narrative: these stem less from the differences between the speakers and more from the inherent contradictions in each participant's story. Bamberg encourages researchers to scrutinise the inconsistencies and contradictions as they mark the teller's 'constant navigation and finessing between different versions of selfhood' (2010: 14).

I am similar yet different – first dilemmatic space of selfhood

Participants integrated and differentiated their sense of self through varying versions of '**we**' in their stories. The We-s ranged from the participant and their significant other, to the often mentioned We of 'me and my tumblr.-friends'.

35 The sampling criteria meant authors of NSFW blogs in English, that have been active for at least 6 months, which are updated on average at least 3 times per week, where captions are added to pictures, videos and audios, and / or which also post merely textual posts, whose 'Ask' boxes are activated, who are legal adults and who give their informed consent to participate in the study. Five bloggers whom the author knew to have a blog that met the criteria, who were popular and had a high status in the community were approached and asked for further contacts.

The 'me and my partner'-We was often constructed in comparison to other couples, seamlessly traversing the contradictions from statement to statement – showing themselves as similar to other couples in one sense (*e.g.* difficulties in living the monogamous norm) and as different in another (*e.g.* sexual lifestyles). This is a layered strategy of social comparison that was common for various categories of sameness/difference in this first dilemmatic space. First, one differentiates from some others and integrates with other others, and then, the same is repeated for the constructed We-entity.

The various tumblr.-We-s usually varied by levels of inclusion. The bloggers navigated their selfhood in the context of people they trust, versus others they are merely comfortable with; the others they engage in OSA[36] with, versus the bigger 'we' that engulfs all sexy bloggers on tumblr. People construct themselves in relation to each other and the group (Baym 2000), thus these different We-s of inclusion are an important aspect for the person's sense of self. Also, systematically differentiating one's tumblr.-We from one's offline-We can be seen as an indication that the online group is important enough and there isn't an offline equivalent to it, thus the online group's values are likely to be incorporated into one's sense of self.

> **Georgina** (41): But um… when it comes to my tumblr. friends, I feel that there's nothing off limits, there's nothing I can't put out there, there isn't anything they will be shocked by or disgusted by, or wonder why I said it.

A wider, **gendered-We** was also evident. Wood (2008) and Muise (2008) have written about the importance of sex-blogging for women in particular, blogs being a 'safe place' and a way to regain control over sexual information. In this case, participants differentiated the genders (men from women) by associating with one's own gender-We or emphasising issues that concerned the other gender but not one's own (for example 'slut-shaming' for women). Those narratives, however, co-existed with differentiations from one's own gender group (common for both men and women), *e.g.* speaking of one's sexual appetite falling outside the norm for one's own gender and age group (or being constructed as abnormal by their partner), *etc.* Additionally, the 'safe place' thread was not limited to women's experiences, but enveloped those of unorthodox sexual lifestyles and preferences (kinky, poly) and the transgender participant.

In addition to the various We-s that the participants' constructed themselves as a part of, there were also the **Me-constructions** – identity claims that pertained to just their sense of self alone and its social comparison to others.

---

36 OSA – online sexual activities.

> **Carl** (60): I was pleased to see not everyone was a randy porn addict /…/ and some were, like me, looking for a discreet forum to freely show some more intimate sides of themselves.

Topics of age, (emotional) maturity, personal ethics and morals, blogging habits, *etc.* were integrated into the Me-narrative. Being able to gain more self-knowledge via the social comparison and the blogging experience was often recognised and reflected on.

Another important category of difference was that of separating some others from other **others**. Hierarchies and typologies of others that make them more and less similar to, or more and less important to, one's sense of self were evoked in identity construction. There are 'the hello people', and the 'share your day with people', as Brian (mid-30s) put it. This othering practice can be seen as a form of identity work, or, using the wikidentity concept, it can be said that a participant is many things to, and with, many people; changing according to purpose, context and form. Differentiations between others were also made according to their tumblr. status, or personal 'consumer' preferences – other bloggers were seen as more and less suitable for particular interactions (*e.g.* this single person is not suitable for OSA, as they will probably get attached) and were categorised by the level of insight, or the quality of content they offer, or by how genuine they seem. Authenticity or seeming/being genuine was curiously a common category of social comparison, and often pertained to blog content (as a consumable good), rather than just the blogger (as a potential interaction partner).

> **Lisa** (26): Some blogs provide more than others, the ones who give you a true glimpse of the person's personality become most popular.

There was also a negative category of others – the **dangerous others**, those, who are either not on tumblr. or not a part of the community, for example, people who read sexy tumblr. blogs, but do not have a sexy blog themselves, or people who comment anonymously.

> **Eric** (late 20s): When someone else in the community ruins their anonymity, or even when someone you know in your real life comes to read your blog and leaves you a comment, calling you out by your real name, that is enough for a lot of the people to just call it quits and end the whole thing.

The relationship between the wider group of neutral outsiders (not-Us) and the specific group of dangerous others was a curious one. At times the bulk of not-Us was constructed as dangerous, while elsewhere the importance of dangerous others was underplayed. It functioned almost as a shadow for the narrative of belonging. When the Me was sharply delineated, the community, and the We, was construed as less important, and the other others as less dangerous. But when one of the tumblr.-We-s was focused on (for example when discussing the limitations of one's offline group of friends and acquaintances) those who were not 'with us' were constructed as 'against us'.

Participants' sense of self was differentiated from others also in terms of the **content of their blog**. The amount of pictures of the individual, reblogs, captions, the level of interaction, these are all important aspects of identity work and social comparison via content. Bloggers also emphasised issues such as the blog having (or not having) a theme (*e.g.* black and white erotica, superhero erotica, food and sex) or a specific voice (*e.g.* personal blog type blogs where the theme is the personality of the blogger). If the theme, or the voice, was strong enough it could warrant a set up of a separate blog for things that didn't fit, so as not to pollute that voice. In the following example Theresa's first blog was dedicated to her overseas lover and she wanted to keep it clean, as that and only that, revoking her own right to post whatever she liked on her blog.

> **Theresa** (37): There was so much good stuff coming across my dash that I'd never use on Blog-Theresa that I set up Blog-Theresa-2, it seemed easy and fun...like tearing clippings out of a magazine and putting them up on a cork board at my desk.

Adding or not adding original captions to the pictures posted was another area of content-based differentiation often mentioned, but posting (sexy) pictures of one's self, and the quantity and quality of those pictures, was one of the most important categories of integration/ differentiation as the bloggers constructed their sense of self.

> **Peter** (37): There are some people, who just post themselves indiscriminately; I want to be a little more artistic.

Some content on tumblr., although arousing, was considered politically or philosophically unacceptable, bringing us to Wood's (2008) claim that sex-blogging allows one to reclaim control over sexual information:

> **Olly** (28): There are blogs I avoid because I find them misogynistic or queer-phobic, even if they are otherwise hot.

Finally, the **blog's function for its owner** – it most often served as a diary or a place for (creative) self-expression – was an important aspect of differentiation. The dichotomy and simultaneity of therapeutic and creative impulses can be conceptualised in the light of what Attwood (2010) wrote about online porn's function for users in general – adding therapeutic discourses to the obvious masturbatory ones.

I am (not) responsible for how this pans out – second dilemmatic space

Lack of agency or ***external agency***, as Bamberg (2010) uses it, was incorporated into people's sense of self via societal norms and pressures, which were especially prominent in descriptions of women (both by men and women). Inhibitions and social repercussions against women, who prosume/produse sexual content online, and wish to engage in certain activities or lifestyles were often mentioned. (Notice the meeting of the first dilemmatic space [integration and differentiation of a gendered We] and the second dilemmatic space of agency in the following example).

> **Daniel** (41): …there is so much judgment of women who expose themselves, so much judgment on women who do things, or talk about things they do, where there isn't that for men. And I know a number of women who have gotten exceptionally frustrated and depressed, by the way they're treated, but I don't know any guys who have that.

A woman running a sex-blog acts at an intersection of external and internal agency, looking for a commons (Wood 2008), or a safe place (Muise 2008), a figured world (Holland *et al.* 1998) to type herself into being as a sexual creature (Ross 2005). An intricate system incorporating social pressures offline, those same pressures mirrored online and a safe space of the pornblr[37] community can be witnessed here. This second narrative illustrates, among other things, the complex decisions made about self-expression and self-disclosure in the experience of sex-blogging. The sense of community, and feedback from other bloggers, seemed to have a dual effect on participants' agency. The positive effects of being heard, belonging, feeling confident; the therapeutic role of interactions with like-minded peers…

> **Olly** (28): Online, finding people with similar preferences, norms, and expectations can create communities that allow for the mutual celebration, validation, affirmation, and comparatively safe modes of showing ourselves off a bit.

…were co-presented with the negative effects of feeling pressure to deliver certain quality and content, especially after having gained a certain status on tumblr.

> **Katie** (30): Like at times when I didn't want to journal and 'ruin' the fairy-tale of non-stop hot sex, I was encouraged by the fact that a) it was so cathartic for me to write about these realities and b) I wanted to be real for those who were reading.

---

37 Pornblr – the common jargon for NSFW tumblrverse (combining porn and tumblr.).

Linking this with the findings presented in the previous section – the wider outsiders and the dangerous-others are constructed as the mouthpiece of the restrictive social norms, while the intergroup-others, and the various We's, can be the source of the external pressure that seeps into the bloggers internal pressure to produce a certain amount of content, perform a certain type of identity. There was a layered strategy of social comparison at work in the first dilemmatic space, and there is a layered strategy of incorporating different levels of external agency into one's sense of self at work here.

Self-censoring is a good example of where external and internal pressures are so intertwined that it is difficult to separate them. A decision to post something (*e.g.* a self picture) is clearly internal, but worrying what others may think, causes self-censorship, and indicates a direct link with external agency. Using a concept of Holland *et al.* (1998) we can view this as self-formation – people are subjects of culturally constructed social worlds, yet at the same time agents capable of remarkable improvisation. Self-censorship was activated when speaking about having special, more intimate relationships with some tumblrites than others, and needing to, *e.g.*, spare them, or hide aspects of one's experience from them. This supports the research that found online and offline relationships highly alike – online self-censorship works similarly to censoring one's actions from an offline significant other (editing the blog content if they have access to it, or editing the content of interactions, if they don't).

> **Anna** (37): Oh... when you have more than one tumblr. boyfriend, you have to be very careful /.../ in what you post. Like for instance, I put something on tumblr. this morning, about hurting people's feelings, and I wrote a caption underneath that said 'eyeballs to person who hurt my feelings very badly last Sunday' and the poor boy who did not hurt my feelings sent me an email about how sorry he was about Sunday. So I was all, 'oh baby no, I was talking about someone at work', because I can't really legitimately tell him, that well, the other tumblr. boyfriend you don't know about dumped me…

In case someone has two blogs, a sexy and a non-sexy one, higher levels of self-censorship and external pressures were evident for the non-sexy ones, mostly due to family members knowing about it.

> **Eric** (late-20s): Whereas on my personal blog, a lot of the times I might want to post something, but I don't, because I'm afraid what people might think about it. And with Eric's Blog I am very aware, that if I keep within certain bounds, I can say and do what I want without anyone, who I don't want to know, finding out.

Looking at this via the concept of identity work we can see an attempt to construct and understand oneself as positively valued in the context of different reference systems. Bloggers are seeking **context-specific coherence**, instead of trying to integrate the different elements of identity into one amalgamated unit.

The agency dilemma was also vivid in participants' thoughts on ***sharing*** their blog with their offline peers (friends, spouses, *etc*.). There were deep seated and contrasting beliefs about whether or not it ought to be shared at all. Often, those who had not shared had made the decision based on fear of judgement. Many also stated that they were not ready to sacrifice that sense of having a place of one's own.

Considering the fear of repercussions from one's offline peers, it is understandable that it is easier for people to show their true-self online (Bargh, McKenna, Fitzsimons 2002; Back *et al.* 2010). This may, however, create a distancing-loop – the pleasure we get from being able to explore and experiment without criticism (Ross 2005; Daneback 2006), increases the likelihood that the online group's values will become integrated (Fulk 1993) into one's project of self, which might result in that self-identity growing into something less and less likely to be shared with those initially excluded for fear of stigmatisation.

Those who had shared with their spouses and lovers often reported a twinge of regret as they now had to self-censor their fantasies, desires, or the full scope of their experiences. For some, sharing resulted in the blog changing in its content or its significance; there were also those who felt they should have shared earlier. Also, interestingly, when talking about how the sharing had come about, an internal-external agency combination was often present, usually following the pattern of mutual disclosure.

Self-presentation (Vazire and Gosling 2004; Back *et al.* 2010) and ***impression management*** (Goffman 1959) were prominently featured in the narrative of agency. Participants' stories featured the desire to be seen as **more**. More, than just a sex blogger; more like themselves; more than themselves. There was a coexisting desire to show their true selves, and yet to protect themselves by maintaining what Anna (37) brilliantly called 'plausible deniability rather than real anonymity'. This is a curious find, because often, when online self-presentation is addressed, the connotation is that what gets presented online, is less real or less truthful (Manago *et al.* 2008). In this case, the 'more' bloggers wished to share, was more in terms of volume, variety and authenticity – non-sexual stuff (that gets shared with people in offline life), in addition to the sexy stuff (some of which is a part of that true-self that doesn't get shared offline).

The dominant criterion in managing which aspects of oneself to present via the blog, was that of authenticity and sincerity 'in as far as it goes', meaning, people reported being true to themselves in what shines through on the blog, but omitting large chunks (jobs, children, exact geographical location, relationship status) for purposes of discretion or thematic coherence.

> **Peter** (37): I am portraying part of myself, rather than the whole, and I do so in a reasonably honest and sincere way to the extent privacy allows. But at the same time, I do sometimes manage the persona as well. But not overtly, and I try not to do so too much.

Sincerity and honesty were also important because of the therapeutic or self-exploratory role blogging played for many. Olly and Georgina both mentioned it just wouldn't work as therapy, if they weren't completely honest in what they posted. Self-exploration and its subsets, like reclaiming one's sexual identity after childbirth, also played a role in a stronger sense of being internally driven. In addition, agency was constructed via content and blogging as an activity; most participants claimed to blog for themselves not others:

> **Katie** (30): but if people stopped watching I'd still be blogging. I find it really helpful and I love having a place that is my own.

Yet going over something that they had posted and deleting it, or realising, after a night of tumblring from a bar, that perhaps not all of it should be there, was often mentioned, as well as differentiating what one likes (and puts a heart on) from what one wants on their blog. Bloggers also reported having to remind themselves that this was their place and they were free to do with it as they pleased.

Passive or ambivalent agency came to the fore when describing relationships gone wrong, either affairs that should not have happened or situations, where one of the parties got more involved than the other considered appropriate. Holland *et al.* (1998) speak of moving between inner and social speech in the space of authoring, which is helpful here. Notice the changing agency from internal to ambivalent, to that of a couple's shared consciousness, and back to passive.

> **Fred** (46): yeah… I got involved in what I might say is an online fantasy romance thing and it… it… got a little more real… let's say than it should have. /…/ and then it… things developed and… we've worked through… we're working through… but there is a trust betrayed.

Also, as a way of self-justification, rationalisation and neutralisation, people (mostly married or involved) almost always portrayed developing a relationship with someone as an accident, or a side product, and never their goal within the blogging experience.

> **Brian** (mid 30s): Absolutely, it's almost accidental, you know. You happen to be walking down the street and you keep bumping into someone accidentally, instead of deliberately going into that shop that you're specifically looking to talk to people at, you know.

Passive agency was also used when people explained how they have become more aware of certain fetishes or sexual proclivities that they had not been aware of before, and might now be more interested in pursuing.

Identity constitution in time and space – third dilemmatic space

Time-space discontinuities and boundaries seem to be used as a strategic self-narrating tool, to manage 'memories and desires to reproduce or transform one's sense of self' (Alvesson *et al.* 2008). There are five themes that emerge more clearly when describing participants' diachronic identity formation – these are space, time, personality, friendships and boundaries.

'Offline' and 'online' were the main differentiated ***spaces*** in terms of identity formation, but other spatial differentiations were also evident, *e.g.* different spaces online (tumblr. versus other SNS's), or sexy spaces versus non-sexy spaces (content driven spatial discontinuities), and, of course, spatial discontinuities between different offline spaces (*e.g.* different schools one has attended or different cities where one has lived).

Participants disclose different amounts and kinds of information in different spaces. Those online spaces that are accessed by one's offline peer group are often more censored than the NSFW blogs. However, the NSFW blogs usually do not include facial images, one's specific location, or information about one's children. Back *et al.* (2010) wrote that self-presentation online integrates private thoughts, images, and social behaviour, all of which can contain valid information about personality; this is undoubtedly true in NSFW tumblrverse as well, although the image a reader gets of the author emphasises aspects that are different from what the authors children, parents or siblings may know. To claim that one is more accurate or 'real' than the other, would however, be an unjust departure from what the bloggers reported.

Time, too, is a key factor in describing the changes in identity, often narrated through a 'before' and a 'now' blog. The blog is seen as a process, the experience portrayed as morphing from one thing into another (*e.g.* entertainment to therapy), or at least starting out as one thing, and then turning into an unexpected (mostly better) experience. The 'before' and 'now' of blogs is described in terms of the functions it serves for the author, thus, the discontinuities mark (trans)formative shifts in terms of one's self-identity, again showing that, as Davies (2003) writes, individuals are constantly constituted and reconstituted through the discursive practices to which they have access.

> **Brian** (mid 30s): What started out as a curious adventure for a friend, turned out to be something completely different. It has been moving, enlightening, stimulating and revealing. Both about people, and myself.

One's sense of ***personality or their preferences***: 'I'm bisexual everywhere' (Katie, 30), were often constituted as continuous on-, and offline (although 'more shy offline' was a parallel strand to claims made in favour of continuity), which can be linked to the need for coherence in identity work. At the same time, a common thread of time *and* space discontinuity surfaced in terms of specific elements of one's personality. Tumblr. was repeatedly granted the role of having enhanced the participants' levels of confidence, self-awareness, and body-positivism.

> **Carl** (60): I think I am now more open, actually I discussed this with my wife, she told me, now I see that you are more prepared to accept behaviour that is different from what you would like...

A beautiful juxtaposition of acknowledging or denying the blogging experience's role in transforming one's identity was evident in many cases, where, despite outlining the previously mentioned effects it has had on confidence levels, and the like, the participant, when asked directly, reported no significant change. This may be a case of impression management during the interview, or can be attributed to identity work – trying to see one's identity as more coherent and positively valued.

When talking about specific elements of one's self-identity, *e.g.* sexual preferences, the narrative often made the offline-online leap from the blog and online interactions into the bedroom, or at least the 'sexual bucket list'. Starting from the assumption that one can explore (stigmatised) identity elements safely online (Ross 2005, Daneback 2006), we can ask if, in the case of successful online explorations (the feedback from the community makes a practice or a preference seem 'normal', the blogger becomes aware of others who like it, and becomes more sure that they themselves do, actually, like it), one is more confident to try and explore them offline.

> **Peter** (37): I mean there are certain… um… I guess proclivities that… uh… that I may not have thought about before, didn't even realise that I find interesting, um… like spanking… or hair pulling. I did not realise that there are plenty of women who like that… so through tumblr. /…/ it's definitely been a self exploration.

> ***Interviewer**: Right, and have you been able to try any of these things in your offline life?*
>
> **Peter**: [sighs] um… a little bit, um… the spanking [sounds shy] a little bit, yeah. I've incorporated that into my life, the hair pulling not so much. Other than that, not really, I mean, my wife, as much as I love her, is fairly vanilla and not terribly adventurous, uh… and isn't… uh… open to a lot of experimentation, so um… not as much as I probably would like.

The same could occasionally be observed in the case of political or activist ideas becoming internalised – feminist thought in particular seems to disseminate via sex-blogging. Some participants also mentioned having picked up new, or reheated an old, form of self-expression via their tumblring experience (photography, art).

Another theme apparent in the third dilemmatic space was that of ***relationships and friendships*** – here a narrative of continuity was very common. It was important for people to show that they, as friends, are the same online and offline and that the depth of their emotions is also similar.

> **Georgina** (41): They're quite similar actually… I wouldn't want to… I wouldn't want to give up my daily life friends for my online friends, but I wouldn't want to give up my online friends for my daily life friends.

When speaking about the relationship cycle, continuity was also stressed, *e.g.*, participants considered online breakups to be similar to offline ones. However, stressing discontinuity was a common alternative, online relationships were awarded both more, and less, intensity based on different personal experience. A discontinuity was also underscored in what one can, and can't, do with online friends versus offline friends (offline friends were mostly seen as more suitable for secret, taboo, private discussions).

Finally, I want to briefly address the question of ***boundaries***. Purposeful boundary management was apparent in case of many interviewees, participants worked to keep online and offline apart, either out of fear of repercussions, or out of a need for a private place.

> **Brian** (mid 30s): It's almost like the way you get in the matrix – there's this other world that you can plug into and you become like this superhero of some sort, and then you plug out of it, and all of the sudden you're back in this hum drum day to day lifestyle.

The latter, a desire for a place of one's own, to which no one from their offline lives has access, in which they can indulge, and experiment, with the more fun aspects of their personalities, emerged as one of the more consistent narratives throughout the interviews.

Conclusion

Analysing the interviews of NSFW bloggers with a specific focus on (de)constructing their narrative identities proved fruitful in my quest to understand identity and the role the online experience plays in it. I built the empirical analysis of this chapter on *3 dilemmatic spaces* (Bamberg 2010), through which one navigates their selfhood: a dilemma of constant comparisons with others, a dilemma of agency, and transformation of selfhood in time and space.

It is important to stress that even though the offline-online divide was instrumental for bloggers, as they chose which facets of oneself to demonstrate, and the levels of positive affirmation they could find, I would vehemently argue against separating out a so-called 'online identity' from an 'offline identity'. Some researchers have pointed out (Orgad 2009) that boundaries between offline and online are blurring. I would argue that there are no discrete identity-entities, which go specifically off-, or online. **Avatars, profiles and blogs are not our alternative identities, they are temporally fluctuating expressions of a part of an assemblage identity**. Based on this research, there is a collection of self-related elements that get selectively shown, or reflected back, to different people in different communicative contexts, which also constantly change in time. The choice of what specifically gets activated/ included in one's project of self, today, is largely informed by the discursive practices available, the cultural context surrounding it, and mainly, the interactive resources at hand. Constructing one's (sexual) self (both on-, and offline, although it's more visible online), I would argue, is a dia-, or even multilogical, and layered act– and identity element might not be activated at a particular time in a particular setting, but it informs the ones that currently are. All the while, the lifestyle, or the cultural context, that provides some of the discourses is also unfixed, unstable, contradictory, complex and a product of choice, placing people, in a way, into an endless loop of choice. New elements are brought in by other people, selected by the communication medium, filtered by the collectively constructed social reality of an online community.

Bloggers attempt to index their sense of self as distinct, coherent, and positively valued (Alvesson *et al.* 2008) within an intricate system of offline social pressures, those same pressures mirrored online, and a safe space of the NSFW community. NSFW blogging helps with valuing oneself positively, especially the aspects that may not have been valued thus offline. This happens via new elements being assembled into one's identity, and previously existing ones being redefined as positive. It also happens via the sense of belonging with a specific group of online others. The newly incorporated identity elements (or the ones allowed out of the murky subconscious) also play a part in indexing oneself as distinct, *e.g.*, compared to one's offline others. In search of coherence, bloggers' emphasise the offline-online continuities in areas like personality traits, and preferences, friendship building and maintaining mechanisms. Still, this is a context-specific coherence the bloggers are seeking. Each assemblage has to work in a particular context, not throughout one's entire experience of being human. Claims of authenticity and sincerity, that were prominent in most bloggers reflections on their blogging experience, can also be viewed as coherence building tools and multi-layered, context-hopping ones at that. There was a desire to be seen as more like themselves, and simultaneously more than themselves, in the bloggers' narratives, a coexisting desire to show their true selves, and yet to protect themselves by maintaining plausible deniability.

The identity narratives of NSFW bloggers showed that the variety of elements that can, at any given moment, be included in one's identity, grew as a result of the experience, while the online community/ interactions/ reality helped to integrate, and in some cases neutralise, those elements. The way internal and external agency coexisted in the bloggers' daily interactive and expressive decisions on tumblr., and their use of ambivalent agency as a neutralisation technique in morally questionable interactive situations (marital indiscretions; multiple, simultaneous, secretive online affairs), are also functions of identity work and impression management (Goffman 1959), and help us, as people, experience our selfhood as positive and coherent despite constant change.

Acts of identity work were also evident in bloggers' narratives of how they navigated the first dilemmatic space of constant social comparison, and the third dilemmatic space of stressing coherence across time and space, despite the obvious discontinuities in what one reveals on-, and offline; in different online settings (tumblr. versus Facebook), and to different people (offline friends/ spouses/ online friends/ blog readers). I witnessed an almost compartmentalised approach to selfhood in the choice of which content, relationships, desires, dreams, preferences and aspects of personality were made visible, and simultaneously, a fluid, coherent sense of self, arching over people, relationships and spaces.

Finally I'd like to stress that, based on my research; social media is a space of active social reality construction, and provides us with the people, interactions, and cultural resources we involve in our identity. The interview analysis done for this chapter highlighted some additional interesting questions, such as, 'can we talk about a sexual filter bubble in NSFW communities?', 'is there a positive feedback loop of openness and tolerance that will eventually destabilise the system by prompting exponential growth?', and 'what are the hedonistic and therapeutic sex related discourses?'. These will have to be answered in another place.

References

Aberton, H. (2010). 'The material enactments of identities in everyday community practices.' In EASST 2010 Practicing Science and Technology Performing the Social.

Albright, J. (2008). 'Sex in America online: An exploration of sex, marital status, and sexual identity in internet sex seeking and its impacts.' *Journal of Sex Research,* 45: 175–186.

Alvesson, M., Ashcraft, K. L. and Thomas, R. (2008). 'Identity matters: Reflections on the construction of identity scholarship in organization studies.' *Organization*, 15: 5-28.

Attwood, F. (2010). *porn.com: Making Sense of Online Pornography*. Lang, Peter Publishing Inc.

Back M. D., Stopfer J. M., Vazire S., Gaddis S., Schmukle S. C., Egloff B., Gosling S. D. (2010). 'Facebook Profiles Reflect Actual Personality, Not Self-Idealization.' *Psychological Science*, 21: 372-374.

Bamberg M. (2011). 'Who am I? Narration and its contribution to self and identity.' *Theory & Psychology*, 21: 3-24.

Bamberg, M. (2003). 'Positioning with Davie Hogan: Stories, Tellings, and Identities.' C. Daiute and C. Lightfoot (eds). *Narrative Analysis: Studying the Development of Individuals in Society*. London: Sage, 135-57.

Bamberg, M., Georgakopoulou A. (2008). 'Small Stories as a New Perspective in Narrative and Identity Analysis.' *Text & Talk*, 28: 377-96.

Bargh, J. A., McKenna K. Y. A. (2004). 'The Internet and Social Life.' *Annu. Rev. Psychol.* 55: 573-90.

Bargh J. A., McKenna K. Y. A. and Fitzsimons G. M. (2002). 'Can You See the Real Me? Activation and Expression of the 'True Self' on the Internet.' *Journal of Social Issues*, 58: 33-48.

Bauman Z. (2001). *Community, Seeking Safety in an Insecure World.* Cambridge: Polity Press.

Baym, N. K. (2000). *Tune In, Log On: Soaps, Fandom, and Online Community.* Thousand Oaks, Sage.

Baym, N. K., Markham, A. N. (2009). Introduction. Making Smart Choices on Shifting Ground. *In Internet Inquiry, conversations about method.* Markham, A. N., Baym, N. K. (eds.) Thousand Oaks, Sage.

Beck U. (1998 [1992]). *Risk Society: Towards a New Modernity*. New Delhi: Sage.

Ben Z'ev, A. (2004). *Love online. Emotions on the Internet.* Cambridge University Press.

Binik, Y. M. (2001). 'Sexuality and the internet: Lots of hyp(otheses) – only a little data.' *Journal of Sex Research*, 38: 281-282.

boyd, d. (2007). 'Why Youth (Heart) Social Network Sites: The Role of Networked Publics in Teenage Social Life.' *MacArthur Foundation Series on Digital Learning – Youth, Identity, and Digital Media Volume* (ed. David Buckingham). Cambridge, MA: MIT Press, 119-142.

boyd, d. (2007). 'Social Network Sites: Public, Private, or What?' *Knowledge Tree*, 13.

boyd, d. and Heer, J. (2006). 'Profiles as Conversation: Networked Identity Performance on Friendster.' Proceedings of the 39th Hawaii International Conference on System Sciences – 2006.

Brand, M., Laier, C., Pawlikowski, M., Schächtle, U., Schöler, T., Altstötter-Gleich, C. A. (2011). 'Watching pornographic pictures on the Internet: role of sexual arousal ratings and psychological-psychiatric symptoms for using Internet sex sites excessively.' *Cyberpsychology, behavior and social networking,* 14: 371-7.

Bruns, A. (2006) 'Towards Produsage: Futures for User-Led Content Production'. Sudweeks, F., Hrachovec, H., Ess, C,. (eds).*Cultural Attitudes towards Communication and Technology*.Proceedings Cultural Attitudes towards Communication and Technology. Tartu, Estonia.

Cooper, A., Månsson, S. A., Daneback, K., Tikkanen, R. and Ross, M. W. (2003). 'Predicting the future of Internet sex: Online sexual activities in Sweden.' *Sexual and Relationship Therapy*, 18: 277-291.

Creswell, J. (1998). *Qualitative Inquiry and Research Design; Choosing Among Five Traditions.* London, New Delhi, Thousand Oaks, Sage Publications.

Daneback, K. (2006). *Love and sexuality on the internet. A qualitative approach.* Report from the Department of Social Work at Gothenburg University.

Daneback, K., Cooper, A. and Månsson, S.-A. (2005). 'An Internet study of cybersex participants.' *Archives of Sexual Behavior*, 34: 321-328.

Daneback, K., Månsson, S.-A. and Ross, M. W. (2007). 'Using the Internet to find offline sex partners.' *CyberPsychology & Behavior,* 10: 100-107.

Davies, B. (2003). *Shards of glass: Reading and writing beyond gendered identities* (revised ed.). New Jersey: Hampton Press.

Döring, N. M. (2009). 'The Internet's impact on sexuality: A critical review of 15 years of research.' *Computers in Human Behavior,* 25:1089-1101.

Ferree, M. (2003). 'Women and the web: Cybersex activity and implications.' *Sexual and Relationship Therapy*, 18: 385-393.

Freedom House. (2012) 'Freedom on the Net 2012. A Global Assesment of Internet and Digital Media'.

Fulk J. (1993). Social Construction of Communication Technology. *The Academy of Management Journal.* 36: 921-950.

Goffman, E. (1959). *The Presentation of Self in Everyday Life*. Garden City: Doubleday.

Georgakopoulou, A. (2006). 'The Other Side of the Story: Towards a Narrative Analysis of Narratives-in-Interaction.' *Discourse Studies* 8: 265–87.

Georgakopoulou, A. (2007). *Small Stories, Interaction and Identities*. Amsterdam: Benjamins.

Giddens A. (2010 [1991]). *Modernity and Self Identity, Self and Society in the Late Modern Age.* Cambridge: Polity Press.

Gergen, K. (2000 [1991]). *The Saturated Self: Dilemmas of Identity in Contemporary Life.* New York: Basic Books.

Griffiths, M. (2001). 'Sex on the internet: Observations and implications for internet sex addiction.' *Journal of Sex Research*, 38: 333-342.

Gubrium, Jaber F. and James A. Holstein (2008). 'Narrative Ethnography.' Hesse-Biber S. B., Leavy, P. (eds). *Handbook of Emergent Methods*. New York: Guildford P, 241-64.

Haferkamp, N., Krämer, N. C. (2011). 'Social comparison 2.0: examining the effects of online profiles on social-networking sites.' *Cyberpsychology, behavior and social networking*, 14: 309-14.

Holstein, J. A., Gubrium, J. F. (1995). *The Active Interview.* Thousand Oaks. Sage.
Holland D., Lachicotte W. Jr., Skinner D. and Cain C. (1998). *Identity and agency in cultural Worlds.* Cambridge: Harvard University Press.
Hookway N. (2008). ''Entering the blogosphere': some strategies for using blogs in social research.' *Qualitative Research*, 81: 91-113.
Joinson, A. N. (2008). ''Looking at', 'Looking up' or 'Keeping up with' People? Motives and Uses of Facebook.' Social Networks, Proceeding CHI '08 Proceedings of the twenty-sixth annual SIGCHI conference on Human factors in computing systems. ACM, New York.
Lampe, C., Ellison, N. and Steinfield, C., (2006). 'A Face(book) in the crowd: Social searching vs. social browsing.' Proceedings of CSCW-2006. New York: ACM Press, 167-170.
Leary, M. R. and Kowalski, R. M. (1990). 'Impression Management: A Literature Review and Two-Component Model,' *Psychological Bulletin*, 107: 34-47.
Leiblum, S. R. (2001). 'Women, sex and the internet.' *Sexual and Relationship Therapy*, 16: 389-405.
Mallan, K. and Giardina N. (2009). 'Wikidentities: Young people Collaborating on Virtual Identities in Social Network Sites.' *First Monday*, 14 (6).
Manago, A. M., Graham, M. B., Greenfield, P. M. and Salimkhan, G. (2008). Self-presentation and gender on MySpace. *Journal of Applied Developmental Psychology*. 29: 446-58.
McCullagh, K. (2008). 'Blogging: self presentation and privacy.' *Information & Communications Technology Law*, 17: 3-23.
McKenna, K. Y. A., Green A. S. and Gleason M. J. (2002). 'Relationship formation on the Internet: What's the big attraction?' *Journal of Social Issues,* 58: 9-31.
Muise, A. (2011). Women's Sex Blogs: Challenging dominant discourses of heterosexual desire. *Feminism & Psychology*, 21: 411-419.
Orgad, S. (2009). Question Two: How Can Researchers Make Sense of The Issues Involved in Collecting and Interpreting Online and Offline Data? Markham A. M, Baym N. K. (eds.) *Internet Inquiry, conversations about method.* Thousand Oaks, Sage.
Pluempavarn, P. and Panteli, N. (2007). 'The creation of social identity through weblogging.' [Online]Available:University of Bath School of Management Working Paper Series. October 2007. http://www.bath.ac.uk/management/research/pdf/2007-10.pdf.
Ricoeur, P. (1991 [1984]). *Time and narra*tive. Vol 1, Chicago: University of Chicago Press.
Ricoeur, P. (1985) *Time and narrative.* Vol. 2 Chicago: University of Chicago Press.
Ricoeur, P. (1988) *Time and narrative.* Vol. 3 Chicago: University of Chicago Press.
Ricoeur, P. (1992) *Oneself as Another*. The University of Chicago Press: Chicago.
Ross, M. W. (2005). 'Typing, doing and being: sexuality and the Internet.' *Journal of Sex Research,* 42: 342-52.
Ross, M. W., Rosser, B. R. S., McCurdy, S. and Feldman, J. (2007). 'The Advantages and limitations of seeking sex online: A Comparison of reasons given for online and offline sexual liaisons by men have you have sex with men.' *Journal of Sex Research*, 44: 59-71.
Sevcikova, A. and Daneback, K. (2011). 'Anyone who wants sex? Seeking sex partners on erotic contact websites.' *Sex and Relationship Therapy.* DOI: 10.1080/14681994.2011.567260
Siibak, A. (2011). 'Online Peer Culture and Interpretive Reproduction on the Social Networking Site Profiles of the Tweens.' Colombo, F.; Fortunati, L. (eds.). *Broadband Society and Generational Changes*. Berlin: Peter Lang Publishers House, 121-132.

Smith, B. and Sparkes, A. (2008). 'Contrasting perspectives on narrating selves and identities: an invitation to dialogue.' *Qualitative Research*, 8: 5-35.

Statistics Estonia. (2012). Database: 'Majandus – Infotehnoloogia ja side – Infotehnoloogia leibkonnas, 2012' ['Economics – Infotechnology and connectivity – Infotechnology in the household, 2012'], [Online]. Available: http://www.stat.ee/sab-uuendus?db_update_id=11053, accessed October 2012.

Sundén, J. (2003). *Material Virtualities*. New York: Peter Lang.

Tan, L. (2008). 'Psychotherapy 2.0: MySpace blogging as self-therapy.' *American Journal of Psychotherapy*, 62: 143-63.

Trammell, K. (2005). 'Examining the New Influencers: A Self-Presentation Study of A-List Blogs.' *Journalism & Mass Communication Quarterly*, 82: 968-982.

Vazire, S. and Gosling, S. D. (2004). 'e-Perceptions: Personality impressions based on personal websites.' *Journal of Personality and Social Psychology*, 87: 123-132.

Weiss, R. (1994). *Learning From Strangers; The Art and Method of Qualitative Interview Studies*. New York, The Free Press.

Whitty, M. T. (2003). 'Pushing the Wrong Buttons: Men's and Women's Attitudes toward Online and Offline Infidelity.' *Cyberpsychology and Behavior*, 6: 569-579.

Whitty, M. T. (2008). 'Revealing the 'real' me, searching for the 'actual' you: Presentations of self on an internet dating site.' *Computers in Human Behavior*, 24: 1707-1723.

Wood, E. A. (2008). 'Consciousness-raising 2.0: Sex Blogging and the Creation of a Feminist Sex Commons.' *Feminism & Psychology*, 18: 480-87.

Appendix

Table 1: Basic information about participants A-F

	Anna	Brian	Carl	Daniel	Eric	Fred
Gender, age, location	Female, 37, USA, Texas	Male, mid-30s, USA, Chicago	Male, 60, Belgium, Brussels	Male, 41, USA, NYC	Male, late 20s; USA, Midwest	Male, 46; New Zealand
Relationship status	Single offline, dating online	Married w/ kids offline, single online (flirting and sexual interactions)	Married w/ kids offline, no relationships online	Divorced w/ kids offline; single online (flirting and sexual interactions)	Single offline and online (flirting and sexual interactions)	Married offline and online
Sexual identity & lifestyle	Heteroflexible[38], more bisexual online and somewhat kinky[39]	Heterosexual edge of vanilla	Heterosexual, vanilla[40]	Heterosexual, somewhat kinky	Heterosexual, vanilla	Heterosexual, vanilla
Occup / educat	Education grad. degree	Graphic design uni. degree.	Admin Phd.	Finance uni. degree.	IT, grad. degree.	Civil engin. uni. degree.

38 A person who is mainly heterosexual, but open to experimentation.

39 A person who's sexual preferences involve nontraditional, fetish related practices, for example elements of BDSM (bondage, discipline, dominance, submission, sadism, masochism).

40 vanilla is a term used in sexually open discourse to categorise people who engage in traditional, one on one, heterosexual, non-fetish sex.

Table 1 cont.: Basic information about participants G-T

	Georgina	**Katie**	**Lisa**	**Olly**	**Peter**	**Theresa**
Gender, age, location	Female, 41; Nebraska; USA	Female, 30; Toronto, Canada	Female, 26; UK	Trans-gender, 28; Kansas, USA	Male, 37; Pennsyl. USA	Female, 37; NYC, USA
Relation-ship status	Married w/ kids offline and online (flirting online)	Consensual non-monog. marriage online and offline, w/ kids, (kids not referenced online)	In a rela-tionship offline; doesn't reference online apart when asked, used to flirt and have sexual in-teractions online, not any more	In a rela-tionship offline and online	Married w/ kids offline and online; (kids not referenced online) flirt-ing and sexual in-teractions online;	Married online and offline;
Sexual identity & lifestyle	Hetero-sexual, edge of vanilla	Bisexual, kinky	Bisexual, kinky	Queer / pan-sexual; kinky and polyamor-ous[41]	Hetero-sexual, edges of vanilla	Bisexual, poly-curious[42]
Occup / educat.	Software develop-ment, high-school.	Child and youth coun-selor; di-ploma de-gree, cur-rently working on a BA.	Technical writer BSc.	Baker/ student therapist; working on second uni-versity de-gree.	Lawyer, grad. degree	Fundraising; uni. degree.

41 A person who is simultaneously in many emotional/ sexual relationships.

42 A person who is curious about the polyamorous lifestyle, perhaps experimenting, unde-cided.

Strategies for managing difficulties related to employment: narratives of Russian-speaking women in Estonia

Kadri Aavik

Introduction

When looking at how gender and ethnicity simultaneously affect people's labour market position, it becomes evident that, statistically, the highest and most prestigious positions in the Estonian labour market tend to be occupied by Estonian men, while the most marginal jobs are held by Russian-speaking women. This is also reflected in salaries – of all groups located at the intersection of gender and ethnicity, Russian-speaking women earn the least (Statistics Estonia 2010). However, if the intersection of gender and ethnicity is not addressed through analysis of labour market segregation, these inequalities often remain unnoticed and unproblematised.

This chapter seeks to understand qualitatively how the group at the intersection of gender and ethnicity who, according to previous studies, seems to be the most disadvantaged – Russian-speaking women (Hansson and Aavik 2012) – narrates their career paths and copes with employment-related difficulties. I seek to understand how the disadvantage of a specific group of Russian-speaking women in the Estonian labour market – those with higher education and good Estonian language skills – is being sustained and reproduced (and/or challenged). I explore the following questions: How do the participants construct and perform their identities in their narratives of employment experiences? How are gender, ethnicity, age and other categories presented, and how are they intertwined in the narratives? What strategies do the participants use to cope with unemployment and other difficulties in the labour market, and how do they challenge existing constraints in the labour market?

Estonian context: gender and ethnic inequalities in the Estonian labour market

Estonia is an interesting case for the exploration of inequalities. Although the country has a long history of female employment, recent data on inequalities indicate that the Estonian labour market has the largest gender disparities in the EU, at both occupational and sectoral levels. The concentration of women in certain occupational areas, such as healthcare and social services, is disproportionately large (Sotsiaalministeerium 2010: 35). Such segregation of the labour market is one of the major causes of the gender pay gap in Estonia, which is currently among the highest in the EU as well – according to different statistics, men earn on average 22.9% (Statistics Estonia 2012) to 30.3% (Eurostat 2009) more than women[43].

The collapse of the Soviet regime and transition to a market economy in the early 1990s led to significant changes in the labour market position of groups at the intersection of gender and ethnicity in Estonia. The process created new economic sectors and jobs, for example, the service sector emerged as one of the largest sectors of the economy, which contributed to increased gender and ethnic segregation in the Estonian labour market.

Hansson and Aavik (2012) found that between 1993 and 2008, important changes occurred in Estonia in the labour market position of four groups at the intersection of gender and ethnicity, in terms of average net monthly wages, job security and job satisfaction. Estonian men have clearly emerged as the most successful and privileged group in the Estonian labour market, while already in 1993, Russian-speaking women were in a more disadvantaged position compared to other groups. By 2008, their disadvantages, compared to other groups, seem to have increased further, as they report the lowest income, lowest job satisfaction, and lowest job security.

Interactions of gender and ethnicity, as well as of ethnicity and occupational status, influenced net earnings more significantly in 2008 than 1993, reflecting the increasing gender and ethnic segregation in the Estonian labour market (Hansson and Aavik 2012). Women, especially Russian-speaking women, increasingly became employed in undervalued and underpaid sectors, such as education, healthcare, manufacturing and wholesale/retail trade. In these sectors, employers' gendered and ethnicised assumptions (Acker 2006; Padamsee 2009) towards employees interact, and Russian-speaking women might be considered by employers as 'ideal workers' (Williams 2001; Acker 2006) in the lower ranking jobs in these sectors.

One of the few previous studies that have focused on Russian-speaking women in the Estonian labour market (Anspal and Kallaste 2007), looks at the position of minority women in the labour market compared to Estonian men and women, and minority men, focusing on their employment rates, access to high positions, and salaries, by analysing quantitative data. The authors, for instance, find that minority women experience an ethnic disadvantage, which is more pronounced than gender disadvantage, as the unemployment rates of minority women have been roughly the same as those of minority men. The study also finds significant pay gaps (over 20%) between the incomes of Estonian and minority women in the capital Tallinn, as well as between ethnic Estonian and mi-

43 For more on the gender system in Estonia see Pajumets and Hearn, and Pilvre in this book.

nority employees. The authors conclude that minority women experience a 'double' pay gap, due to their identity as minority women (Anspal and Kallaste 2007: 20).

Although statistical data indicates that the current labour market position of Russian-speaking women is more precarious than that of other groups, existing data or research does not show specificities of their disadvantage, and their construction of identities as workers (as well as citizens), and interpretation of their employment situation. This chapter attempts to fill the gap.

Theoretical framework

Intersectionality

Intersectionality is a theoretical concept, and methodological approach, that has attained an increasingly important position in the work of feminist scholars in the last two decades (see McCall 2005; Bowleg 2008; Lykke 2010; Hancock 2007; Shields 2008; Yuval-Davis 2006; Choo and Ferree 2010). Intersectionality suggests that, along with gender, other socially constructed identity categories contribute to social inequality, and thus, gender should not be taken as the sole, or primary category in which to study social inequality. Intersectionality is therefore conceptualised as 'the interaction between gender, race, and other categories of difference in individual lives, social practices, institutional arrangements, and cultural ideologies and the outcomes of these interactions in terms of power' (Davis 2008: 68).

Intersectionality helps to uncover experiences of disadvantage (as well as privilege). The disadvantages that people experience at the intersection of social categories are not cumulative, but interactional – 'for example, racism is infected and changed by sexism for black women, and vice versa – the sexism they encounter is infected and changed by racism' (Bagilhole 2009: 50). In other words, intersectionality means mutually constitutive relations among social identities, that is, how 'one category of identity, such as gender, takes its meaning as a category in relation to another category' (Shields 2008: 302-303).

The participants of my research – Russian-speaking women with higher education and good Estonian language skills – are located at the intersection of multiple social categories, which shape their experiences, thus the narratives of their experiences cannot be studied by prioritising one primary category of difference, such as gender or ethnicity, and therefore, an intersectional approach should be used.

The principal task of intersectionality researchers is to make 'the intersections between ethnicity, sex/gender, sexual orientation (just to name a few), and the social inequality related to these identities, explicit' (Bowleg 2008: 322).

Three main methodological approaches to conducting intersectionality research are outlined by Leslie McCall (2005). In this research, I use the 'intra-categorical approach' (McCall 2005), also called the 'group-centred approach' (Choo and Ferree 2010). This approach often deals with 'particular social groups at neglected points of intersection /.../ in order to reveal the complexity of lived experience within such groups' (McCall 2005: 1773-1774).

Although the intersection of gender and ethnicity is an important focus in my analysis, I do not limit the analysis to only these two categories. I follow the suggestion of McCall 'not to deny the importance – both material and discursive – of categories but to focus on the process by which they are produced, experienced, reproduced, and resisted in everyday life' (2005: 1783).

I rely on a constructionist approach, which suggests that intersectionality is something that people do, rather than something that they are, or have (Staunaes, quoted in Lykke 2010: 74). This idea follows from the constructionist assumption that gender, race and ethnicity (and other categories) 'are constructed in communicative processes', hence, 'doing intersectionality' means 'the doing of the relation between categories, the outcome of this doing and how this doing results in either troubled or untroubled subject positions' (*ibid*). It is important to ask, then, 'how do intersecting power differentials produce life-history narratives in which the effects of genderisation, racialisation, ethnification, class stratification and so on can be seen as interwoven?' (*ibid*). Importantly, this approach pays attention to individual agency.

In intersectional research, a specific method of studying identity categories in relation to each other in involves 'asking the other question' (Davis 2008: 70; Choo and Ferree 2010: 135). This involves identifying how, in a particular situation, categories or dimensions of inequality are 'crisscrossed with other axes of power and exclusion that are less well articulated' Choo and Ferree (2010: 135).

Narrative identity and the construction of experience

Contemporary preoccupations with identity have made narrative an increasingly popular research genre (Riessman 2008: 7), as individuals construct their identities through storytelling – 'our very 'selves' are 'storied'' (Sclater 2003: 317). According to contemporary approaches to narrative, 'we come to know, understand and make sense of the social world /.../ and constitute our social identities' through narrativity (Somers 1994: 606).

Sclater (2003: 317-318) summarises this position by quoting Andrews (2000): 'We become who we are through telling stories about our lives and living the stories we tell'. We construct our identities by locating ourselves 'or being located within a repertoire of emplotted stories, /.../ "experience" is constituted through narratives.' (Somers 1994: 614). Chase (1995: 7), points out that 'narration is a cultural practice; in making sense of experience, any narrative draws on, and is being constrained by, the culture in which it is embedded'.

In the narrative identity approach, actors are inserted 'within relationships and stories that shift over time and space' (Somers 1994: 621). For example, individuals' experiences as workers are intricately tied to other relations that structure their lives – '...their regional location, the practical workings of the legal system, family patterns – as well as the particular stories (of honour, of ethnicity, of gender, of local community, of greed, *etc.*) used to account for the events happening to them' (Somers 1994: 625).

In this chapter, I draw from Joan Scott's (1991) conceptualisation of experience as the origin of knowledge, or as evidence. Scott emphasises that the experience of subjects should not be taken as self-evident, as experience itself is constructed and stresses the need to explore 'how difference is established, how it operates, how and in what ways it constitutes subjects who see and act in the world.' (Scott 1991: 777). The workings of the ideological system and its categories of representation, what they mean, and how they operate, have to be critically examined. Particularly, it must be understood how difference is relationally constituted: 'it is not individuals who have experience but subjects who are constituted through experience' (Scott 1991: 779). It is important to ask 'how conceptions of selves (of subjects and their identities) are produced' (Scott 1991: 782). Consequently, categories, such as man, woman, black, white, *etc.* must not be taken as given characteristics of individuals or naturalised; rather, we must examine how they are produced (*ibid.*).

Data and method

In total, I conducted 11 interviews[44] in the period of December 2011 to March 2012 with Russian-speaking women aged 32 to 62 (three of the women were in their 30s, others were above 40), all except one currently living in Tallinn and Tartu, the two largest cities in Estonia. Eight participants were born in Estonia, and three were born elsewhere in the Soviet Union, and migrated to Estonia with their families in their childhood. Thus, this group cannot be classified as recent migrants, but an ethnic minority in Estonia. All participants, except one, finished Russian-speaking high schools in Estonia. They then continued their educational paths in universities in different fields of study (some in long distance programmes, to combine studies with work), predominantly in Russian-speaking

44 One interview was conducted via email, as the participant refused a face-to-face and Skype interview.

programmes, the most common specialty being accounting and finance. Thus, the group studied is highly educated, however, in the case of older participants, their educational qualifications obtained in the Soviet period might no longer be relevant or valued in the Estonian labour market today.

At the time of the interview, most participants were unemployed, while others were working in jobs that were below their educational qualifications. All of them have at some point in the past, or were at the time of the interview, registered as unemployed in the Estonian Unemployment Insurance Fund (EUIF), a state institution whose task is to provide basic unemployment benefits and assist in finding new employment.

Participants were asked to narrate their employment (and educational) paths so far, starting from their high school, and to describe their current job or, if they were unemployed, their last job and experiences relating to unemployment. The interview design was open and participants were able to and encouraged to raise and pursue topics that they considered important, relating to the general theme of the interview.

Interviews were conducted in Estonian, as all participants had Estonian language skills that ranged from upper intermediate to proficient. However, participants were often self-critical and insecure about their Estonian language skills. Participants were found via personal acquaintances, and with the help of the Tartu office of the EUIF. Prior to conducting the interviews, participants were informed via e-mail or phone about the topic of the interview, the procedure of conducting the interview and issues of confidentiality. Interviews took place at locations in Tallinn and Tartu proposed either by participants or the researcher.

I chose to focus on women with higher education and fluent Estonian to exclude the lack of Estonian language skills or insufficient education from the obvious causes of their difficulties in the labour market. I chose to interview women above 30 years of age because I was interested in how they narrate their career paths in different structural conditions and life stages.

Several approaches exist within narrative analysis, which are not mutually exclusive and can be combined (Riessman 2008). In this research I mainly use thematic analysis, where the focus is on the content of the text, and which identifies common thematic elements in the narratives of several research participants, guided by research questions. However, the context of the text is equally important, that is the wider institutional and cultural settings and discourses, as 'narrative analysis can forge connections between personal biography and social structure – the personal and the political' (Riessman 2005: 6). Thus, I conduct thematic narrative analysis using an intersectional approach.

In this chapter, I predominantly present my findings using representative cases. However, in the last part of the next section, I draw from several stories of the participants to highlight ways that they present ethnicity-based exclusion in the labour market, as issues of ethnicity are consistently present in somewhat different ways in almost all stories.

Presentation of career paths and rationalisation of current labour market situation

When asked to narrate their career paths since high school, participants often summarised their educational qualifications and did not extensively narrate their years of study and early work experiences, rapidly shifting to their present employment situation, or other issues they considered important in their present-day lives.

Although, at the time of the interviews all participants were experiencing difficulties finding (suitable) employment, the presentation of their career paths as well as their rationalisation of the present situation differ somewhat. I have grouped the stories into two types of work narratives. This allows me to explore how the participants locate their personal narratives in relation to the changing political, social and economic environment in Estonia, and how they see these structural conditions influencing the development of their careers.

The first and most frequent type of narrative could be called that of gradual downward mobility, or declining success in the labour market, with the passing of time. It has to be noted that the emergence and dominance of this type of narrative may be derived from the background information that the participants received prior to the interviews – they were approached as Russian-speaking women experiencing difficulties in the labour market. Thus, this type of narrative was most readily available to them, and its emergence is of no particular surprise. With this narrative, the participants 'confirmed expectations' by telling stories of occupational decline and increasing difficulties related to employment.

The second type of story is one characterised by ups and downs, or stability in career advancement and status on the labour market. In this type of story, the work path is presented as one of fluctuations, successes followed by failures and disappointments, ending with the latter. Some participants did not emphasise significant change in their labour market position or employment status over time or, if they referred to some change in their position or job security, it was less explicitly articulated.

In explaining their current difficulties in the labour market, participants referred to different factors, which can be categorised as internal and external to themselves, as reasons why they are experiencing difficulties with employment. Often, these personal and structural/societal circumstances they speak of are intertwined in their narratives. However, the narratives differ in terms of how much (both implicit and explicit) emphasis is placed on external factors/ structural conditions determining the current labour market situation of the participants. I use two narratives to illustrate how career paths are presented and the current labour market situation rationalised.

Olga

Olga's (55) story is representative of the first type of work narrative, that of gradual decline in occupational status and income. In rationalising her current labour market situation, Olga represents those (especially older) participants who primarily blame themselves, and their personal misfortunes and insecurities, for their difficulties and do not explicitly criticise external structures and conditions.

Olga is a good example of the participants who have already been in the labour market for decades, but are currently unemployed or unable to find work that matches their qualifications. When looking at her work narrative as a whole, it is evident that the collapse of the Soviet Union, and the subsequent restructuring of the labour market had a negative impact on her career, although she does not explicitly highlight this herself. After having completed a vocational degree in accounting, she combined work with further studies at the end of the 1970s and early 1980s, receiving her university degree in the mid-1980s in finance and credit. Up to 1991, her position in the job hierarchy was gradually improving. However, transition to market economy with new institutional settings coincided with the birth of her first child and parental leave, as Olga explains:

> My last job was that of an auditor in the state bank. But then, in 1991, I went on parental leave and then there was the Bank of Estonia [the bank was restructured]. I was not dismissed. But after, I stayed home with my child for 3 years and had to go back, they say that they don't have a job /.../.Well, I didn't have proficiency in Estonian. State officials need to speak proficient Estonian, I only had category D[45]. And also, I didn't have the blue passport [Estonian passport]. But two months later, I got the blue passport... [laughs] /.../ Then I thought ok, my children are small, I already had 3 children, let me stay home for a while and try afterwards. After that I didn't work in the bank any more. Then I had several jobs... I did accounting for small companies, these were cooperatives.

In this story, Olga refers to ethnicity, as well as mothering as reasons why she was unable to return to work, explaining her job loss with her not having Estonian citizenship and not speaking Estonian to an adequate level. She sees new requirements regarding language and citizenship, which had been institutional-

45 Intermediate level.

ised while she was on parental leave, as having suddenly constructed her as an 'unsuitable worker'. While for her, ethnicity is an important factor here, she also refers to gender, specifically her long parental leave. As a mother of three children, she took parental leave, as women are implicitly considered the primary care-givers of children (also, at the time, men were not yet entitled to parental leave). Just as in Olga's case, male partners were missing from all narratives of taking care of children and the need to reconcile work with family, but were often mentioned in the context of supporting the family financially.

After having lost this job, she no longer worked in the field of finance. In narrating her subsequent work-related experiences, she refers to a personal misfortune that she seems to associate with many of her later difficulties in the labour market:

> Four years later my husband died. I took my three children and moved to the countryside. For 8 and half years I was the housekeeper of a manor house /.../ Well, this was good for the children. Then all of them went to Estonian-language school and I didn't have to pay rent, I lived for free. I rented out my apartment in Tallinn. Well, at that time I already had a very difficult financial situation.

Although she does not talk explicitly about gender and economic status in this story, it is evident that these categories are intertwined – her economic situation and status as a single mother, with three children, considerably narrowed her choices regarding which jobs to accept. After working eight years as a housekeeper, she remained in the same village, working as a guard in night shifts for a lumber company:

> Well, there was really no employer in [name of the village], it was only [this lumber company]. When we moved there, the village had a school, a kindergarten, a post office, and when we moved away, everything was closed – the post office, the shop, the kindergarten, and the school were all closed /.../ The biggest problem was that I wanted my children to finish school there. If it was just me, I would have maybe left earlier to a city, like Tallinn or Tartu.

In this narrative, Olga emphasises her location in the rural area as the greatest obstacle for finding a (good) job. She presents staying in the countryside as her personal choice, made out of the necessity to prioritise the needs of her children, yet also refers to difficulties of life there with very restricted opportunities, in terms of employment and so forth. Chase (1995: 8) has pointed out that prevailing metanarratives in Western cultures about women 'emphasise women's selflessness, orientation to and development through others, and preoccupation with family and domestic affairs'. In articulating her experiences on this period of her life and work, Olga makes use of this hegemonic narrative plot, as she is no longer able to build a positive self-image through paid work, which might have led her to prioritise more her gendered identity as a good mother.

In reasoning about her current difficulties in the labour market, Olga singles out the category of age, as well as her status as a mother as the most obvious obstacles in finding any kind of employment:

> They [employers] don't want you to be too young and they don't want you to be too old either, but they want you to have experience, they want your children to be grown up /.../. Well, I have written in my CV that my children are... well, they are living their own lives [laughs]. My sons live with me, but they are all grown up.

Although Olga does not speak of gender explicitly, her story evokes gendered expectations of employers, and society at large, according to which women are the primary care-givers of children, and having young children is detrimental to women's performance as committed workers.

Out of the factors or circumstances that explain why Olga is having difficulties in the labour market, she herself refers most explicitly to her age. Gender and ethnicity appear more implicitly in her narrative as factors that might create or sustain her disadvantage. However, she does not explicitly highlight the intersection of these categories as disadvantaging her.

Ekaterina

Ekaterina's (32) story exemplifies the type of narrative where the career path is represented as successive upward and downward fluctuations. Ekaterina is rather explicit in identifying and articulating external factors that, according to her, contribute to her disadvantage in the labour market, yet simultaneously she often devalues herself as a competent and worthy employee.

She is one of the many participants who articulated issues of ethnic identity spontaneously, and explicitly, in their narratives. For example, issues of ethnicity and language occupy a central place in her account of her school years, as she emphasises her and her family's conscious, and systematic, efforts to learn the Estonian language, and highlights her strong identification with Estonia as her 'homeland'.

The following extract is a good example of her experiences in the labour market, represented as a series of fluctuations. She begins with her first job after university in 2003 in a small private company:

> I was hired unofficially, without a contract, because the manager didn't know what my professional knowledge, let alone experience, is. At that time, the minimum salary in Estonia was around 121 Euros, I don't remember the exact number, and I got

> 90 Euros net unofficially. I was very happy that I got a job matching my qualifications. But, with great shock we discovered together with the manager that I know nothing. The theoretical knowledge that I had received in the university, didn't match with practical life. I owe a thousand thanks to the manager, because he taught me and gave me a lot of knowledge. I worked in his company around half a year, and then, in December, I expressed my wish to have a slightly bigger salary and officially. The manager said he would think about it. But this is how the young blood is – you want everything right now.

Ekaterina left the job and found a new one immediately, describing it as follows:

> There I also had minimum salary, but I could use the opportunity of having the employer pay my student loan. At the same time, I received 10% extra for knowing 3 foreign languages and using them in my work. And of course, I was influenced by the fact that this was a state institution, prestigious, and I personally felt proud to work in such a place. I worked for 2.5 years, during that time I received a certificate of honour and my salary was raised a bit, it was no longer the minimum. I felt very good, I was useful to people and my work was valued in the institution.

Initially, she speaks of herself as an employee without explicit references to any category except age, suggesting that it was the impatience of young age that triggered her to ask for a pay rise, not the unjust conditions in which she was working. Such self-presentation suggests that she devalues herself as a worker, which is also evident in her not contesting the manager for paying her the minimum salary unofficially, instead seeing blame in her own lack of experience. Despite earning a low salary in the second job, she feels valued there. She does not see gender as a factor influencing her treatment by employers. Ethnicity is explicitly missing from this account too, however, the fact that Ekaterina emphasises the pride she felt for working in a 'prestigious' Estonian state institution, suggests that with this she is responding to, and wants to resist, the prevalent metanarrative in the Estonian public discourse, according to which members of the Russian-speaking minority might not always be loyal to the Estonian state. The issue of economic status is also implicitly present in this narrative, in her mention of paying back the student loan as an important factor in preferring one job to another.

The turning point, which led to a decline in her career path, is divorce from her husband, and moving out of his apartment. As a single mother she was no longer able to manage with the salary. Her negotiations with the employer about a raise failed, and she quit the job, finding a new job in a private company, followed by another rise and fall:

> I rented an apartment, enrolled my child in the kindergarten and did my work. It seemed that my life was going well and everything worked out. /.../. The trial period of 4 months passed quickly. I liked my new job, my great colleagues and the prestig-

> ious reputation of the company. As soon as I finished the trial period, I asked for a pay rise, but as a result of this, they started pressuring me – they wouldn't raise my salary, but added more work, and demanded that I work faster, and that if I wanted additional payment, I should work more /…/. To get X amount in brut, I would have had to work 300 hours per month. You understand that as a single parent with a small child, it is not possible to work like this. Also, they started to point out some grammatical mistakes and to fine me for this. I think these accusations were unfounded.

Ekaterina refers to impossible demands from her employer, emphasising how these demands put her at a disadvantage as the primary caregiver of her small child. She mentions her financial need as a single parent as a justification for a raise. She does not refer to her gender but, interestingly, uses the word 'parent', instead of 'mother'. Ethnicity is also present in this story, as she feels unjustly treated by her employer due to not speaking Estonian as a mother tongue.

Currently, Ekaterina is unemployed and has moved to the countryside to live with her mother, continuing to look for work via the EUIF. She sees her current location in a rural area as one of the main obstacles in getting a job:

> I live with my mother in a small rural area, there are no jobs around here. A trip to Tallinn (60 km one way, that is 120 km there and back), you have to have a personal car, because the first bus going to Tallinn that passes our village leaves at 9.30! Which employer wants an employee who turns up at work at noon. And the last bus leaves the city at 18.20. You need at least 250 Euros per month for fuel, plus you need to buy the vehicle and it needs maintenance, changing of tires, etc. Thus, if I am being offered a job with the minimum salary of 290 Euros, I am not able to accept this offer.

Rather than saying that she deserves a salary larger than the minimum because she is worth it as an educated and competent employee, she refers to a practical need that she elaborately justifies, just as in the previous story she emphasised the need for a larger salary because of her status as a single parent.

At the same time she refers to structural factors as causing her situation and blames the EUIF and the general labour market situation:

> Every time I come to the EUIF, the service person makes a sour face, checking what I have managed to find in one month and what replies I got [from employers]. If I haven't found any job ad in one month, I am a bad person, therefore I am not looking for work and I should not be registered as unemployed. It is not my fault that my field occupies such as small niche in the labour market and there is no demand for such specialists. If I arrive [at the EUIF] half an hour earlier, it's my mistake. If I'm a bit late, they threaten to delete me from the database of the unemployed. But I cannot always come at the right time, sometimes the bus is late, or sometimes my good neighbour takes me to the city and back by car, when it's convenient for her.

> Psychologically, this is very depressing. I asked for training opportunities, if it's possible to study something extra and thereby to increase my competitiveness on the labour market. The EUIF replied to me that they don't have money.

While gender is not present in these stories, in another part of the interview, she explicitly problematises gender inequality in the labour market, implicitly seeing this as one of the reasons for her situation. She does not refer to a personal experience, but rather to a general pattern that she has observed:

> I have noticed that if a man and a woman with the same education and age apply for a job, employers prefer to hire the man. It is not he who stays home with sick children, he won't take parental leave, and there is no need to find a replacement employee. Also, about the salary – if a male jobseeker asks a 1200 euro salary when applying for the position of a specialist, this is considered normal, whereas if it's a woman, the employers are staring their eyes out.

To summarise, the factors that Ekaterina sees as contributing to her current difficulties in the labour market are: unfair treatment by labour market institutions, her ethnic identity, location in the rural area, divorce from her husband and being a single mother.

Narratives of ethnicity-based exclusion in the labour market

The participants often brought up issues of ethnic and/or linguistic identity in presenting their career paths, and rationalising their current labour market situation. In this section, I focus on how ethnicity-based exclusion is articulated and identify how the broader cultural and institutional context is reflected in the narratives.

The participants refer to, and often construct, their identities as workers in response to two metanarratives, or mechanisms of exclusion that they see as operating in the Estonian labour market. While the first of these is explicitly articulated in the stories, the second appears more implicitly.

Exclusion from Estonian-speaking workplaces and networks

Significantly, and perhaps, counter-intuitively, at first glance, several participants explicitly indicated their desire to find employment in an Estonian-speaking workplace, as opposed to a Russian-speaking one. First, working in an Estonian-speaking workplace would help to improve Estonian language skills, as Julia (41) points out:

> It is very difficult for a Russian person to find a job in an Estonian-speaking workplace. I think that if I found work in an Estonian-speaking workplace, then I would

> learn to speak Estonian faster... /.../ and I think it's a big problem that they [Estonian-speaking employers] don't take... [Russian-speakers].

Julia, like several other participants, who speak good Estonian, lacks confidence in her Estonian language skills which, along with her perception that Russian-speakers are not welcome in Estonian-speaking workplaces, might be one of the reasons why she indicates her willingness to accept less skilled positions than her qualification merits, willing to work as a secretary or manager's assistant. The second reason depends on how several participants construct Estonians and Russians as having different mentalities in the context of work, as expressed by Oksana (58):

> I am always saying that I have never been, and will never go, to work in a Russian-speaking workplace. /.../ I just know the Russians, I know them more, for them, everything is based on emotions, they could just say to you NO, just because they have bad mood and tomorrow they can say to you YES, just because they are in good mood /.../ and this affects work in a negative way. With Estonians, it is much more concrete. It's like that.

One of the reasons why several participants prefer to work in an Estonian-speaking workplace might be their wish to be accepted, and included, in the Estonian society, in the context of work and as citizens more generally. One way to express this is to differentiate themselves from 'other Russian-speakers', and present themselves as 'desirable' workers by identifying with the image they construct of Estonians as employees.

In the Estonian public discourse, the Russian minority is constructed as 'other' – as oppositional to Estonians and the 'Estonian ethnic identity'. The narratives of the participants are a reaction to this prevailing metanarrative, as they emphasise how Estonia is their home, construct themselves as culturally different from Russians in Russia, speak about their preference to find a job in an Estonian-speaking workplace, and their efforts to learn Estonian and teach it to their children, which suggests that they wish to be considered citizens with equal rights and opportunities in Estonia.

Despite the articulated desire to be employed in Estonian-speaking workplaces, several participants feel that they are not welcome there, as is evident from the statement made by Julia, but also others. Anna (50) describes the result of her last job interview as follows:

> They invited me and made an interview with me and then they decided that well... she... well... when they saw that I speak Estonian like a Russian, it became clear to them that I am Russian... and I think there were many people who wanted that

> job... and of course they would take someone who...speaks Estonian. Well, an Estonian.

It should be noted here that both Anna's surname and family name are Estonian. Anna sees not getting this job as having to do with her Russian ethnic and linguistic identity, which was 'discovered' at the interview by the employer. Although she speaks very good Estonian, she too is critical of her Estonian language skills, and embarrassed about her accent, which she perceives as an obstacle for getting employed.

Similarly, Svetlana (49), when explaining why she has not worked as a lawyer, in the field she has studied, refers to ethnicity-based barriers as well as established networks present in this field:

> I tried [to work in this field]. I mean, one thing, which is immediately obvious, is that you have a long surname. And second, I can say this out loud, if you don't have acquaintances, if you don't interact with this group.. I mean they created some lawyers' club in 93 or 97 or something /.../ then it is impossible for you to enter.

As the meaning 'a long surname' was not clear to me, I asked her to elaborate on this later in the interview and she confirmed that she was referring to the recognisability of Russian names, and the possible disadvantage she thinks this might create for Russian-speakers in the Estonian society.

The fact that she used the expression 'a long name' for the first time without further explanation, may indicate that she is referring to a certain common or shared understanding in the Russian community in Estonia about ethnicity-based barriers in the labour market. In this case, it became evident that I, as an 'outsider' who has not experienced ethnic discrimination in the labour market, did not share this common understanding and had to ask for her clarifications to understand what she meant.

In their work on gender and ethnicity based segregation in the British labour market, Clarke *et al.* (2003) point out that 'recruitment and promotion are very much based on informal networks', especially in some sectors. This is also true for the Estonian labour market, where non-Estonians' weaker and fewer social networks, compared to the majority nationality, have been cited among the causes of the marginalisation of minorities in the labour market (Marksoo and Järv 2008: 18; Krusell 2007). Krusell (2007: 2) suggests that higher unemployment among minorities may be the result of intra-network processes, as non-Estonians are 'likely to have less knowledge about the work opportunities available in the wider labour market'. Krusell (2007: 7) concludes that 'the differences in pay and occupational position can also be explained in part by segregated networks'. The category of gender is also important in the context of networks, as men are more likely to find jobs via social networks than women in Estonia (Jeenas 2011). Networks based on gender and ethnicity simultaneously (such as the political and business elite in Estonia, consisting almost exclusively of ethnic Estonian men), might operate to exclude other groups from resources of power.

When speaking about ethnicity-based exclusion, it is important to consider the historical context and changes in the labour market position of Russian-speakers. The narratives of the older participants suggest that the intersections of social categories began to increasingly shape the work paths and lives of the participants, starting from the time of the restoration of the Republic of Estonia in 1991, and the transition to market economy. The narrative of Olga that I presented earlier about the loss of her job in the bank is a good example of this.

In stories where participants referred to ethnicity-based exclusion, other categories of identity were usually missing, and ethnicity was given priority as the only category shaping these experiences. This prioritisation of ethnicity and simultaneous exclusion of other categories of difference from these narratives, is a good example of how the participants typically see one category at a time as shaping their experiences in particular contexts, while exclusion of other categories, such as gender, is obscured. I discuss possible reasons for this in the concluding section of this chapter.

Gendered and ethnicised ideal worker for unskilled jobs

The narratives point to implicit gendered and ethnicised assumptions shared by labour market institutions, and in society at large. More specifically, participants refer to the implicit expectation of either EUIF, or employers, that the participants should be willing to accept menial jobs for a very low salary, regardless of their educational qualifications. When encountering these assumptions, participants use different strategies to challenge these expectations.

One of the most interesting examples of this is Marina's (35) and Olga's (55) experiences of communicating with EUIF officials:

> The psychologist in the club for the unemployed told me that if I want to work, for instance, in a shop, I should not write in my CV that I have higher education /.../. If the job is simple, as they say in the EUIF, then employers don't want higher education... Too smart [laughs]... and want too much, they perhaps thought. And that's why she said that we shouldn't write such things like higher education.
>
> Well, the EUIF suggested that I go to work in a laundry service... /.../ to clean some dirty laundry or something. The payment was 1 euro 70 cents. I said no thank you... /.../. This was the hourly wage.

This account and other similar narratives of my participants suggest that Russian-speaking women in Estonia might be considered 'ideal workers' (Williams 2001, Acker 2006) for the unskilled jobs (many of which do not require significant Estonian language skills) that they have been offered, such as shop-assistant, cleaner, cook's assistant, seamstress, *etc*. It is important to note that, besides being gendered and ethnicised, this image of the 'ideal worker' in these particular jobs, has an educational, as well as, age aspect that usually means older Russian-speaking women with lower educational levels are preferred in these jobs.

However, the participants do not themselves articulate the idea that they are being marginalised by labour market institutions as *Russian-speaking women*. Rather, they speak of themselves as *individuals* without referring to social categories, which could be an example of internalisation of the prevalent individualist discourse in the Estonian society.

The narratives of dealing with labour market institutions, and the statements and attitudes about them, are indicative of (mostly implicit) ways in which these institutions are implicated in creating, and sustaining, their disadvantaged labour market position.

Strategies for coping with employment-related difficulties and exclusion

While there are several common strategies that the participants use to cope with difficulties in the labour market, significant differences emerge depending on whether the participant has accepted/is willing to accept an unskilled job or not. Following either of these paths produces somewhat different subsequent strategies, and discursive justifications. While this might be considered a choice, it is an intersectional one, and strongly influenced by the economic situation of the participants and other factors, such as age, or being a single mother. In addition to these two paths, a third option that the participants used was to seek temporary semi-skilled employment, e.g., as a census official, which gives temporary income and social security. I illustrate the first two paths by two cases, both of which feature strategies that the participants use.

Tatyana

When presenting her younger self in her previous jobs as electrical engineer, the field she had specialised in, Tatyana (62) highlights her knowledge and skills. However, she emphasises that with age she has become less confident in her abilities. Due to this, as well as for other reasons she mentions (problems with her husband, health issues *etc*.), she no longer feels she is able to work as electrical engineer. She talks about several unskilled jobs she has held in the last few years, such as salesperson in a kiosk, manager's assistant, *etc*. At the time of the interview, she was working as dishwasher and cook's assistant (the salary is paid to her unofficially), and presents herself in this job as follows:

> This grating and peeling is a normal work, it's quiet. You sit, if you don't want to stand, and you peel. Well, you need to peel a lot, but they have special knives which enable you to do it very quickly… and so I learned this work… well, I didn't use to do it so much, I mean how much do you peel at home… But there… the owner was satisfied that I work so fast and he is saying that I'm a real professional here. And then I compared myself with an ad on TV where they showed how to peel carrots and I thought, I am not slower than this… So yes, this is easy work for me, no one comments or demands to do it faster or something like this. So, very normal work, for an old hag like me. And I… [laughs] I… try to somehow live with this money.

This narrative suggests that although she has resorted to unskilled work, she tries to cope with this situation, by attempting to maintain her dignity by presenting herself as a valuable and loyal worker in this job.

In this account, Tatyana refers to the intersection of categories of gender and age, using the expression 'old hag'. She does not mention ethnicity here. However, the wider institutional and cultural settings, which often construct Russian-speaking women as ideal workers for menial jobs for minimum salaries, regardless of their educational qualifications and experience, as outlined in the previous section, could be taken into account when interpreting this story. This account suggests that Tatyana has internalised these expectations and constructs her current self as suitable for this work. It appears quite often in the stories of the participants that they frequently underestimate either their professional competencies, or Estonian language skills, and, therefore, construct themselves as unsuitable for more demanding jobs, and thus are willing to accept unskilled work, if necessitated by their economic situation.

Anna

The second case is the story of Anna (50), who is unemployed, but in contrast to Tatyana, resists accepting unskilled jobs. She is confident about her professional knowledge and skills in accounting and finance, and emphasises this, but is at the same time unsure about her Estonian language skills, and sees this- her ethnicity and her age- as the main obstacles for not getting a suitable job.

One of the strategies she uses is to attempt to increase her competences in her field, in order to improve her chances of suitable employment. She attends further training courses, is active in online job portals, and frequently sends out her CV. These two strategies frequently used by the participants are also strongly promoted by the EUIF, which focuses on the unemployed as a 'problem group', whose competences should be improved for them to become more 'desirable' for employers. Anna, like many other participants, emphasises asking for specific training courses from the EUIF on her own initiative, and presents herself as a hardworking person, and an active job seeker.

Another major strategy that she uses is attempting to set up her own company. At the time of the interview, she had just submitted an application for EU support for new businesses and was waiting for the response. She presents setting up her own accounting company as a response to not being wanted by the employers, despite her knowledge and experience. Also, she refers to formal requirements she needs to fulfil to be able to work as an accountant, and feels that setting up her own company would help meetings these:

> I am [registered] in CV Centre [online job-seeking portal] and I was all the time reading [job offers]..and sending [CV], because I have such a CV that I myself would like to hire myself [laughs]. Well, I think all of them see how many years I have, I am already old [laughs]... everyone wants young ones.
>
> The law requires that I have bookkeeping software [for doing accounting work], but I am not able to buy it because it's too expensive /.../ I'm setting up my own company, because the euro [EU] helps people who want, and who can, do things, but don't have money [laughs] /.../ I asked from my consultant [in the EUIF] if I can submit this business project, she said yes you can do it, you have everything necessary... you have the education, experience of being a board member /.../, training courses, entrepreneurship courses, you can do this /.../ So I am waiting for their response, if there is positive response, then I will open my company and buy this bookkeeping software, because there are companies who want to, and are waiting to [use my services].

In this account, Anna refers to her age as an obstacle to employment, which drives her to seek self-employment. This self-presentation is typical among my participants, as they rarely refer to more than one category at a time when speaking of their labour market situation, and strategies to cope with difficulties, or if they do, they speak of these separately, and do not see them as intertwined.

Compared to Tatyana, Anna has the advantage of being 12 years younger and also, her field of accounting and finance, compared to Tatyana's specialty of electrical engineering, is more relevant in today's labour market. These factors are likely to influence the two participants' self-presentations and coping strategies.

Discussion and Conclusions

The analysis suggests that due to restricted opportunities, and the disadvantaged conditions in which they exert their agency in the labour market, it is difficult to speak of lifestyle choices in the case of this group of Russian-speaking women.

In rationalising their current situation in the labour market, the participants place a different degree of responsibility for their situation on themselves and external circumstances. While some participants more explicitly problematise external institutional and cultural factors, others mostly refer to internal factors, and see themselves as problematic, appealing to individual responsibility for their situation. I illustrated common strategies that the participants use to cope with difficulties in the labour market, based on two cases, which differed depending on whether or not the individual had accepted an unskilled job. These cases suggest that the intersection of categories, such as age and educational qualifications/occupational field, might play a role in how participants present themselves and their coping strategies – older age and acquired education/profession that is less relevant in the contemporary labour market, compared to the Soviet period, might produce a less confident self-presentation.

In interpreting individual narratives it is useful, as Bowleg (2008: 320) suggests, to view them 'within a larger sociohistorical context of structural inequality that may not be explicit or directly observable in the data'. Locating the narratives in a specific social and historical context helps to understand why participants might articulate certain categories more explicitly than others. As Yuval-Davis (2006: 203) notes: 'in specific historical situations and in relation to specific people there are some social divisions that are more important than others in constructing specific positionings'. I have attempted to do this in locating the narratives within the context of the contemporary Estonian labour market and wider cultural and social structures as well as outlining metanarratives that reproduce and sustain inequalities and/or privilege for certain groups.

An important focus in the narratives is on ethnicity-based exclusion that the participants perceive, and express, both explicitly and implicitly, referring to difficulties in being accepted to Estonian-speaking workplaces. More implicitly, the narratives refer to certain gendered and ethnicised shared assumptions, or metanarratives, about suitable jobs for Russian-speaking women in the Estonian labour market. In these narratives of exclusion, the participants most often prioritise one category of difference, and appeal to their ethnic identity. However, in other contexts, for example, when talking about suggestions that they should accept unskilled jobs, they speak of themselves as individuals, not constructing themselves in terms of categories of difference.

In thinking why ethnicity is prioritised over other categories of difference in the narratives, it is useful to consider that social categories have different ontological bases, 'as each prioritises a different sphere of social relations' (Yuval-Davis 2006; Verloo 2006), different origins and mechanisms of reproducing inequality (Verloo 2006). Thus, it is important to understand how particular categories are constructed in a given social context. One of the reasons why gender as a category is often explicitly missing from the narratives of my participants, while ethnicity is much more explicitly articulated might have to do with how 'compared to gender and sexual orientation, class and race/ethnicity are represented as more firmly located in the public sphere, in the spheres of citizenship and employment' (Verloo 2006: 218). In the Estonian context, ethnicity is a more politicised category in prevailing metanarratives, compared to gender and age, as discrimination on these latter grounds might be seen as more 'natural'. Ethnicity in the Estonian public discourse is certainly a tension-filled topic and, as such, it is more available as a source of critique to my participants compared to other categories.

One category that was articulated both explicitly, as well as implicitly, in the narratives was age. It was identified, along with ethnicity, by several older participants as the primary source of disadvantage in the labour market. However, this factor, intersected with gender, also shaped the narratives of younger participants who spoke of childcare responsibilities negatively impacting their careers. Furthermore, it seems that with increasing age, several participants felt less secure about their professional competence, which affected their self-presentations.

One of the categories least explicitly mentioned in the narratives was gender, as none of my participants explicitly state that their gender might be one of the factors that keep them from finding (good) jobs. However, gender is often implicitly present in narratives of difficulties in the labour market, and coping with these as well as when participants mention jobs that they are ready to accept. Even if these are not unskilled jobs, they are often below the educational qualifications of the participants, and clearly gendered, such as secretary or assistant to the manager, overwhelmingly populated by women, and underpaid. Thus, they rarely challenge the 'hegemonic metanarrative' (Dahl and Thor 2009: 7) according to which the ideal worker (Williams 2001, Acker 2006) in these jobs is a Russian-speaking woman.

There are several possible reasons why gender is not explicitly articulated, while much more attention is paid to other categories, such as ethnicity. One of these reasons might be the participants' perception of their positioning vis-à-vis me as the interviewer – while they might have constructed themselves similar to me in terms of gender, they differentiated themselves on the basis of ethnicity, and perhaps felt the need to (re)present themselves to me primarily as *Russian-speaking citizens* not as *Russian-speaking women*. Another reason that the category of gender was obscured in the narratives might have to do with the legacy of the Soviet period, when, especially in the work context, citizens were constructed as genderless 'comrades'. Although gender inequalities, including, and perhaps even especially, in the context of work, have received more coverage in the public discourse since Estonia joined the EU, this has not translated into how the participants view themselves as workers, and see their opportunities in the labour market. In addition, the Russian-speaking community in Estonia has been found to embrace a more conservative gender ideology compared to the Estonian population (Kasearu 2011), which might make it harder for Russian-speaking women to identify gender as a source of discrimination.

An explanation as to why people do not often explicitly refer to categories of difference, but speak of themselves as individuals, is offered by Chase (1995) who distinguishes two discursive realms in work narratives. The first is that of professional work, where the focus is on the individual. However, in the second discursive realm, that of inequality, 'persons are identified primarily as members of some race, class, or gender group in talk about inequality' (Chase 1995: 20-21). 'Within the discursive realm of professional work, competent and ambitious persons achieve as individuals, not as men, women, whites, Hispanics, or Blacks' (Chase 1995: 19). Despite numerous studies by feminist scholars demonstrating that 'seemingly neutral discourse is often gendered and racialised' (*ibid.*), this has not transformed the use of professional discourse.

It seems that the discursive disjunction outlined by Chase is characteristic also of the narratives of the participants, as they often present their professional lives and work-related efforts in individualistic ways, while appealing to group membership (most often their ethnic identity as members of the Russian-speaking minority) only when talking about perceived inequalities, such as exclusion in the labour market. In the Estonian society, metanarratives that highlight individual achievement in the public sphere, as opposed to appealing to group-identity, are widespread; this might further contribute to the lack of references to categories of difference in the work narratives. According to this prevailing narrative, stemming from neoliberal ideology in contemporary Estonia, everyone has equal opportunities to succeed and if they do not, they are to blame. This narrative usually obscures inequalities based on categories of difference and their intersections that shape people's lives and are likely to create advantages and/or disadvantages for individuals in particular contexts. It is possible that the participants' self-perceptions and consequent narratives are influenced by this prevailing metanarrative.

Another issue that emerges from the data is the tendency to refer to one social division at a time when discussing disadvantage in the labour market, or sometimes to refer to several categories separately, without articulating intersections between them. Thus, my participants do not see their experiences being shaped by intersections of social categories. Certain identities, most notably ethnicity, prevailed (Barat and Sungun 2012: 113).

As the narratives suggest, the participants often devalue themselves as competent workers, and doubt their Estonian-language skills, despite actually having good educational and professional qualifications, and Estonian skills. Their low self-esteem as employees, the mainly ethnicity-based exclusion they perceive in the labour market, and their internalisation of individualist values, is likely to influence their self-perception as citizens, and might reinforce divisions between the Estonian-speaking and Russian-speaking populations in Estonia, and, consequently, hinder successful integration.

References

Acker, J. (2006). 'Inequality Regimes Gender, Class and Race in Organizations'. *Gender and Society*, 20 (4): 441-464.

Bagilhole, B. (2009). 'For Diversity Against Discrimination: From Gender Mainstreaming, through Multiple Discrimination, to Intersectionality'. Franken, M. *et al.* (eds). *Teaching Intersectionality: Putting Gender at the Centre.* ATHENA3 Advanced Thematic Network in Women's Studies in Europe. University of Utrecht and Centre for Gender Studies, Stockholm University.

Barat, E. and Sungun, E. (2012). 'The French Ban on Headscarves: Rendering Racism Respectable'. Hipfl, B. and Loftsdottir, K. (eds). *Teaching "Race" with a Gendered Edge.* ATGENDER, The European Association for Gender Research, Education and Documentation, Utrecht, Central European University Press, Budapest-New York.

Bowleg, L. (2008). 'When Black + Lesbian + Woman ≠ Black Lesbian Woman: The Methodological Challenges of Qualitative and Quantitative Intersectionality Research'. *Sex Roles*, 59: 312-325.

Chase, S. (1995). *Ambiguous Empowerment: The Work Narratives of Women School Superintendents*. Amherst: University of Massachusetts Press.

Choo, H. Y. and Ferree, M. M. (2010). 'Practicing Intersectionality in Sociological Research: A Critical Analysis of Inclusions, Interactions, and Institutions in the Study of Inequalities'. *Sociological Theory*, 28 (2): 129-148.

Dahl, I. and Thor, M. (2009). 'Oral history, constructions and deconstructions of narratives: Intersections of class, gender, locality, nation and religion in narratives from a Jewish woman in Sweden'. *ENQUIRE*, 3.

Davis, K. (2008). 'Intersectionality as buzzword: A sociology of science perspective on what makes a feminist theory successful'. *Feminist Theory*, 9 (67): 67-85.

Eurostat (2009).*The unadjusted gender pay gap 2009.* http://epp.eurostat.ec.europa.eu/ (January 10, 2010).

Hancock, A. M. (2007). 'When Multiplication Doesn't Equal Quick Addition: Examining Intersectionality as a Research Paradigm'. *Perspectives on Politics,* 5 (1): 63-79.

Hansson, L. and Aavik, K. (2012). 'The effect of gender and ethnicity and their intersection on work satisfaction and earnings in Estonia, 1993-2008'.*Studies of Transition States and Societies,* 4 (2): 3-19.

Jeenas, P. (2011). Töökoha leidmine sotsiaalsete võrgustike abil: meeste ja naiste erinevused Eesti tööjõu-uuringu tulemuste põhjal [Finding a job through social networks: differences between men and women]. *Ariadne Lõng,* 1/2.

Kasearu, K. (2011). Individuaalnesooideoloogia – millest see sõltub? [What does individual gender ideology depend on?]. *Ariadne Lõng,* 1/2.

Krusell, S. (2007).'Noorte eestlaste ja mitteeestlaste tööturupositsioonid' ['A comparison of the respective labour market positions of Estonian and Non-Estonian young people']. Purju, A. (Ed.). *Sotsiaaltrendid* 4: 56-62. Eesti Statistikaamet [Statistics Estonia].

Lykke, N. (2010). *Feminist Studies. A guide to Intersectional Theory, Methodology and Writing.* New York, London: Routledge.

Lykke, N. (2010).'Theorising Intersectionalities. Geneologies and Blind Spots'. Lykke, N., *Feminist Studies: a Guide to Intersectional Theory, Methodology and Writing.* New York: Routledge, 67-86.

Marksoo, Ü. and Järv, K. (2008). 'Risk Groups of the Labour Market.Marksoo', Ü (Ed.). *Employment and Working Life in Estonia 2007.* Series of the Ministry of Social Affairs 5/2008 eng, 10-18.

McCall, L. (2005). 'The Complexity of Intersectionality'.*Signs*, 30 (3): 1771-1800.

Padamsee, T. J. (2009). 'Culture in Connection: Re-Contextualizing Ideational Processes in the Analysis of Policy Development'. *Social Politics: International Studies in Gender, State and Society*, 16 (4): 413-445.

Riessman, C. K. (2005). 'Narrative Analysis'. Riessman, C. K., *Narrative, Memory and Everyday Life.* Huddersfield: University of Huddersfield, 1-7.

Riessman, C. K. (2008). *Narrative Methods for the Human Sciences.* Los Angeles, London, New Delhi, Singapore: SAGE Publications.

Sclater, S. D. (2003). 'What is the subject?' *Narrative Inquiry,* 13 (2): 317-330.

Scott, J. (1991). 'The Evidence of Experience'. *Critical Inquiry*, 17 (4): 773-797.

Shields, S. A. (2008). 'Gender: An Intersectionality Perspective'. *Sex Roles*, 59: 301-311.

Somers, M. (1994). 'The Narrative constitution of identity: A relational and network approach'. *Theory and Society,* 23: 605-649.

Sotsiaalministeerium (2010). *Soolise võrdõiguslikkuse monitoring 2009. Uuringuraport.* [*Gender Equality Monitor 2009. Research Report*]. Sotsiaalministeeriumi toimetised 1/2010.

Statistics Estonia (2010). *Equalised Yearly Disposable Income By Ethnic Nationality And Sex.*

Statistics Estonia (2012). *Gender pay gap by economic activity.*

Verloo, M. (2006). 'Multiple Inequalities, Intersectionality and the European Union'. *European Journal of Women's Studies*, 13 (3): 221-228.

Williams, J. (2001). *Unbending Gender: Why Family and Work Conflict and What To Do About It.* Oxford, New York: Oxford University Press.

Yuval-Davis, N. (2006). 'Intersectionality and Feminist Politics'. *European Journal of Women's Studies,* 13: 193.

Just how political is the personal? Estonian eco-village activism as lifestyle and as life politics

Airi-Alina Allaste, Mikko Lagerspetz

Lifestyle in a late modern society

In his *Modernity and Self-Identity*, Anthony Giddens (1991) sketches a portrait of what he calls late modernity – a social order characteristic of the industrialised Western world of today. It is born out of the modernisation processes, not through a rupture, but as a logical continuation of previous developments. A crucial precondition of modernity was systematic and critical reasoning, which cast doubt on the sureties of tradition and habit (*ibid.*: 2). But whereas modernity started as a rationalising process, an Enlightenment, it may now be seen as having turned its inspecting gaze towards itself; late modernity is characterised by reflexivity, which also questions the modernity's foundations, its faith in rationality and progress. This points to an internal contradiction within the modernisation project, which has of course already been observed by numerous thinkers both before and after Giddens. Late modernity has, then, not replaced tradition with the certitude of rational knowledge, but rather with a consciousness of a constant need to make numerous, ultimately subjective choices between a 'puzzling diversity of options and possibilities' (Giddens 1991: 3). This applies to both the political and economic decision-making at various levels, and individuals who face the challenge of constructing a self-identity through moral, lifestyle, and consumption choices. At the same time unpredictable risk factors, which originate from global trends, affect all strata and may render the planned individual strategies impossible. For certainty and predictability, people turn to authorities, such as the expert systems, but also ideologies and social movements. Different social movements have strengthened their position by taking initiative in defining the risks and offering solutions to them (Beck 1992).

Late modernity's urgency of lifestyle choices brings forward a change in politics. Giddens (1991: 210) conceptualises the change as a movement from *emancipatory politics* to *life politics*. Emancipatory politics, which has resulted in the creation of the modern capitalist welfare state, is concerned with freeing the individual from oppression or patronage, be it by religion, tradition, upper classes, or a rigid gender system. The essence of that type of politics has not, according to Giddens, been guidance in moral or lifestyle choices, but to give the individual the autonomy that is needed in order to enable those choices in the first place. He cites theorists such as Marx, Rawls and Habermas as examples of those who expressed the ideas of emancipatory politics. Giddens rightly points out, that they have set as their goal to state the *forms and ruling principles* of a just social order, but not the *substance* of choices made by individuals within that order. The latter is, however, the central essence of life politics. Life politics is no more about the conditions of individual freedom and autonomy, but a politics about the values guiding our choices once we have reached the possibility of making them.

> The necessity of life politics arises, above all, from global issues. The foremost example of the interconnection between the global and the private is about the environment. Our chances of minimising global ecological risks are dependent on lifestyle changes in the industrialised world: Lifestyles based on an expectation of never-ending economic growth should be substituted by a 'cultivation of potentialities for self-expression and creativity' (Giddens 1991: 223).

The view on the contemporary world sketched above leaves many questions open. On one hand, late modernity appears to be a social order in which common values and norms disappear, leaving after them almost a state of anomie, in which atomised individuals struggle in order to make sense of their lives – and do it through their lifestyle choices, rather than by political participation. On the other hand, these lifestyle choices should be of a certain kind in order to save the planet – and all this should be reached by life politics. Giddens suggests that life-political issues (such as decisions concerning nuclear power) will acquire greater and greater importance in institutional politics. However, the mechanism that transforms lifestyle choices into elements of political agenda is left vague:

> Several movements have played a basic role in bringing life-political issues to the fore, and forcing them on public attention. *Whether such movements are harbingers of organisational changes in the domains of political activity is a moot question.* /…/ Life-political problems do not fit readily within existing frameworks of politics, and *may well* stimulate the emergence of political forms which differ from those hitherto prominent, both within states and on a global level (Giddens 1991: 226-228; our italics).

Critics have pointed out, that the view of individul citizens that Giddens presents in this, and other writings, discussing the 'third way' may be unduly optimistic (Rojek 2001: 123). Among other things, he does not consider the importance of media as socialising agencies, or the impact of their undemocratic control (Mouzelis 2001: 452). Objections of this kind are related to a more general criticism of his notion of life politics. According to Mouzelis (*ibid.*), its continuity with emancipatory politics should not be underestimated: It can be seen as a broadening of the latter's rights discourse to include not only civil, political and socio-economic, but also cultural rights (such as the right to define one's identity). Consequently, it will need to confront the macrostructures of modern capitalism in ways not dissimilar to previous emancipatory struggles.

In our view, efforts at alternative lifestyles 'may well' remain isolated from political activity, maybe changing individual lives radically, but without any chance of influencing the arenas where decisions are made on taxation, environmental norms and planning, energy politics, trade policies, *etc.* – decisions necessary for lifestyle changes on any large national, regional or global scale. By joining together in alternative lifestyle communities, people make efforts at building 'islands of freedom' in the middle of the capitalist consumer society. The question is whether one would expect that these islands would be in strategic contact with each other, to jointly form an archipelago, and later perhaps a new continent – *i.e.*, whether and by what means they can initiate major changes in society's values and practices as a whole (*cf.* Hirsch 1980: 180). The efforts at building alternative communities inside capitalist societies are, on one hand, a reaction against such phenomena as large-scale unemployment, destruction of nature and cities, alienation and consumerism; they are ways of experimenting with new forms of work, social organisation and political participation (*ibid.*: 172f.). On the other hand, they risk becoming mere refuges in the margins of capitalism, compensating for its shortcomings, but, in this way, also watering down the possibilities for political and ideological protest (*ibid.*: 179). One can also perceive the alternative communities and their culture of resistance simply as channeling the resistance in a way that is harmless to the existing order (Heath and Potter 2006).

Dilemmas of this kind were debated among the Western European Leftist and Green movements in the 1970s and 1980s, but the questions posed are equally valid when discussing contemporary prospects of 'life politics'. In what ways can lifestyles become 'political'? The question is both theoretical and empirical. In this article we will describe and analyse the emergence and development of alternative lifestyle communities in Estonia. With this concept we refer here to collective efforts at creating social organisations and spaces, that consciously strive for ecological sustainability, non-hierarchical organisation, and intimacy among participants. They call themselves eco-villages (*ökokülad*). Our discussion is partly based on interviews and field work from 2008-2009 (see Allaste 2011). We begin however with a brief overview of the emergence and development of these initiatives; among other things we will discuss the ways in which they are embedded in the overall context of Estonia's post-socialist transformation. We will also point at some often forgotten similarities between the ideas of Western alternative movements of the 1970s and 1980s, and those of the Central European 'dissident' thinkers of the same period.[46]

The dream of a non-alienated society

Central and Eastern Europe's transition to democracy in the late 1980s and early 1990s did not only mean mechanically copying the democratic institutions of the West. From the point of view of our present discussion, two aspects are of specific interest. Firstly, the authoritarian Communist regime and its destruction of independent institutions caused both a popular distrust of the state and a reliance on informal networks in everyday life. Secondly, resistance against the Communist modernisation project found expression in a widespread nostalgia and, later on, in a view of the systemic change as 'a return' (Lagerspetz 1999). The political cultures of post-socialist countries are heavily influenced by anti-statism, anti-institutionalism, and anti-modernism, and these sentiments are also mirrored in the present interest for alternative lifestyles.

As many researchers have observed, several aspects of 'real socialist' societies were structured around informal networks (*e.g.*, Wedel 1990, Ledeneva 1998; Jensen and Miszlivetz 2006: 134f.). They displayed a peculiar mixture of resistance, autonomy, and system-compatible complementarity (see Benda and al. 1988). Some of the 'dissident' writers saw in them even a kind of embryo of new, non-alienated forms of governance (*e.g.*, Havel 1992 [1984]: 271). What has received less attention is the similarity between 'dissident' utopias of the 1980s and those of their contemporary social movements in the West (Lagerspetz 2001). Both were sensitive of environmental issues and critical of industrialisation and modernisation; in fact, the revolutions around 1989 were in several countries triggered by environmentalist protest. This was the case at least in Hungary, Bulgaria, Latvia and Estonia. In Estonia, a controversial plan of phosphorite mining led to the emergence of a large-scale environmental movement in 1987 (see Gerner and Hedlund 1993: 70). There are even more similarities. Importantly, the East Central European oppositionist thinkers put their hope in communities that are 'open, dynamic, and small', and based on 'values like trust, openness, responsibility, solidarity, love' (Havel 1992 [1978]: 210). The personal was linked to the political, but in a way that was contemptuous of what officially constituted politics. For Havel and his soul mates, the key to a non-alienated society was not the introduction of political institutions of the Western

46 As to the quotation marks, *cf.* Václav Havel's (1978/1992: 167-175) discussion of the term 'dissident' as the result of a stigmatization process.

type, but overcoming the divide between private and public morals. This anti-institutionalism is amazingly reminiscent of that of the new social movements in the West (Wainwright 2004: 106).

The systemic change of late 1980s - early 1990s in Central and Eastern Europe led both to the introduction of competitive multiparty systems and the abandonment of (a supposedly) planned economy in favour of market economy. Despite most of the previously 'real socialist' countries' ever deeper integration with Western Europe, some important differences remain. The popular legitimacy of institutional politics is constantly lower than in the 'old democracies' of the West; this conclusion can be drawn from a large number of surveys (Lagerspetz 2009). Also, citizens are less prone to participate in organised civic activities, such as voluntary associations or trade unions. As to the economic policies chosen, there is considerable variation between different Central and Eastern European countries. Estonia and Slovenia are sometimes depicted as representing the two opposite ends of a continuum from, respectively, a liberal-market and a corporatist welfare-state model (Adam, Kristan and Tomšič 2009). In Estonia, the policies pursued have led to a rising social inequality, while the social security system has not been able to effectively fight poverty and marginalisation. Despite changes in the ruling party coalitions, during the country's now 21 years of restored independence, the different government cabinets in office have consequently pursued neo-liberalist economic policies. There are, however, signs of popular disappointment and concern about the path chosen, evidenced by the success of Social Democrats in the 2011 parliamentary elections and in subsequent opinion polls.

One more note is needed about the specificities of Estonian pre-revolutionary oppositional thought. In Estonia (and in neighbouring Latvia and Lithuania), the overthrow of the Soviet regime also brought forward an ethnic-national liberation of the 'titular nationalities' of these Soviet republics. In them, the Soviet version of modernisation, urbanisation and industrialisation was carried out in a way that included a large inflow of employees from other Soviet republics. As a result, the industrialisation (as its most intensive, in the 1960s and 1970s) coincided with a rapid decline of the share of ethnic Estonians in the republic's population (from 88% in 1934 to 61% in 1989, according to population censuses). As a reaction, the anti-modernist sentiments typical of Central and Eastern European popular dissent, here combined a nostalgia of the period of independent statehood (1920-1940), with a view of rural life as genuinely Estonian.

The Eco-village Movement worldwide

The Estonian eco-village movement emerged nearly two decades after the regime change, and has been heavily influenced by foreign examples and by an international discourse. However, when ideas travel, their implementation often result in something quite different than expected, especially if the recipient society differs from the donor society with respect to values or other important structural conditions (Watson 2001: 199). We maintain that the specific focuses, forms, and practices adopted by Estonian eco-village movement can only be understood in the social, political, and cultural context discussed above. They have emerged in a meeting of an international discourse with the sounding-board of domestic values, habits and expectations, making some ideas resonate and some others not.

The global eco-village movement has its roots in the 1960s' resistance culture. New Age thinking inspired the founding of such, now well-known, eco-villages as Findhorn in Scotland, The Farm in the U.S., and Auroville in India. The term eco-village was coined in 1975 by *Mother Earth News,* an alternative U.S. magazine, and around the same time as *'Ökodorf'* in West Germany (Spada 2010: 35). The movement took more solid forms from 1987, when the Denmark-based Canadian businessman and environmentalist Ross Jackson initiated the foundation *Gaia Trust.* Jackson's and the foundation's purpose was to support an ecologically sustainable lifestyle. A report published by the foundation popularised the concept of eco-village, and described the already active villages (Gilman and Gilman 1991). They were applauded as 'lifestyle laboratories' supporting human spiritual growth, and a harmonious and sustainable relationship with nature. By disseminating their experiences, they could stand as a model for a new society. For this purpose, *Eco-villages' Global Network* (GEN) was founded in October 1995. It is divided into three regional networks, one of which operates in Europe. Information and experiences on how to proceed if one wants to establish an eco-village are, since 2000, being spread through a special training program, *Gaia Education*. The manual of the education program is free to download for everybody. As is stated in the manual, The Global Eco-village Network (GEN) believes the most promising and effective way to deal with [the challenges of our time] is through education – not a typical education, but a new kind of global education, specifically designed to meet the challenges and opportunities of the 21st century. This is an education where a thorough and objective assessment of the state of the planet is followed by regional, community, and place-based solutions (Gaia Education 2005:2-3).

Empirical Case Study –Eco-village Movement in Estonia

The article relies on 16 open-ended interviews conducted with Estonian activists in 2008-2009. Analyses of the interviews have been supported by participant observation and secondary analyses of literature. The first author participated in an eco-village community's (Lilleoru) winter camp in Estonia, attended meetings of the Union of Estonian Eco-communities, local Gaia education working groups, and a conference of the Global Network of Eco-villages. Background data also include secondary analyses of relevant written materials – homepage materials, the Gaia education handbook, books written by eco-village activists, and books commonly read by Estonian eco-villagers. The people interviewed were members of an existing eco-village or a network planning to establish one. Of the interviewees, seven were male and nine female, their age ranging between 23 and 64 years. Most of the people interviewed were in their early thirties, but some in their twenties and others in their fifties or sixties as well. Most of the interviewed activists had higher education and in many cases held (or had held and given up) a well-paid job. Two of the informants were inhabitants of the Lilleoru community.

According to the interviewees, in Estonia, people started experimenting with alternative communities already in the 1990s, the most famous being Lilleoru (*'Flower Valley'*) near Tallinn (the largest city in Estonia). Lilleoru was established in 1992 as a centre for practising yogic self-development techniques. At first, the community was mainly a *new age* centre and connections with the eco-village movement were established only in late 1990s, when the community was already an established open network of people sharing a common worldview. In a way, this repeats the early stages of the eco-village movement worldwide: already existing spiritual communities were united by the ideas and networks of eco-villages. As many community members living elsewhere would have preferred to live in Lilleoru, in 2004, designing of the buildings for living started, and many houses have been inhabited by now. The number of people actually living there is around 20; approx. 60 are registered members of the association and visit the location frequently. People involved in the wider community (60) have very different background concerning age (from very young to 70 years old), education (from primary education to PhD degrees), and occupation (clerks, businessmen, academics, art-related professions, labourers). Today, the estimated number of community members who do not visit Lilleoru every week, but still visit it periodically, is around 200, but the total number of visitors of different events in Lilleoru exceeds this number by far. Since 2006, Lilleoru has been a full member of the Global Eco-village Network.

According to the interviewees, with the exception of Lilleoru, the eco-village movement has developed since the mid-2000s. Estonian eco-village enthusiasts started participating in the European GEN meetings and visited eco-villages in other countries. They were encouraged by their experiences and started to form networks for establishment of eco-villages in Estonia. A gathering of five eco-village enthusiasts took place at Lilleoru in 2005, and the first larger-scale gathering took place in 2006. The Estonian Eco-villages' Association (Eesti Ökokogukondade Liit, see www.kogukonnad.ee) was formed in 2008. The Association is a member of GEN and has received operating funding from, among others, SIDA, and the Open Estonia Foundation funded by George Soros. The Association's journal is published four times a year.

The Association's web site states, that it brings together 'members of either existing or prospective eco-villages with registered associations and individuals working for similar goals.' They are required to support the 'environment conservation, sustainable living, cooperation and personal growth, or have an interest in it.' Based on interviews and participant observation, the people involved in eco-village movement in Estonia could be divided into two groups – the visionaries and the adaptors. These categories are ideal types, and, in practice, differences between them are rarely clear-cut. Since Estonia is characterised by rationality and survival values, in contrast to self-expression values (Inglehart and Welzel 2005), and the success-oriented, materialistic mentality prevails, 'spiritual growth and a sustainable relationship with nature' is an alternative life choice. The visionaries are generally rather successful, according to those prevailing values in Estonia. It could be said that, in their case, survival values have been satisfied and self-expression values have become more important. They consider life in the mainstream society boring and unsatisfactory, and are looking for new challenges. However, in most cases they have not given up their position in the society, and have combined it with alternative values. The adaptors, on the other hand, have limited opportunities for success from the point of view of the mainstream society. Their choices are narrowed down materially, and they depend on networks of mutual assistance (similarly to many people of the lower strata in Estonia). For them, belonging to the community also has a practical value in terms of their private economies and life arrangements. Moreover, belief in the eco-village ideology gives higher meaning to their everyday life.

The reasons behind getting connected to the eco-village movement are different, as is the background of the people. While some of the members have reached the movement through esoteric circles or beliefs, others have approached it through green movements and beliefs. Through these people, the eco-village movement has connections to various spiritual and alternative enterprises (*e.g.* Steiner school, aura transformers) and green movements and organisations. However, the most explicitly articulated co-operation partners mentioned both in the interviews and the Association's official sources are different communities (traditional village communities, residential neighbourhood associations, *etc.*). Although the eco-village movement currently unites many people believing in the core ideas of GEN ideology, and engaging in various joint activities, Lilleoru remains the only larger eco-village actually inhabited by some of them. Other rural places called eco-villages have only a couple of inhabitants, although they function as space for movement meetings and seminars.

Both the global and domestic discourse emphasise three key aspects. According to the Union of Estonian eco-villages the establishment of an eco-village involves 'a fusion of social, ecological and spiritual aspects; one of the eco-village movement's main principles is that these three are inseparable from each other.' In our presentation of the Estonian eco-village activism, we follow this three-way division.

The spiritual: New Age

For many (but not all) movement activists, yoga was the gateway to eco-villages. Even Lilleoru was originally formed by a yoga teacher and his adepts. Another active network, which planned to set up an own eco-village, consisted of 'the children of a common yoga teacher.' For these people, a natural and community-based lifestyle was an organic continuation of yoga. Some had been in contact with other esoteric ways of thought, such as alternative medicine:

> **Martin** (34): When I was a child, I remember it so well, my stomach ached /…/ And then [an esoteric healer] took out some kind of Chinese teaching in Russian translation, squeezed somewhere in my sole, and the pain disappeared after about three minutes, click, just like that. /…/ I have experienced that, apart from doctors and conventional thinking, there also exist some kind of non-traditional forms /…/ I think most of those who now think of an eco … village way perceive that there exists also other values than those around us and visible.

Before Estonia's independence, yoga, esoteric and different forms of religion could be perceived as forms of resistance against the Soviet regime, while they remained largely invisible to the public. A situation where religion is relegated to the private sphere put special obstacles before the major Christian churches as institutions, while faiths stressing the importance of a personal, private, religious experience had a better chance of adapting to the circumstances. When the public mission work became possible again at the end of the 1980s – with the introduction of Gorbachev's policies of *glasnost* and *perestroika* – it was not the Lutheran church, but the smaller Protestant denominations, and the New Age movement, which grew rapidly (Altnurme 2005: 80-86). Estonia is currently, according to the *Eurobarometer,* the most secular country in Europe: only 16% of the population profess to believe in God (Eurobarometer 2005); at the same time it is common to have other, more diffuse notions of the supernatural (Altnurme 2005: 100). For the eco-village activists, an esoteric spirituality was an alternative to the materialistic values dominant in society; it bore witness that the consumption-oriented lifestyle was not the only possibility. The revolutionary development, which had started as a protest against national oppression and the Soviet type of modernisation, had in fact paved way for its Capitalist version; the activists now distanced themselves from that as well.

The international eco-village movement has frequently used the concept of *Gaia*, which refers to a vision of the world as a living organism, whose 'organs are connected to each other through certain frequencies. You yourself are an organ of this organism. Through your thoughts, words and deeds you send out certain frequencies which serve peace or war.' (Duhm 2007). Within the Estonian movement, one can discern both a core for which the spiritual message is crucial, and other, less dogmatic members. The latter emphasise the importance of living in harmony with one's surroundings, and understanding the social and environmental consequences for one's actions. They prefer not to explicitly oppose science and its institutions.

The ecological: The Environment

One of the reported reasons for the establishment of eco-villages was an awareness of environmental problems, and a desire to live with as small an 'ecological footprint' as possible. Several informants had an education in biology or other natural sciences. This awareness was coupled with a critique of the industrial society – life in a community in a rural area was perceived both as an alternative to the alienated technocratic society, and as a way of taking responsibility for the nature and the environment.

> **Tiina** (28): When you live in the countryside, the eco-friendly solutions come much easier: there are no ready-made packages, and you grow everything yourself and eat it. [I see the eco-village as] a way of living in peace with your conscience, so that you are not a burden to the environment.

In comparison to life in a Western European city, life in the Estonian countryside is still characterised by traditional economising. This was particularly the case during the Soviet times when the supply of consumer goods was less.

> **Tiina** (28): You see, when you live in the countryside, so (pause 2 seconds) well, maybe less now, but I think in the past, in Soviet times or so, you re-used everything for the second and third time, as long as it was good for something.

At the same time, many of the eco-village's residents work in the city and have the organic cultivation only as a hobby. Some of the participants, above referred to as visionaries, have highly skilled jobs that allow them to work at a distance. In this regard, the eco-village can also be seen as an example of the 'mix of urban and rural lifestyles', which characterises the 'post-modern rural' that has emerged near urban centres (Eklund 2007). Their abandonment of the urban lifestyle is by no means total; rather, they tend to pick up the best things of both worlds. They make use of modern household commodities, such as washing machines, but due to the collective lifestyle of the eco-village, the machines are sometimes shared by different households. They try to choose a technology that is environmentally friendly, which sometimes is also more expensive than the alternatives.

The Social: The Community

The eco-village movement's ideology emphasises equality and participation, not only in the context of the spiritual activities, but also more generally. Both in the eco-villages and in meetings of activists who do not themselves live in the village, activities, rituals and space are designed in order to support these ideals. They eat together, meditate together, dance and sing together; physical contact is encouraged in the form of various games. Meetings are arranged without any pre-determined team program, and follow what is called open space technology. Eco-village activists often emphasise that they have no leaders, and distance themselves from ideas of hierarchical structure, which they consider to be typical of other social spheres.

> **Mari** (41): The reason is that the systems that we have experience of in fact had authoritarian leadership. And then we maybe feel that we should have no leaders at all, because it is so bad and authoritarian, and most of us have no experience of leadership of a different kind.

However, it is an exaggeration to say that the movement would not have any leadership. Especially the so-called spiritual leaders enjoy authority, and this is recognised both by themselves and the others. They have no formal status, but act as charismatic authorities. Also visionaries have often more impact in the decision-making processes while they tend to be better informed compared to other people.

The sense of community is supported also by other boundaries towards the rest of society. At a training meeting within the Gaia Education program, participants often mentioned the 'common man' who is not assumed to possess any true understanding of the world. In order to help the common man to understand the movement principles, everything must be made easy to comprehend, they assumed. For the same reason, one should also avoid giving too much visibility for the most extreme ideological positions, but try to present one's views in a way that is comprehensible and also potentially acceptable for an outsider. The difference between the eco-village activists and others also becomes concrete in a comparison between the most highly educated, city-moved village members, and the rest of the rural population:

> **Martin** (34): With the traditional community, we also have the problem that … there are no high-quality [*suure kvaliteedimärgiga*] people. Some drink, some are … so to speak, simply socially excluded, or victims of some social processes. In this respect, it would be … something different to try to revive and develop a traditional community, in fact perhaps more difficult. If you … build something from scratch, based on people with similar interests or who are on the same wavelength, it is perhaps even better, or simpler, easier.

The ideal is to create a community with equal and friendly social relations, and economic independence (some eco-villages outside Estonia have introduced their own currency in order to run the local economy), which would serve as a model for outside world. However, currently, even successful eco-villages are economically dependent on the outside world; while they may be a 'separated island' in terms of lifestyle, they also remain tied to the market of consumption goods. An important part of Lilleoru's budget originates from fee-paying courses, tourism and voluntary contributions. Lilleoru was built, and exists today, largely because of the support of people living and working outside.

> **Aime** (33): Our first house, which still remains the main building, was built without money. /…/ We had a team who worked on the construction, we tidied up on weekends. /…/ People have valuable professions and it would, in a way, not be such a good idea to decide that we all will live there from now on. /…/ So we agreed on a system of monthly voluntary donations.

Eco-villages as life politics?

From the experiences of social movements, and from numerous biographies of dissenters, we know that borders between resistance, collaboration, and system-compatible complementarity are lines drawn in water. The existence of realms of fictitious, or partial liberty, within authoritarian socialist regimes did, at least according to some of the participants of oppositional movements, in fact weaken the opposition (*e.g.*, Richter 1988/1990: 16 f.). But even if exclusive, consumerist or deficient in other ways, they also did represent an element of pluralism of values, even of power. In another key, the discussions within green, leftist and other alternative movements in the West in the 1970s and 80s, witness the same duplicity.

A comparison of that resistance culture and its later outgrowth, the eco-village movement, illustrates well Giddens' theory on lifestyle issues' increased importance at the expense of other forms of emancipatory politics. If one only takes into account the number of members of the existing eco-village, the Estonian eco-village movement appears marginal. Meanwhile, its supporters and the like-minded are many more. Its operating ideology also has links with key features of social consciousness. The movement's scepticism towards formal institutions and formal hierarchies is being fuelled by the anti-institutionalism that characterises the entire post-socialist Central and Eastern Europe; in its critique of modernisation, it resembles the anti-modernism inherited from Soviet-time 'dissidents'. A nostalgia, and a yearning for an (idealised) local community with non-hierarchical, non-alienated social relationships are widespread. According to surveys from 1992-2005, the market liberalism that has prevailed after the systemic transformation does not find support in popular attitudes (Saar and Helemäe 2011: 518). At the same time, the quest for increased quality of life in the countryside near a city coincides with a global trend among urban middle classes (Eklund 2007). The spirituality characteristic of the movement fit well with the diffuse, syncretistic beliefs of many others. Estonia is a small country, where neo-liberal policies have prevailed ever since the new independence in 1991, without having been seriously challenged within institutional politics (see Lagerspetz and Vogt 2004). One can therefore think that the attempts to introduce alternative ways of life could have a better chance of being noticed than in old democracies, with their well-established 'repressive pluralism'.

Despite this, Estonia's economic and political development has been based on completely different values than those advocated by the movement or, for that matter, Giddens. Rapid economic growth has brought increased inequality and change of economic structure, which has hit the traditional local communities hard (Annist 2011). The question is whether these trends actually have a chance to be reversed by the greater ecological awareness eco-village movement represents. The participants have first-hand experience of the post-Communist revolutionary change initiated by Green, democratic and nationalist movements in 1988-1991, but probably less insight on late capitalism's actual capability of resisting change. As Susan Sundback (1996) points out, New Age spirituality is, in all its individualism, actually very well adapted to the modern commercial society, and lacks strong political implications. The 'frequencies' sent by individual thoughts, words and deeds, according to the Gaia ideology, are not what we understand as ways of influencing society. Despite their strong mental commitment, the Estonian eco-village movement is for most participants a leisure time activity, not an alternative to their occupational lives. Not only the ecologically conscious, but also the affluent tend to withdraw from the society to their own, privately financed, and well-guarded worlds (*e.g.*, Lasch 1995). Just as was the case with the private networks in the Soviet period, it is also now difficult to draw clear dividing lines between resistance and adaptation to the system.

References

Adam, F., Kristan, P. and Tomšič, M. (2009). 'Varieties of Capitalism in Eastern Europe (with special emphasis on Estonia and Slovenia).' *Communist and Post-Communist Studies,* 42 (2009): 65-81.

Allaste, A.-A. (ed.) (2011). *Ökokogukonnad retoorikas ja praktikas.* [Ecological communities in rhetoric and in practice.] Tallinn: Acta Universitatis Tallinnensis: Socialia.

Altnurme, L. (2005). *Kristlusest oma usuni. Uurimus muutustest eestlaste religioossuses 20. sajandi II poolel.* [Summary: From Christianity to own belief. A study about the changes in the religiosity of the Estonians in the 2nd half of the 20th century.] Tartu: Tartu Ülikooli Kirjastus.

Annist, A. (2011). *Otsides kogukonda sotsialismijärgses keskuskülas. Arenguantropoloogiline uurimus.* [*Seeking community in post-Soviet Estonian centralised villages.*] Tallinn: Acta Universitatis Tallinnensis: Socialia.

Beck, U. (1992). *Risk Society: Towards a New Modernity*. London: Sage.

Benda, V.; Šimečka, M.; Jirous, I. M.; Dienstbier, J; Havel, V.; Hejdánek, L. and Šimsa, J. (1988). 'Parallel Polis, or An Independent Society in Central and Eastern Europe: An Inquiry.' *Social Research,* 55 (1-2): 211-246.

Duhm, D. (2007). *Future without War: Theory of Global Healing*. Belzig: Meiga.

Ecovillage Design Education. Available: http://www.gaia.org/mediafiles/gaia/education/EDE_V3.pdf (accessed 26 July, 2012).

Eesti ökokogukondade... (2011). *Eesti ökokogukondade ühendus. Estonian Eco-village Movement.* Available: www.kogukonnad.ee (accessed 5 September, 2011).

Eklund, E. (2007). 'Modern och postmodern landsbygd.'[Modern and post-modern countryside]. *Prosum,* 2/2007: 23.

Eurobarometer (2005). *Social Values, Science and Technology.* Special Eurobarometer 225/ Wave 63.1. [Brussels:] European Commission. Available: http://ec.europa.eu/public_opinion/archives/ebs/ebs_225_report_en.pdf (accessed 5 September, 2011).

Gerner, K. and Hedlund, K. (1993). *The Baltic States and the End of the Soviet Empire.* London and New York: Routledge.

Giddens, A. (1991). *Modernity and Self-Identity: Self and Society in the Late Modern Age.* Cambridge: Polity.

Gilman, R. and Gilman, D. (1991). *Eco-Villages and Sustainable Communities. A Report for Gaia Trust by Context Institute.* Holte: Gaia Trust.

Havel, V. (1992 [1978]). 'The Power of the Powerless.' Václav Havel: *Open Letters: Selected Writings 1965-1990.* New York: Vintage, 125-214.

Havel, V.(1992 [1984]). 'Politics and conscience.' Václav Havel: *Open Letters: Selected Writings 1965-1990.* New York: Vintage, 249-271

Heath, J. and Potter, A. (2006). *The Rebel Sell. How the Counterculture Became Consumer Culture.* West Sussex: Capstone.

Hirsch, J. (1980). *Turvavaltio. 'Saksan malli', sen kriisi ja uudet yhteiskunnalliset liikkeet.* [The Security State. The 'German Model', Its Crisis and the New Social Movements.] Tampere: Vastapaino.

Inglehart, R. F. and Welzel, C. (2005). *Modernization, Cultural Change and Democracy: The Human development Sequence.* New York: Cambridge University Press.

Jensen, J. and Miszlivetz, F. (2006). 'The second renaissance of civil society in East Central Europe – and in the European Union.' Peter Wagner (ed.): *The Language of Civil Society.* New York and Oxford: Berghahn, 131-158.

Lagerspetz, M. (1999). 'Post-socialism as a return: Notes on a discursive strategy.' *Eastern European Politics and Societies*, 13 (2): 377-90.

Lagerspetz, M. (2001). 'From 'Parallel Polis' to 'The Time of the Tribes': Post-socialism, social self-organization and post-modernity.' *Journal of Communist Studies and Transition Politics*, 17 (2): 1-18.

Lagerspetz, M. (2009). 'Still Citizen vs. State? Post-Communist prospects for democracy in Europe.' Annamari Konttinen (ed.): Civic Mind and Good Citizenship. Comparative Perspectives. Tampere: Tampere University Press, 147-168.

Lagerspetz, M. and Vogt, H. (2004). 'Estonia'. Sten Berglund, Joakim Ekman and Frank H. Aarebrot (red.): *The Handbook of Political Change in Eastern Europe. Second Edition.* Cheltenham, UK and Northampton, MA, USA: Edward Elgar, 57-93.

Lasch, C. (1995). *The Revolt of the Elites and the Betrayal of Democracy.* New York: W. W. Norton.

Ledeneva, A. V. (1998). *Russia's Economy of Favours:* Blat, *Networking and Informal Exchange.* Cambridge: Cambridge UP.

MINA Koolituskeskus (2011). *MINA Koolituskeskus – Self Awareness Training Center.* Available: www.lilleoru.ee (accessed 5 September 2011).

Mouzelis, N. (2001). 'Reflexive modernization and the third way: the impasses of Giddens' social-democratic politics.' *The Sociological Review 2001*: 436-456.

Richter, E. (1988/1990). 'Warum kommt es in der DDR zu keiner der sowjetischen Analogen Umgestaltung?' [Why is there no analogy to the Soviet *perestroika* in the GDR?] *Alles ist im untergrund oberauf, einmannfrei...ausgewählte beiträge aus det zeitschrift KONTEXT 1-7.* [Selected readings from the journal KONTEXT 1-7]. Berlin: edition KONTEXT: 15-17.

Rojek, C. (2001). Leisure and Life Politics. *Leisure Sciences,* 23 (2): 115-125.

Saar, E. and Helemäe, J. (2011). 'Conclusions and Discussion.' Ellu Saar and Jelena Helemäe (eds.), *Towards a Normal Stratification Order: Actual and Perceived Social Stratification in Post-Socialist Estonia,* Frankfurt am Main etc: Peter Lang.

Spada, C. (2010). 'The Social Construction of Norm. The Experience of the Valley of the Elves and the Proposal of the Italian Eco-villages'. *PhD Thesis presented and defended at Università degli Studi di Milano, 4 October 2010.*

Sundback, S. (1996). 'New Age och religiositetens förändring i Norden' [New Age and the change of religiosity in the Nordic countries]. *Sosiologia,* 33 (3): 216-226.

Wainwright, H. (2004). 'Western Europe: Democratic civil society versus neoliberalism.' Marlies Glasius; David Lewis and Hakan Seckinelgin (eds.): *Exploring Civil Society: Political and Cultural Contexts.* London and New York: Routledge, 101-110.

Watson, A. (2001). *The Evolution of Western Private Law. Extended edn.* Baltimore, MD: Johns Hopkins University Press.

Wedel, J. (1990). The Ties that Bind in Polish Society. Stanislaw Gomulka and Anthony Polonsky (eds.): *Polish Paradoxes.* London: Routledge, 237-260.

Drinking culture among young Estonian adults

Maarja Kobin

Introduction

Recent studies (Beccaria 2010) have indicated that there is a trend towards more diversified drinking cultures in both traditionally 'southern' European and 'northern' European drinking regions. Estonia, above all, has been described as a country with a heavy drinking tradition, representing the Northern drinking culture. In order to fully understand drinking patterns in different countries, one needs to understand the underlying motives, beliefs, values and norms that constitute alcohol culture in everyday drinking situations, and which legitimise drinking habits. Everyday drinking is seen as something that is self-evident – drinking that is considered socially normal and acceptable. What is considered normal or abnormal depends on cultural traditions and different cultural contexts where drinking is practiced.

From a micro-sociological perspective, and through in-depth research, this chapter explores the drinking practices of young people who, on the one hand, continue to be influenced by previously existing norms and values, but on the other hand, are the ones who are the most open-minded and receptive to new ideas and fashions, who are also integrated into different youth cultures and, therefore, are also capable of changing and creating new norms and values concerning alcohol consumption. The chapter explores the distinctive characteristics of present-day, socially accepted alcohol consumption practices in Estonia among young adults. More specifically, the purpose is to analyse the ritualistic function of drinking. The ritualistic function of drinking and ritualistic drinking practices in this article are seen as a 'liminal phase' that offers a 'time-out' from reality (Gusfield 1987; Turner 1969 cited in Beccaria and Sande 2003) or a 'passage' (Gusfield 1987; Järvinen 2003), where everyday life with its rules and regulations can be put aside, and the transition to leisure or festive time starts. Looking at the drinking practices, and the ritualistic function of drinking, it is possible to draw out what kind of drinking practices are considered socially acceptable, and what their bases are. The choices about how to drink reflect young people's lifestyles and their identity construction.

The context of Estonia and drinking cultures in Europe

Alcohol consumption in Estonia

By the end of the 1970s during the Soviet era, alcohol consumption had increased rapidly in Estonia, reaching a very high level by international comparison at the time (Kollom 2010). In 1985, Mikhail Gorbachev initiated a battle against drunkenness through a massive anti-alcohol campaign that used a variety of measures. The campaign diminished overall alcohol consumption, and alcohol-related harm, but was largely perceived as authoritarian, repressive, and was generally seen as a failure (*ibid.*). It was very unpopular among consumers, the government suffered from the sharp decline in tax revenues, prevention was practically non-existent, and illegal production markets increased dramatically (Tarschys 1993, cited in Kollom 2010: 169-170). After the re-establishment of Estonia´s independence in 1991, borders opened towards the West, and the varieties, as well as the production and quantities of alcohol sold, increased explosively. Estonian alcohol policies remained considerably more liberal than in most Nordic countries. (*ibid.*: 169-171). Alcohol policy changes between 1990-2004 were minuscule, and lacked clear direction, and more restrictions started to appear around 2005 after Estonia had joined the EU in 2004 (Raudne 2012: 53). Attention has now been drawn to alcohol-related problems in public health strategies. More restrictive measures have been implemented, such as a ban on alcohol retail sale between 10 pm and 10 am all over Estonia, alcohol advertising is now only allowed from 9 pm onward (since 2008), and the excise tax on alcohol has been raised several times in the last years (Kollom 2010; also Raudne 2012).

Alcohol consumption has grown consistently in Estonia from year-to-year, and current research has shown a continual rise both among men and women; consumption of both light and strong alcoholic drinks has increased[47] (Hein *et al.* 2008). Among women, especially among younger and more educated women, drinking heavily has increased (Tekkel, Veideman and Rahu 2009; Tekkel and Veideman 2011). According to the ESPAD 2011 study, heavy episodic drinking during the past 30 days was more commonly reported by Estonian students aged 15-16, compared with the average in Europe; heavy drinking has increased throughout the years among girls (32% in 1995 and 52% in 2011),

47 Light alcoholic beverages are alcoholic beverages with actual alcohol strength by volume below or equal to 22%. Strong alcoholic beverages are alcoholic beverages with actual alcohol strength by volume exceeding 22%. (Hein et al 2008: 20). Examples of strong beverages could be vodka or cognac, light beverages ciders or mixed spirit beverages.

and the figures in heavy episodic drinking between boys and girls have become very similar (54% versus 52% in 2011). Damage arising from alcohol is at a very high level, which is demonstrated by the numbers of alcohol-related psychoses, injuries, suicides, and traffic accidents that result from driving under the influence of alcohol (Kasmel 2005, Kõlves *et al.* 2006, cited in Kollom 2010: 166). During the last 15 years, alcohol consumption (100% alcohol) litres per capita has risen from 5.6 litres in 1996 to 9.9 litres in 2002 , and up to 12.6 litres in 2007 (Hein *et al.* 2008: 49; Orro et al 2011: 51). Since 2008, alcohol consumption has decreased moderately in Estonia. This could, on the one hand, be seen as a result of strengthened alcohol policy since 2005 (adaptations of, and regulations due to, Estonia´s accession to the EU in 2004), and on the other hand, by the economic downturn that influenced both the income and employment rate, which further impacted the affordability of alcoholic beverages (Lai and Habicht 2011). Estonia used to be a predominantly spirit-drinking country, but since the beginning of this century, it has been primarily a beer-drinking country (Pärna and Rahu 2010).

Drinking cultures in Europe

The most common way of describing drinking cultures in Europe is the distinction between 'dry' and 'wet' societies, stereotypically also described in terms of the difference between the northern European 'spirits' or 'beer cultures', and the southern European 'wine cultures' (Room and Bullock 2002: 620). In the 'dry' cultures drinking is held apart from everyday working life as a special commodity for special contexts: drinking has traditionally been sporadic, often at festivals or weekends (Room and Bullock 2002: 620, Beccaria and Sande 2003: 111), episodic drunkenness occurs among males, who use spirits predominantly without food, seeking drunkenness as an unhealthy but physically necessary escape (Heath 1998: 119). In the 'wet' cultures, drinking is integrated into everyday life and routines, frequently accompanying meals (Room and Bullock 2002; Beccaria and Sande 2003)[48]. Although there are no studies conducted in Estonia that would give information from a micro-level perspective about the drinking practices that were present during the Soviet time, Estonia has been described as a country that encompasses the 'hard-drinking traditions' common to 'spirit-

48 Though as also mentioned before, 'wet' drinking cultures have typically been represented by the Mediterranean countries and 'dry' drinking cultures by the Nordic and Anglophonic countries. However, in today's Europe, this criterion ('dry' vs. 'wet' based on the level of consumption in the population) is problematic because it no longer separates cultures that are supposed to vary (Beccaria *et al.* 2010: 12).

drinking countries' (Room 2007: 26). Though, as Leifman (2001) has pointed out, many of the spirits countries (Estonia, Finland, Latvia, Lithuania, Norway, Poland and Sweden) could be described as 'former spirit-drinking' countries, since in 2001 the recorded consumption of spirits is still dominant only in Latvia (cited in Room 2007: 26). Room (2007: 26), points out that these countries still remain representative of the hard-drinking traditions of northern and parts of eastern Europe, despite their changes in beverage preferences. In her study on drinking culture among Estonian workplace-based groups of men, Raudne (2012) writes that the centrality of intoxication for men supports the categorisation of describing the Estonian drinking culture as relatively 'dry'.

Recent qualitative studies have found similarities between the northern and southern European youth drinking practices – drunkenness has always played an important role in Finnish alcohol culture and is, by now, also part of the modern drinking culture among young people in Spain or in Italy (Pyörälä 1995, Beccaria 2010). In Finland, the role of alcohol as an intoxicant at seasonal feasts is still strong, but in addition, drinking is nowadays present during a wide range of everyday occasions (Beccaria *et al.* 2010: 18). In Finland, one of the most significant aspects of this change encompasses the changes in the drinking habits of women, the increase in women's drinking (*e.g. ibid.*). It is not possible to know exactly what the gender differences in drinking were during the Soviet time in Estonia, but it can be assumed that men´s drinking practices were heavy, and intoxication was more accepted for men than it was for women. Gapova (2002: 653) has written that, during the Soviet era, men's health was weaker than women's, and they had a shorter life expectancy; in addition to other things, they were engaged in self-destructive practices, such as smoking and drinking.

'Everyday life frame' and ritualistic drinking

Drinking practices, like any other social practice, rely on inter-subjectivity, *i.e.* on shared assumptions about the world (Alasuutari 1990: 66). Any kind of research on culture, such as alcohol culture, can be seen as an endeavour to understand meanings. In this sense, culture can be seen as a system of symbols, through which life is organised into an understandable set of actions and events (Gusfield 1987: 75).

This chapter is more specifically concerned with an analysis of the socially accepted drinking practices among young people – with the symbolic and social meaning, as well as the function of drinking in the temporal organisation of daily, weekly, monthly or yearly life among young Estonian adults. Socially accepted drinking practices rely on drinking that is self-evident – the so-called normal drinking, which everybody does without asking any questions. Self-evident drinking can be interpreted on the basis of the *everyday life frame* (Alasuutari 1990: 6-8). The everyday life frame is structured by the alcoholism frame, based on the normal/abnormal dichotomy (*ibid.*) – the first one referring to socially accepted and the other one to socially unaccepted drinking. Self-control/loss of control and self-initiative are the main distinctions between a normal drinker and an abnormal drinker (socially accepted drinking habits versus drinking habits that are not socially accepted). Self-control acts like a cultural immuniser, which makes sure that a person stays away from abusing alcohol (Järvinen 2003). According to Room (1984), the loss of control concept serves as a culturally acceptable, and humanely oriented governing image, strictly separating normal drinking from alcoholic drinking (cited in Järvinen 2003).

In understanding the concept of frame, I rely on Alastuutari (1990), and on his use of this concept. Alasuutari relies most of all on Giddens (1984, 1987), who emphasises the cognitive nature of frames. The concept of the *everyday life frame* should be handled as an aggregate of more specific frames, within which people drink or interpret drinking (Alasuutari 1990: 6-7). When a drinking situation is perceived as normal, or within an everyday life frame, the actor does not use or apply a particular frame consciously, but he/she understands what is going on as a competent culture member. In this sense, ordinary drinking is not even understood as normal drinking on a daily basis. Rather, as Alasuutari (1990) has pointed out, ordinary drinking consists of usual everyday life occasions, such as 'having a party' or 'going to the tavern'; others could be 'having fun with friends' or 'just relaxing'.

Socially accepted drinking practices, as understood within the 'everyday life frame', could be seen as a form of ritual (see also Gusfield 1987), encompassing ritualistic functions in the present-day lives of young adults. Instead of speaking of a ritual as something that is a special activity inherently different from daily routine, and closely linked to the sacred in traditions and organised religion, it is more accurate to speak about ritualised activities (therefore, the ritualistic function of drinking) – the ones that are somewhat less established as public events, less codified by tradition, and less likely to appeal to divine beings. (Bell 1997: 138-139). The ritualised activities might often be explained with such reasoning as 'we have always done this', or 'we do it because it makes such-and-such positive thing happen'– therefore, they appear to address a very specific and obvious need or have a sufficiently long history that, in and of itself, justifies them (Bell 1997: 167). Rituals could be understood as a 'time-out' from reality, and represent a transformation of individuals between social categories and different realities (Gusfield 1987; Turner 1969 cited in Beccaria and Sande 2003: 101). Victor Turner (1969) focuses on the liminal phase of rituals, as a creative way of playing with the structure of reality and society, and the separation and aggregation phase representing the structure and authority of the society (cited in *ibid.*). This liminal phase constitutes a time-out from normal social roles, responsibilities, rules, orders and even modes of thoughts (Rothenbuhler 1998: 15.), and the liminal phase offers fun, playing, games, carnivals, partying and celebration (Beccaria and Sande 2003: 102) but not always – it could also offer consolation.

In his work on drinking habits among Americans, Gusfield (1987) wrote about how drinking could serve as a significant marker, symbolising the shift from work to play as a transformation of daily life. Järvinen (2003) has nicely summarised Gusfield's different types of ritual functions for alcohol. The most obvious function of alcohol is *mood setting* – the effects of drinking, such as relaxation and disinhibition, cannot be attributed to the physiochemical properties of alcohol alone; mood setting is always related to the social definitions of drink. Another central function of alcohol is *passage*, where drinking marks the transition from work to leisure, from the public to the private sphere, from the everyday to the festive. In Gusfield's description, the combination of mood and passage makes alcohol the opposite of the serious and mundane world. The third ritual function of alcohol is *sociability*: drinking solidifies personal relationships, and it is a dissolver of social hierarchy and formality. It signals the exposition of self to others within an atmosphere that is also protective. (cited in Järvinen 2003). Drinking alcohol often serves a ritualistic function, and marks the transitions from one status or stage to another (Fox and Marsh 1998). These transitions could be life cycle, lifestyle or habitual (*ibid.*). I have looked at my data in terms of these categories as they appear to be central to understanding drinking culture among young Estonians.

Research method and data

Data collection and analysis have been done from the perspective of constructing a grounded theory (Charmaz 2006). The theoretical standpoint was not fixed, and theoretical analyses took place in parallel with data gathering and analysis. The empirical part of this chapter relies mostly on open-ended individual interviews (19; 10 carried out in rural areas and 9 in urban areas) and focus group interviews (7; 4 in rural and 3 in urban areas). Two of the focus groups were single-sex and the other five were mixed-sex. Altogether, 20 men and 28 women were interviewed. In general, interviews lasted 1½ to 2 hours, the longest one being four hours in length. All interviews were carried out in 2010, recorded, and transcribed. In addition, some participation observation, visiting different events or parties where alcohol was consumed, was conducted in order to have a broader view and interpretation of the data.

The age range of informants was 18-36, most of them in their 20s and/or early 30s, and both from rural (24; 11 men and 13 women) and urban areas (24; 9 men and 15 women) in Estonia. Rural areas mean small towns, villages and/or hamlets – often with one bar/pub, or none at all, and no theatre and cinema. Urban areas refer to bigger towns in Estonia, such as Tallinn (capital city), Pärnu, Tartu, and Kohtla-Järve. Interviews were carried out in the homes of the informants or in cafes. Before conducting the interviews, a full explanation about the nature of the study and its purposes was given; informants were guaranteed anonymity and confidentiality.

An interview schedule was used for open-ended interviews that covered the topics I wished to discuss – for example, the first time consuming alcohol, changes in one´s drinking practices, the meaning of drunkenness, *etc.* – which also allowed for new topics to emerge. In focus groups, topics like gender and drinking, the meaning of drunkenness, and others were explored. The contacts with individual and focus group interviewees were initially collected through different personal acquaintances, which then led on to new people to interview (snowballing). Snowball sampling is best used to study hidden populations (Faugier and Sargeant 1997: 792) and is suitable for studies that are explorative, qualitative, and descriptive in areas that involve sensitive, illegal or deviant issues (Hendricks and Blanken 1992, cited in *ibid.*). The snowballing technique has proven to be useful, especially in reaching young people from rural areas who would be willing to be interviewed. The focus groups consisted of informants who knew each other. The latter can be seen as a good basis for open conversation. The focus group interviews give us an idea of how collective knowledge or an understanding about a phenomenon, such as drinking alcohol, is created, and how certain understandings have an influence and how they are established as collective truths in the groups (Barbour 2007). The disadvantages of focus groups are that the 'collective truths' are a result of negotiations, where some participants have more to say than others; also since people knew each other, those who do not wish to confront the group majority with an alternative view on alcohol use may be left hidden (Demant and Järvinen 2011: 100).

The interviews were coded with the help of a qualitative software program NVivo 8. The aim of the coding was to identify relevant, central topics. Comparing and analysing the codes allows for an interpretation of the phenomenon under research – drinking practices – that originates from (is grounded in) the data (Charmaz 2006). Categories were combined with relevant literature/theoretical background to provide an explanation of the phenomenon.

Ritualistic function of drinking

Drinking habits could be understood as a routine way of action that the agents have internalised through interaction with their environment (Törrönen and Maunu 2007b: 179). Analytically, it is possible to speak about two broad categories of drinking habits that are considered socially acceptable among young Estonian adults, as was evident in my data: 1) moderate, frequent drinking in small amounts and 2) excessive drinking, in bigger amounts, on special occasions. However, in everyday life the forms of moderate as well as excessive practices are dependent on the drinking context and are open for negotiation (see also Demant and Törrönen 2011). Within these two broad habits, I looked at three transitions as analytical categories, in order to interpret the meanings and purposes of drinking; however, these transitions should not be taken as an exhaustive overview, but rather an attempt to understand the purpose of drinking among young Estonians. Often these transitions overlap, and the same phenomenon can mark different transitions at the same time.

Life cycle transitions

Ritual-like activities are done in such a way that performing, in and of itself, gives the acts a special or privileged status. The style of doing creates a type of framework around the act that communicates the message 'this has extra significance' (Bell 1997: 166). One of the transitions that ritualistic practices carry are life cycle transitions, marked by special occasions and life-changing events, such as a wedding or a significant/landmark birthday that is celebrated by heavier drinking. For a 20-year-old, expressing and declaring heavy drinking in front of the parents is a way to declare independence and adulthood.

> **Maria** (24): I turned 20 and it was the first time when I went home and I was totally drunk. I went home, and mom and dad were still up. Mother said hello and declared that I'm drunk. I said I am and that I'm old enough.
>
> ***Interviewer***: *What happened eventually?*
>
> **M**: Nothing happened. I went off to bed.

For young people, the symbolic and reflexive focus is on individual choice and game-play, with the rules and norms of normal society. In the modern local and global youth culture, the use of alcohol for intoxication purposes is the key symbol for 'free flow' in the phase of transition from childhood to the individual life project of making one´s social identity (Beccaria and Sande 2003: 116). Drinking and getting drunk with, or in front of someone, are highly symbolic behaviours, which are important ways of performing and expressing distinction or belonging to a community (Room 1994, 1995, cited in Room 2007: 19).

An example of life cycle transitions could be also graduation, mostly celebrated among young Estonians by heavier drinking, both by young men and women. In the following quotation, Laura recalls how she got heavily intoxicated and managed to cope with a severe hangover the next day during the graduation ceremony. She contested the rules of the adult society and discovered her own limits.

> **Laura** (23): It was the end of primary school and I was so sick /…/ But it was really, I drank many things together and that's why. I puked a lot. /…/ At the graduation the next day, it was hot and the whole time it felt like I'm going right now, I'm going [puking]… But luckily I held out.

Drinking because of dramatic and negative life-changing events, such as funerals, or the loss of a partner, may offer comfort or consolation. In this case, alcohol is perceived as a way to escape reality for a short while. The latter could also be important for those who have experienced the loss of a job and have become unemployed. Drinking alcohol is seen here as something that helps in the aftermath or as consolation in coping with the sudden change in one's personal and social life, as evidenced by Peeter in the next quotation below, from a focus group – a young man who had been unemployed for more than six months.

> ***I**: So, when you don't have a job, you drink?*
>
> **Peeter** (30): Yes
>
> **David** (20): Because of depression also.
>
> **Tiina** (21): You don't have any kind of obligations. For instance, I know that I'm on work tomorrow and I know that I can not start drinking because how am I going to work with a hangover?
>
> **P**: The unemployment is so long… a month passes, two or three, maybe a year, and then we have drunkards. A person goes, in order not to think, and buys a bottle from somewhere and gets himself drunk and does not think about it anymore. People get depressed.
>
> **D**: Yes…
>
> ***I**: Could it not be that a person is sober at that time – in order to wait and be ready if anything should come up?*
>
> **D**: There is very little of this…
>
> **P**: People give up very easily. I had it also at some point when I was unemployed… You give up on everything. You can't and you can't find another job and then a person eventually gives up on it.

In this sense, drinking does not only constitute the world, but also makes an intelligible, bearable world, which is much more how an ideal world should be than the painful chaos that threatens all the time (Douglas 1987: 11). Alcohol can provide an escape from the present reality and help neglect the external world, at least for a short period of time. Though usually 'drinking for the sake of drinking', and drinking alone, has little to do with the main functions of being intoxicated (such as collective cheerfulness, relaxation in good company), and is seen as a lack of social capital (Demant and Järvinen 2011: 97; see also Kobin 2012). However, there is still enough space for individual deviation from these norms (Demant and Järvinen 2011). In the focus group extract, the informants perceive that drinking because of feeling down could be dangerous, as it might lead to the development of more serious drinking practices and risk behaviour – drinking that is no longer controlled. Those who have started drinking in larger amounts and/or more frequently because of losing their job are not always condemned. They are pitied and understood: 'This could happen to anybody'. This also means that others did not distance themselves from Peeter and did not exclude him from the group, but rather 'accommodated the norms of the group to the behaviour of the 'deviant', thus reassigning normative social capital to him' (*ibid.*: 97).

Lifestyle transitions

Different life cycle events, such as a landmark birthday, do not always bring along a change in one's lifestyle, but they possibly could. I have interpreted lifestyle transitions in two broad categories. First, I have distinguished the transition within a broader time frame, which, among young people, marks the shift from childhood (leaving home, going to the city) to adulthood (achieving independence, finishing university, settling down, finding one's own path/acquiring education and new acquaintances), and it encompasses drinking practices that are seen as an inherent part of the process of growing up, entering the adult world and playing with one's identity. During college years, young adults often mark this kind of transition with a lifestyle that consists of heavy drinking and partying. The liminal phase of drinking is revealed through partying with friends during the week, or during weekends, to weaken, for example, the pressures arising from studies or leaving the parents' home. Drinking during the college years could be seen as a particular set of practices and experiences that many young people experience, therefore, it can be treated as a separate lifestyle (transition) on its own that accompanies life cycle events, such as leaving home. As pointed out before, different transitions could overlap with each other. In the next quotation, Oliver talks about this transition and shows the dynamics of this shift – both leaving the parental home and studying at the university – and how this college drinking lifestyle is later changed, when he moves on to adult life, where he must act responsibly.

> **Oliver** (25): When I went to the university, a very good friend of mine… with whom we had been university students for three years during our BA studies, we did not go through that much trouble with learning. Our studies were all fine, maybe we had an open mind, which helped. During these three years, we managed to go to all kinds of parties during the week. When I think back, it seems completely unbelievable. Girls from my class have told me that it was impossible to see me sober during this time. This is how life was; it was just a phase of life. After that we have not been drinking that much, there is no time for that. I am the owner of a business, a manager, and we are collaborating internationally, you can´t allow yourself these things…. I´m not saying that we don´t meet or drink, of course, we meet on the weekends to go to the sauna or something, and all the anniversaries and things, but we don´t have this kind of full-on-drinking during the week, cause there is too much to lose.

Second, lifestyle transitions could be looked at from a narrower point of time, paying attention to the celebration of concrete, but less significant events (Fox and Marsh 1998). In a consumer culture, individuals display their individuality and sense of style by choosing, for example, different behaviours, clothes or goods that they combine together in a lifestyle (Featherstone 1991: 84). These goods or events that are then celebrated could be, for example, making a good business deal, as well as buying a new house or a new car, as perceived by the informants. Celebrating of a new car carries symbolic meaning, which helps to create a link between the current act (buying a new car) and possible future well-being.

> **Artur** (25): Once, when I bought this new car, we celebrated it together with friends. It is like blessing the car – you take a drink for a wheel or for a gear stick or for the left tyre. It would, like, be for the good future of the car and myself.

However, opposite opinions are also present in terms of celebrating lifestyle changes/events. This kind of distinction could be seen as a cultural diversification in drinking practices among young Estonians, when distancing from hard drinking traditions and drinking that celebrates 'nothing' (just to drink). In his interview, Paul reflects on what has been called 'heroic drinking' that is common, for example, in the Finnish alcohol culture among boys/men – it celebrates being confident in their powers and is intoxication-oriented drinking style (see *e.g.* Demant and Törrönen 2011). Paul speaks about filling up shot glasses to 'see who would win' behind the table.

> **Paul** (28): We don't have these things like toasting cars. Perhaps it is just said that one should do it now [have a party and celebrate], but eventually nobody does it actually. In my opinion, this is some sort of misconception that you must toast to everything. You might as well do it for anything, buying new bread, for example. We

> don't have these kinds of things that we should all drink now for one reason or another. /.../ Everybody also drinks in the way they want and what they want to drink, they make cocktails the way they want. Usually we drink also only cocktails; we don't like sit behind a table, fill up shot glasses and then start taking shots to see who would win. We don't have any of these things. In my opinion, this is also a kind of habit that belongs in the Soviet time.

Distancing helps create a more 'cultural' and 'European' self-presentation in one's drinking image, and drinking here has become more of a symbolic way of performing these distinctions (see also Pilvre in this book). In the Soviet cultural space at large, masculinity was perceived as a problem in connection with alcoholism and other self-destructive practices, and alcohol was ubiquitous during the Soviet time (Raudne 2012). New drinking styles in the youth culture are most often defined in contrast to the drinking styles of preceding generations (Room 2007: 24). This kind of distinction also refers to what Demant and Törrönen (2011: 1252) call 'playful drinking', which does not emphasise traditional, inflexible masculine identity and is not as unyielding and exclusive of a form of drinking, since young adults are expected to play and shift between different self-presentations. In this case, lifestyle means a way of being in which aspects of locality – local traits, knowledge, mannerisms, *etc.*, are reflexively managed, and creatively combined with a range of appropriated cultural resources, in the construction of identity. Therefore, there is a dynamic interplay between the individual and the circumstances of everyday life, where the local has become a point of reference for the individual (Bennett 2005: 64). In this context, a possible interpretation could be that the legacy of Soviet-time drinking, and its images among young people, are seen as a backdrop for distinction, and it is a cultural marker that helps to distinguish. The identification is based on the desired drinking practices that are, on the one hand, perceived as part of the global (European) lifestyle, and on the other hand, distinctions from representations of Soviet drinking practices as the Soviet way of life.

Habitual transitions

Habitual transitions help define, facilitate, and enhance far less momentous transitions, such as the daily or weekly transitions from home to work or from work to play, or even the beginning and completion of a specific task (Fox and Marsh 1998). Habitual transitions are the ones that cover also moderate drinking in small amounts. Drinking serves as a pastime (passage according to Gusfield 1987) while doing habitual activities – different housework, such as chopping wood, mowing the lawn or making bread. From this young woman′s point of view, making bread is accompanied with a cocktail, which transforms the waiting time for the bread to be finished into a time that has a special character – drinking makes the transition 'comfy' and helps relax.

> **Anna** (30): On Saturday evening, it happened accidentally that making bread prolonged late into the night. Well, it happened spontaneously, and then it went on until half past 12 at night, and I had to start baking it. And then I thought what are we going to do here [together with her husband], sitting behind the table the two of us, and waiting for the bread to be ready. So we made to ourselves rum cocktails. Actually it is so comfy. Just the two of us… and then one cocktail… to drink.

Among young men, it is common to drink a few beers while watching television, after getting home. Here, beer drinking could be seen as a transition from work to home. It is also commonly agreed that drinking a couple of beers can not be considered drinking at all – it is not taken seriously since it hardly impacts a person's coordination or the ability to understand their surroundings adequately. This is especially important in the broader cultural context, where heroic drinking is mostly seen as a norm among men, as it is in the Finnish alcohol culture (see *e.g.* Demant and Törrönen 2011). Beer drinking could be seen as one component in the definition of unproblematic or abnormal drinking (Järvinen 2003). The need to comment on what 'drinking' means also refers to the position of alcohol in the Estonian society. Drinking carries, in and of itself, negative connotations and is most of all based on the assumption that drinking involves intoxication, and alcohol is perceived as an intoxicant not as a food and, therefore, needs to be clarified (as in the Finnish alcohol culture, Beccaria *et al.* 2010: 230).

> **Mart** (32): And two beers, this is not like drinking, it is more like a refresher. /…/ It is like drinking Fanta or Coke.

Drinking after work during the week is also present among women. As Maria explains, a drink dissolves the working routine and helps to transition into a time that is for yourself and for relaxing.

> *I: Why do you drink alcohol?*
>
> **Maria** (24): After a hard day of work it is a nice relaxation. /…/ Like today, in this beautiful weather, well… a cold cider is perfect.
>
> *I: You finished your working day?*
>
> **M**: Yes, at 4 o'clock.

Drinking on weekends marks, most of all, the transition from work to play. The weekend can be seen as a contrast to the week (Gusfield 1987: 73). This implies a routine scheduling of time in which a period of work and a period of play exist in contrast. The weekend symbolises, or has become, a release from the rules and the tasks of daily routine. (*ibid.*). Alcohol has a ritualistic function – it separates work time from leisure time. Drinking is associated with recreation and irresponsibility. Alcohol helps break the routines of everyday life, forget about responsibilities and promises. The world of drinking means spontaneity, areas of release and actions for their own satisfaction, rescue from self-imprisonment (*ibid.*: 74). This does not mean that young people allow themselves the sensuous indulgence of consuming alcohol but always do it in a planned, carefully controlled way, and drinking occurs at specific times, in specific places, and with certain company and intensity (Brain 2000; Measham 2004; Szmigin *et al.* 2008; Kobin 2012). This implies also what has been called the 'work hard-play hard' lifestyle, common among British youth, where intoxicated weekends are vital to the desired harmony and good fit between work and play, concentration and relaxation, dealing with problems and worries, and 'time out' from this process (Parker 2007: 128). Drinking as a 'time out' is a common finding in many studies that look at young people and drinking (*e.g.* Szmigin *et al.* 2008; Seaman and Ikegwuonu 2010; Törrönen and Maunu 2007a; Brain 2000), as it is also among young Estonian adults.

> **Artur** (25): I think you will forget about this reality just for now, for a moment, when you get there. In this sense you are, like, alive then, you are not responsible for anyone else. Though I have two children and a wife… but just then it is so easy. It is like, I think, that for a moment I can be on my own. And in the way that is, for you, much more comfortable or better. Afterwards you maybe sick (laughs)… but at least for a moment it is good, you feel different, much more free. It feels good.

An example of weekly transitions among young Estonians is also the practice of going to the sauna. The ritual of sauna bathing is a common Estonian cultural practice. In the following interview excerpt, going to the sauna is reflected on the background of hard work, where having sauna, combined mostly with beer, helps to beat or neutralise working week pressure.

> **Samuel** (25): Sometimes we have just sat at somebody's home, whether at my place or at friend's or somebody else, everybody has their own saunas. It has somehow become common, at least now, that on the weekends, on Friday we have the sauna evenings, we get together and talk. And these evenings don't last that long, not like until 5 o'clock in the morning, but finish at a decent time, for example, at 1 or 2 o'clock. Because everybody understands that you have a tough week behind you, and that you just don't have the energy.

Drinking also includes practices that in some cases may last for a couple of days in sequence and that are most of all accepted among and by men. These practices may happen during, for example, a vacation, travelling around with friends, or during a weekend, when having a birthday party, or simply celebrating a weekend. This marks the period of play, relaxation and bonding with others. The element of the extreme and wildness offers an opposite for everything 'ordinary', which allows the person to return, with some release, to routines (Choquet 2008).

> *I: Is it common to drink many days continuously?*
>
> **Peeter** (30): Well, 2 days.
>
> **Sirje** (22): … exactly, about 2-3 days
>
> **David** (20): Especially 2.
>
> **Lea** (20): Especially when there is a plan to go for a trip and someone is sober, then in cars on the way. There isn't anything much but drinking only.
>
> **P**: It is fun and a pastime…
>
> **D:** You start drinking in the evening, and in the morning when you wake up, you have as many people as there were yesterday, then you keep drinking. If the rest of us are gone, you're sitting in a group of two or three, then you don't have this mood to keep going on the 2nd day. It is more about company. /…/ When you have a party all night long, you sleep a little bit and then you go on…

Drinking can also act 'as a symbolic punctuation mark differentiating one social context from the next' (Mandelbaum 1965: 282). As seen in the following quotation, for Anna drinking marks the transition from 'special' time (spent with the husband) to more 'ordinary' time (while the husband is gone) (see also *ibid.*; Fox and Marsh 1998). For her, drinking helped to cope with the following context, when she is once again on her own.

> **Anna** (30): My husband was unemployed for 2 months and for those 2 months he stayed at home. It was such a wonderful time. Then he went back to work [in Finland], and I was totally depressed because of it, and one night I drank until I was totally drunk, so it wouldn't hurt so much. It was better at this moment of course, but it was much worse the next day.

Self-control/loss of control – a link from socially accepted drinking practices to problematic drinking

In all of these different transitions, it is possible to see a 'potential risk' in them, which could be seen as a path or a warning sign towards becoming a problematic drinker or developing drinking practices that are no longer understood in terms of the *everyday life frame*. In the case of life cycle events, it is possible to draw a line between the types of events that are celebrated with heavy drinking. For example, in the case of a wedding, as a joyful event, it is hardly unlikely for the event to be conducive to problematic drinking; however, in the case of negative life cycle events, such as losing a job, or the death of someone close which, as perceived, might have an important influence on drinking more heavily and consequently losing control over it.

> *I: What do you think, what might be the reasons for becoming an alcoholic?*
> **Emma** (23): Maybe the loss of somebody or when somebody leaves this world, or then the breaking of a family... I think something like that. These could be those main reasons.

In the case of lifestyle celebrations, the question about using a new car as an excuse to drink raises background suggestions about the need to drink, with a reason that could be perceived by others as more or less legitimate. As was written before, the reason 'just to drink' or celebrate could be found in these kinds of celebrations. Also, habitual transitions are perceived as having the potential to result in more problematic drinking practices. Drinking alone is one of the first aspects of losing self-control and is mostly associated with being an alcoholic, though strong exceptions exist. In other words, drinking alone is mostly accepted when it concerns soft alcoholic beverages (such as beer or cider or a light cocktail), drinking vodka alone is mostly connected with some problems in drinking behaviour – dependence, or abuse. Whether drinking alone is accepted depends strongly on the context – drinking a couple of beers after getting home is accepted, as long as a 'couple' of drinks remain only a couple. The ability to stop drinking at any time is an aspect connected to maintaining control of one's drinking. In the former socialist, now liberal European, Estonia the forms of social control have shifted from the Soviet 'mutual surveillance' and institutional prescriptions, to the individual's self-monitoring and expectation of responsibility. Such control has been internalised and it is present in a number of life domains, including alcohol consumption (Raudne 2012: 119). If a person cannot help but drink, then the desire to drink has turned into a craving, and this is mainly associated with abnormal drinking (Alasuutari 1990). There is an important distinction between drinking for relaxation, for fun based on self-initiative, and because of a (physical) need for it. The latter is associated with being an alcoholic.

> **Marge** (26): I think it is quite common or normal among men in the evening after coming home from work to drink a beer, but at least they can restrain themselves in the weekends. They don't drink because they need it so desperately, but because, well, they are relaxing after work. An alcoholic can not stop, it is like he drinks a beer and in spite of himself, it becomes more and more, and he can find the money from anywhere in order to drink no matter what.

The overall connection between those three transitions – life cycle, lifestyle and habitual – to problematic drinking lies in the capability of having control over one's drinking practices, so that drinking will not start negatively impacting everyday life – such as going to work or any other responsibilities (family, studies).

Conclusion

Among young Estonians, it is possible to distinguish two types of drinking habits that are socially accepted – moderate frequent drinking, and more excessive drinking on special occasions. The ritualistic practices on a daily, weekly, monthly or yearly basis give an opportunity to step out of the routine everyday life and work, to feast and to party, and to relax, and drinking also offers consolation in the context of bereavements, encompassing also the ritual functions that Gusfield (1987; also Järvinen 2003) has pointed out: alcohol is a mood-setter (helps to relax), a passage (like a buffer zone that helps step out of the everyday life), and it facilitates sociability (helps bond with people). For the majority of young people, drinking is a planned release, which balances out the constrained behaviour that young people are subject to in the formal structures of everyday life, whether in the work or family setting (Szmigin *et al.* 2008: 362). Within the 'everyday life frame' (Alasuutari 1990), different transitions when young people drink in order to relax, party, and socialise with friends, or rest after arriving home from work, are seen as a liminal phase (Turner 1969, cited in Beccaria and Sande 2003), which offers a time-out from the everyday normal life, with its rules and obligations.

In understanding socially accepted ritualistic drinking practices, it is important to understand the main logic behind the meaning and norms of the everyday life drinking frame – the distinction between normal and abnormal drinking practices, based on self-control and loss of control, which create the borders for the perceptions of socially accepted practices. 'Drinking alone', 'drinking just to drink', or the ability to stop drinking, are aspects that impact the legitimisation of the functions of the ritualistic practices: having fun, relaxing, collective cheerfulness, stepping out of everyday life, and so forth (also Demant and Järvinen 2011). As these norms form the basis for legitimate ritualistic drinking practices among young adults, it is possible to see how the collectively stipulated norms provide a resource for action (Coleman 1998, cited in Demant and Järvinen 2011: 92) – how to drink, when to drink, and with whom to drink. Demant and Järvinen (2011) argue that social capital is both a background factor, influencing a participant's relationships to alcohol, and an effect of their drinking experience. Social capital incites some forms of drinking ('controlled drunkenness'), while restricting others, such as drinking alone (*ibid.*: 91).

In each of these transitions (life cycle, lifestyle, habitual), it is possible to see drinking practices that give rise to the idea that the Estonian alcohol culture among young adults represents the 'Northern' drinking culture: 'heroic drinking' and heavy drinking in bigger amounts on special occasions, such as graduations or funerals, weekend drinking from 'work to play', or drinking for days in sequence. Besides the traditional 'heroic drinking', 'playful drinking' (Demant and Törrönen 2011) is also present among young Estonian adults. Heavy drinking styles have become more diversified and hybrid formations and competing images can be found. The distinction and distance from heavy drinking practices is connected also to the negative image of *homo sovieticus*, which is not seen as a part of the desired European lifestyle.

Besides the traditional 'Nordic' drinking practices, there are also moderate ritualistic drinking practices such as 'from work to home', or drinking accompanying concrete tasks such as mowing the lawn, which show that everyday drinking has become more 'ordinary' – drinking is not only a weekend habit, and it does not have to include strong drunkenness. Drinking has been integrated into everyday life, which has been traditionally characteristic to Mediterranean drinking cultures (Beccaria and Sande 2003). The ritualistic drinking practices present among young Estonian adults are a result of the transition from a former socialist country to a country with a free market economy, access to internet and travelling, the diffusion of Western hedonistic lifestyles and values, and their integration into youth cultures, including the marketing of alcohol and drinking practices in the media, increased availability and variety of alcoholic drinks. Forces of globalisation – marketing, media, youth tourism and travel – are potential forces that differentiate youth cultures from general national cultures (Room 2007: 24).

As there is a variation of acceptable drinking practices in the Estonian drinking culture among young adults, it can be speculated that the Estonian alcohol culture is showing signs of being a 'mixed' culture, where the 'Nordic' drinking practices are accompanied by the more 'Southern' ones. Similar changes have been found in other 'Nordic' drinking cultures, such as the Finnish (Beccaria *et al.* 2010, Pyörälä 1995). However, these kinds of generalisations should be done with care, and instead of arguing for strong growing cultural similarities, it might be argued that these trends may be a sign indicating that the cultural position of drinking (in Estonia) is undergoing a transformation, similarly to large parts of Europe (Tigerstedt and Törrönen 2007, cited in Beccaria *et al.* 2010: 13). As in other countries in Europe (see Beccaria 2010), the 'mixed' Estonian drinking culture reflects a broader global change.

References

Alasuutari, P. (1990). *Desire and Craving. Studies in a Cultural Theory of Alcoholism.* Tampere: University of Tampere.

Barbour, R. (2007). *Doing Focus Groups.* Thousand Oaks, Ca: Sage.

Bennett, A. (2005). *Culture and Everyday Life.* London: Sage.

Beccaria, F. and Sande, A. (2003). 'Drinking Games and Rite of Life Projects : A Social Comparison of the Meaning and Functions of Young People's Use of Alcohol during the Rite of Passage to Adulthood in Italy and Norway.' *Young,* 11 (2): 99–119.

Beccaria, F. (ed.) (2010). *Alcohol and generations. Changes in style and changing styles in Italy and Finland.* Carocci, Editore, Rome.

Beccaria, F., Prina F., Rolando, S., Simonen, J., Tigerstedt, C. and Törronen, J. (2010). 'Introduction.' Beccaria, F. (ed.) *Alcohol and generations. Changes in style and changing styles in Italy and Finland.* Carocci, Editore, Rome, 11-37.

Bell, C. (1997). *Rituals: Perspectives and Dimensions.* New York: Oxford University Press.

Brain, K. (2000). *Youth, alcohol, and the emergence of the post-modern alcohol order.* Institute of Alcohol Studies. [Online]. Available: http://www.ias.org.uk/resources/papers/brainpaper.pdf (2011, February 28).

Charmaz, K. (2006). *Constructing Grounded Theory: A Practical Guide Through Qualitative Analysis.* London: SAGE.

Choquet, M. (2008). 'Case Study: Young People's Drinking in France.' Martinic, M., Measham, F. (eds.) *Swimming with Crocodiles: The Culture of Extreme Drinking.* London: Routledge, 39-52.

Demant, J. and Järvinen, M. (2011). 'Social capital as norms and resources: Focus groups discussing alcohol.' *Addiction Research and Theory,* 19 (2): 91-101.

Demant, J. and Törrönen, J. (2011). 'Changing Drinking Styles in Denmark and Finland. Fragmentation of Male and Female Drinking Among Young Adults.' *Substance Use and Misuse,* 46 (10): 1244-1255.

Douglas, M. (ed.) (1987). *Constructive Drinking: Perspectives on Drink from Anthropology.* Cambridge: Cambridge University Press.

ESPAD (2011). *The 2011 ESPAD Report. Substance Use Among Students in 36 European Countries.* (2012). Stockholm, The Swedish Council for Information on Alcohol and Other Drugs, CAN.

Faugier, J. and Sargeant, M. (1997). 'Sampling hard to reach populations.' *Journal of Advanced Nursing,* 26: 790-797.

Featherstone, M. (1991). *Consumer Culture and Postmodernism.* London: SAGE.

Fox, K. and Marsh, P. (1998). *Social and Cultural Aspects of Drinking. A Report to the European Commission.* The Social Issues Research Centre. [Online] Available: http://www.sirc.org/publik/drinking_contents.html (2010, October 24).

Gapova, E. (2002). 'On Nation, Gender, and Class Formation in Belarus … and Elsewhere in the Post-Soviet World.' *Nationalities Papers,* 30 (4): 639-662.

Gusfield, J. (1987). 'Passage to play: rituals of drinking time in American society.' Douglas, M. (ed.) *Constructive Drinking. Perspectives on Drink from Anthropology.* Cambridge University Press, 73-90.

Heath, D. B. (1998). 'Cultural variations among drinking patterns.' Grant, M., Litvak, J. (eds.) *Drinking Patterns and their Consequences*. Washington: Taylor & Francis.

Hein, P., Ahermaa, E., Martens, K., Saar, I., Josing, M. and Liivaauk, P. (2008). *Alcohol market, consumption and harms in Estonia. Yearbook 2008.* Tallinn: Estonian Institute of Economic Research. [Online]. Available: http://www2.tai.ee/teated/arenduskeskus/Uudised/Alkoholi_aastaraamat_2008.pdf (2009, July 7).

Järvinen, M. (2003). 'Drinking Rituals and Drinking Problems in a Wet Culture.' *Addiction Research and Theory*, 11 (4): 217-233.

Kobin, M. (2012, forthcoming). 'Managing drinking time, space and networks as strategies for avoiding alcohol related harm among young Estonian adults.' *Studies of Transition States and Societies*.

Kollom, K. (2010). 'Estonian non-governmental organisations in alcohol policy planning.' *Nordic Studies on Alcohol and Drugs*, 27: 165-182.

Lai, T. and Habicht, J. (2011). 'Decline in Alcohol Consumption in Estonia: Combined Effects of Strengthened Alcohol Policy and Economic Downturn.' *Alcohol and Alcoholism*, 46 (2): 200-203.

Measham, F. (2004). 'The decline of ecstasy, the rise of 'binge' drinking and the persistence of pleasure.' *Probation Journal*, 5 (4): 309-326.

Orro, E., Martens, K., Lepane, L., Josing, M. and Reiman, M. (2011). *Alcohol market, consumption and harms in Estonia. Yearbook 2010.* Tallinn: Estonian Institute of Economic Research.

Parker, H. (2007). 'Consumption Beyond Control. The Centrality of Heavy Social Drinking in the Lifestyles of English Youth.' Järvinen, M. and Room, R. (eds.) *Youth Drinking Cultures: European Experiences.* Aldershot: Ashgate, 119-130.

Pyörälä, E. (1995). 'Comparing Drinking Cultures: Finnish and Spanish Drinking Stories in Interviews with Young Adults.' *Acta Sociologica*, 38: 217-229.

Pärna, K. and Rahu, K. (2010). 'Dramatic Increase in Alcoholic Liver Cirrhosis Mortality in Estonia in 1992-2008.' *Alcohol and Alcoholism*, 45 (6): 548-551.

Raudne, R. (2012). *Drinking to Freedom: themes of continuity and change in contemporary Estonian alcohol discourse.* PhD Thesis. Johns Hopkins University.

Room, R. (2007). 'Understanding Cultural Differences in Young People's Drinking.' Järvinen, M. and Room, R. (eds.) *Youth Drinking Cultures: European Experiences.* Aldershot: Ashgate, 17-40.

Room, R. and Bullock, S. (2002). 'Can Alcohol Expectancies and Attributions Explain Western Europe's North-South Gradient in Alcohol's Role in Violence?' *Contemporary Drug Problems*, 29 (3): 619-648.

Rothenbuhler, E. W. (1998). *Ritual Communication. From Everyday Conversation to Mediated Ceremony.* Thousand Oaks, London, New Delhi: SAGE.

Seaman, P. and Ikegwuonu, T. (2010). *Drinking to belong: Understanding young adults' alcohol use within social networks.* Joseph Rowntree Foundation. [Online]. Available: http://www.jrf.org.uk/sites/files/jrf/alcohol-young-adults-full.pdf (2011, February 28).

Szmigin, I., Griffin, C., Bengry-Howell, A., Weale, L., Mistral, W. and Hackley, C. (2008). 'Re-framing 'Binge Drinking' as Calculated Hedonism: The View from the UK.' *International Journal of Drug Policy,* 19 (5): 359-366.

Tekkel, M., Veideman, T. and Rahu, M. (2009). *Health Behaviour among Estonian Adult Population, 2008*. National Institute for Health Development.

Tekkel, M. and Veideman, T. (2011). *Health Behaviour among Estonian Adult Population, 2010*. National Institute for Health Development.

Törrönen, J. and Maunu, A. (2007a). 'Light transgression and heavy sociability: Alcohol in young adult Finns' narratives of a night out.' *Addiction Research and Theory*, 15 (4): 365-381.

Törronen, J. and Maunu, A. (2007b). 'Whilst it's red wine with beef, it's booze with a cruise! Genres and gendered regulation of drinking situations in diaries.' *Nordic Studies on Alcohol and Drugs*, 24: 177-199.

Contributors

Kadri Aavik is a PhD student at the Institute of International and Social Studies at Tallinn University. Her principal research interests are inequalities in the Estonian labour market, more specifically, experiences and perceptions of disadvantage and privilege of people at the intersection of gender and ethnicity (and other categories) in the Estonian labour market. [e-mail: kadria@tlu.ee]

Airi-Alina Allaste is Professor of Sociology and the Head of the Centre for Lifestyles Studies at the Institute of International and Social Studies at Tallinn University. Her research interests focus on young people, subcultures and new social movements. She is currently coordinator of Estonian project on changes in lifestyles and country coordinator of the FP7 project 'Memory, Youth, Political Legacy and Civic Engagement'. [e-mail: alina@iiss.ee]

Andy Bennett is Professor of Cultural Sociology and Director of the Griffith Centre for Cultural Research at Griffith University in Queensland, Australia. His research expertise includes identity and lifestyle, postsubculture theory, popular culture, popular music and youth cultures and he has published numerous internationally recognized books and journal articles on these topics. [e-mail: a.bennett@griffith.edu.au]

Leeni Hansson is a Senior Research Fellow at the Centre of Lifestyle Studies at the Institute of International and Social Studies at Tallinn University. Her main research interests include the issues of the impact of radical social change on the institution of the family and family policies, on informal social networks, as well as on life satisfaction and subjective well-being. She has published articles and books on changing family forms and behaviours, reconciliation of work and family life, different aspects of parenting, on gender issues, *etc.* [e-mail: leeni.hansson@iiss.ee]

Jeff Hearn is Professor of Sociology, University of Huddersfield, UK; Professor of Gender Studies, Linköping University, Sweden; and Professor in Management and Organisation, Hanken School of Economics, Finland. His research focuses on men, gender, sexuality, violence, organisations, and transnational processes. Recent books include 'Men and Masculinities' around the World (2011), and 'Rethinking Transnational Men' (2013). He is Co-Director of GEXcel, Linköping and Örebro Universities Centre of Gender Excellence [e-mail: hearn@hanken.fi]

Eda Heinla is a Associate Professor of the Department of Arts Therapies at the Institute of Fine Arts, Tallinn University. Her research has focused on the child's creative thinking, creativity in the school environment and sociology of values. [e-mail: edah@tlu.ee]

Maarja Kobin is a PhD Student at the Institute of International and Social Studies at Tallinn University where she is researching alcohol culture among young Estonian adults. Her previous research has also been about young people and she has published articles in the field of subcultural studies. [e-mail: maarja.kobin@gmail.com]

Mikko Lagerspetz is since 2006 Professor of Sociology at the ÅboAkademi University, Turku, Finland. Before that, he worked at Tallinn University, Estonia, as Professor and director of the Centre for Civil Society Study and Development. He has published more than 90 scientific publications mainly on civil society, cultural policies, minorities and social problems. In 2004, he received the Estonian Annual State Prize for Research in the Social Sciences. [e-mail: mlagersp@abo.fi]

Liis Ojamäe is Associate Professor and Senior Researcher at the Centre of Lifestyles Studies at Institute of International and Social Studies at Tallinn University, and also affiliated to Tallinn School of Economics and Business Administration, Tallinn University of Technology. Her research fields include residential and urban studies, in intersection with economic sociology. [e-mail: liis.ojamae@tlu.ee]

Katrin Paadam is Professor of Sociology at the Tallinn School of Economics and Business Administration, Tallinn University of Technology; she also teaches urban sociology on a long-term basis at the Tallinn University. Her primary conduct in residential and urban research, with an interest in interdisciplinary perspectives, includes a number of experiences of Nordic-Baltic and European studies in the field. [e-mail: katrin.paadam@ttu.ee]

Marion Pajumets is a Lecturer of Sociology and Researcher at the Centre of Lifestyles Studies at the Institute of International and Social Studies, Tallinn University. She recently defended her PhD theses *Post-Socialist Masculinities, Identity Work, and Social Change: An Analysis of Discursive (Re)constructions of Gender Identity in Novel Social Situations*. Pajumets' main areas of research include (post-socialist) masculinities, gendering migration, and sociology of gender more broadly. She has published widely in the Estonian language, and in the journal *Fathering* (2010). [e-mail: marion@iiss.ee]

Barbi Pilvre is Associate Professor at Tallinn University, Institute of Communication. She has published on gender representations in the media, tabloidization, gender equality. She has been working in Tartu and Tallinn universities since 2000 and has been one of the initiators of introducing gender studies to Estonian universities. Before entering academy she has been a journalist, editor for arts and columnist since 1980s. Among else she has written a chapter on media to the first Estonian gender studies textbook for students, compiled an Estonian version of 'Screening Gender' and published two collections of columns. Recently she contributed to a European project 'Gender Narratives' by EIGE and an international project 'The Worlds of Journalism'. [e-mail barbi@tlu.ee]

Maaris Raudsepp is a Senior Researcher at the Centre for Contemporary Cultural Studies at Tallinn University, Estonia. Her research interests include socio-psychological aspects of environmentalism, interethnic relations and individual coping strategies with socio-cultural change. She has published on regulative role of values in culture and mind. [e-mail: maaris@tlu.ee]

Kristel Siilak is a PhD student in Sociology, Tallinn University and Lecturer at the Tallinn School of Economics and Business Administration in Tallinn University of Technology. Her qualitative research experience includes studies on the transition from higher education to labour market and on her PhD dissertation 'The Social Construction of Home Identities in a Cross-cultural Experience'. [e-mail: siilak@tlu.ee, kristel.siilak@ttu.ee]

Indrek Tart is a Senior Researcher at the Centre for Contemporary Cultural Studies at Tallinn University, Estonia. His main fields of research incorporate methodological aspects of basic human value studies and the role of values in post-socialist social change. [e-mail: itart@tlu.ee]

Katrin Tiidenberg is a PhD student and a Lecturer at the Tallinn University Institute of International and Social Studies. She has attained a Bachelor's Degree in Sociology from the University of Tartu and a Master's Degree in Media and Communication from the University of Tartu. She is an internet researcher with a focus on issues of identity, community, online experience and sexuality online. [e-mail: katrin.tiidenberg@tlu.ee]

Baltische Studien zur Erziehungs- und Sozialwissenschaft

Reihenherausgeber:
Gerd-Bodo von Carlsburg, Algirdas Gaižutis und Airi Liimets

Band 1 Gerd-Bodo Reinert / Irena Musteikienė (Hrsg.): Litauische Gespräche zur Pädagogik. Humanismus – Demokratie – Erziehung. 1999.

Band 2 Gerd-Bodo Reinert / Irena Musteikienė (Hrsg.): Litauische Gespräche zur Pädagogik II. Staat und Schule. 2000.

Band 3 Jaan Mikk: Textbook: Research and Writing. 2000.

Band 4 Gerd-Bodo Reinert / Irena Musteikienė (Hrsg.): Erziehungswandel und moderne pädagogische Verfahren. 2001.

Band 5 Airi Liimets (Hrsg.): Integration als Problem in der Erziehungswissenschaft. 2001.

Band 6 Gerd-Bodo Reinert / Irena Musteikienė (Hrsg.): Wissenschaft – Studium – Schule auf neuen Wegen. 2002.

Band 7 Palmira Jucevičienė / Gediminas Merkys / Gerd-Bodo Reinert: Towards the Learning Society. Educational Issues. 2002.

Band 8 Gerd-Bodo Reinert / Irena Musteikienė (Hrsg.): Bildung im Zeitalter der Informationsgesellschaft. 2003.

Band 9 Dalia Ohlinger: Argumentation in der Erst- und Fremdsprache. Pragmalinguistische und grammatikalische Aspekte anhand von Argumentationen deutscher und litauischer Studierender. 2003.

Band 10 Inga Šukevičiūtė: Interkulturelle Interferenzen im Bereich Wirtschaftskommunikation. Zur Analyse von Geschäftsbriefen im Vergleich Deutschland, Litauen und Russland. 2004.

Band 11 Gerd-Bodo Reinert von Carlsburg / Irena Musteikienė (Hrsg./eds.): Innovation durch Bildung. Innovation by Education. 2004.

Band 12 Gerd-Bodo von Carlsburg / Palmira Jucevičienė / Gediminas Merkys (eds.): Learning and Development for Innovation, Networking and Cohesion. 2005.

Band 13 Gerd-Bodo von Carlsburg / Irena Musteikienė (Hrsg./eds.): Bildungsreform als Lebensreform. Educational Systems Development as Development of Human Being. 2005.

Band 14 Gerd-Bodo von Carlsburg (Hrsg./ed.): Entwicklung erziehungswissenschaftlicher Paradigmen: Theorie und Praxis. Development of Educational Paradigms: Theory and Practice. 2007.

Band 15 Gerd-Bodo von Carlsburg (Hrsg./ed.): Bildungs- und Kulturmanagement. The Management of Education and Culture. 2008.

Band 16 Jaan Mikk / Marika Veisson / Piret Luik (eds.): Reforms and Innovations in Estonian Education. 2008.

Band 17 Gerd-Bodo von Carlsburg (Hrsg./ed.): Qualität von Bildung und Kultur. Theorie und Praxis. The Quality of Education and Culture. Theoretical and Practical Dimensions. 2009.

Band 18 Denkkulturen. Selbstwerdung des Menschen. Erziehungskulturen. Festschrift für Professor Dr. Dr. h.c. Dr. h.c. Heino Liimets. Herausgegeben von Airi Liimets. 2010.

Band 19 Ellu Saar (ed.): Towards a Normal Stratification Order. Actual and Perceived Social Stratification in Post-Socialist Estonia. 2011.

Band 20 Marika Veisson / Eeva Hujala / Peter K. Smith/ Manjula Waniganayake / Eve Kikas (eds.): Global Perspectives in Early Childhood Education. Diversity, Challenges and Possibilities. 2011.

Band 21 Airi Liimets / Marit Mäesalu (eds.): Music Inside and Outside the School. 2011.

Band 22 Gerd-Bodo von Carlsburg (Hrsg./ed.): Enkulturation durch sozialen Kompetenzerwerb. Enculturation by Acquiring of Social Competences. 2011.

Band 23 Reet Liimets: Ich als raumzeitliches Konstrukt. Die Fiktionen vom Leben der estnischen und deutschen Jugendlichen. 2012.

Band 24 Raivo Vetik (ed.): Nation-Building in the Context of Post-Communist Transformation and Globalization. The Case of Estonia. 2012.

Band 25 Airi-Alina Allaste (ed.): ‚Back in the West'. Changing Lifestyles in Transforming Societies. 2013.

www.peterlang.de

Kolibri 360 GmbH
Ferdinand-Jühlke-Straße 7
99095 Erfurt, Deutschland
produktsicherheit@kolibri360.de